STUDY GUIDE

for use with

D1249795

MICROECONOMICS

David C. Colander
Peter S. Sephton

Prepared by

Susan Kamp
University of Alberta
Douglas W. Copeland
Johnson County Community College
Richard Trieff
Benjamin Shlaes
Both of Des Moines Area Community College

Represented in Canada by:

Times Mirror
Professional Publishing Ltd.

IRWIN

Toronto • Chicago • Bogotá • Boston • Buenos Aires
Caracas • London • Madrid • Mexico City • Sydney

ISBN 0–256–17576–4

1 2 3 4 5 6 7 8 9 0 ML 3 2 1 0 9 8 7 6

Preface

INTRODUCTION: STUDYING ECONOMICS— THE REWARDS

The rewards of studying economics are many and varied. You have the opportunity to learn what makes the economy tick as well as why it sometimes misses a beat. You will gain awareness of economic institutions and develop insights on how they affect our lives. Perhaps most importantly, the study of economics may enable you to become a more critical thinker and a more effective decision maker. Economics is all about making choices in a rational and systematic manner. We all, of course, are faced with choices every day. While the choices that are considered in the study of economics may not look much like those you deal with in everyday life, the study of economics does have something practical to offer you.

The technique of choice making in economics can be applied to any sort of decision-making task with which you are confronted. Effective decision making requires that all of the important questions be objectively recognized and weighed. All possible outcomes of the choices available must be determined as far as possible. This is what the study of economics has you do on a continuing basis.

Some people are naturally better decision makers than others, just as some people are better swimmers or card players than others. But anybody can improve skills through practice. In this way, then, the study of economics is a mental exercise in thinking critically. You are required to identify, analyze, apply, and evaluate information. You make choices and evaluate their outcomes. This sort of activity is part and parcel of all decision making. You probably will not retain all of the economic ideas and concepts that you are exposed to in this course. But you will never run out of opportunities to critically evaluate choices and make tough decisions. The exercise you get in this course will develop intellectual muscles that you can use whenever you need to analyze and evaluate problems.

Critical thinking does not mean cynical thinking. Just as one should not accept as true everything one is told, neither should one immediately reject perspectives that do not conform to one's existing beliefs. A critical thinker engages in a systematic assessment of the strengths and weaknesses of the evidence that provides the basis for a belief. Economic thinking is an exercise in critical thinking.

Economics is important beyond the intellectual discipline it fosters. It is no accident that so many programs of study require introductory economics. The concepts and institutions that you will be exposed to in economics are necessary background information in a wide range of subject areas and vocational pursuits. A familiarity with economic concepts will provide solid grounding for your success elsewhere in your other academic and career pursuits.

The study of economics will also make you a more responsible and effective citizen and consumer. If you are not aware of the underlying principles of economic behaviour, then you are missing out on an important influence on the workings of our society. Your personal consumer choices and political choices will be improved if you make them from the basis of more complete understanding.

USING YOUR TEXTBOOK

Always Preview and Review

Pick up your textbook and look at the table of contents. Carefully examine the topics that David Colander and Peter Sephton have laid out for study. Reviewing the table of contents periodically throughout the course (perhaps when you finish reading each chapter) is a good idea. This review helps you keep in mind how what you just read fits in with what you have done before. It also makes more meaningful the subjects you are going to investigate next. Regular review of the table of contents may sound like a simple technique, but I cannot over-stess how keeping things in perspective will help you make sense out of your study of economics. This review doesn't take much time.

Read the author's introduction in the textbook. They are your guides on this economic exploration. You will benefit by having a good feel for what Professors Colander and Sephton want to accomplish and what they want *you* to accomplish.

Review the Learning Objectives at the start of each chapter. These outline the skills you need to master in the chapter at hand. Keep these objectives in mind as you read.

Preview each chapter before getting down to actually reading it. Once again, this helps you to keep things in perspective. Leafing through the chapter before you begin your concentrated reading will give a feel for the road that you will be travelling.

Retaining your sense of perspective as you deal with various concepts will help you see how each concept is relevant. This will help you maintain motivation and concentration, which will lead to a successful learning experience.

Interact with Your Textbook

Read your text assignments before the information is dealt with in class. You are sure to have heard this advice before, because it is good advice to follow. Knowing something about the material allows you to ask for clarification on topics you may not understand.

Mark Up Your Textbook

After previewing the assigned chapter, read it carefully, marking up your textbook as you go. You don't need to go into a highlighting frenzy. Professors Colander and Sephton have provided convenient margin notes to encourage you to focus on important passages in the text.

Every time you come across something that isn't clear to you, mark it. Make notes in your textbook that explain the problem you are having with the troublesome section. Take a few minutes right before class to review your text markings so that you have fresh in your mind what confuses you in the chapter that you have read. If the classroom presentation fails to clarify matters, then you have a good basis for posing questions to improve your comprehension.

USING YOUR STUDY GUIDE

This Study Guide has been designed to fulfill two major goals. First, by complementing the material presented in David C. Colander's and Peter S. Sephton's **MICROECONOMICS**, First Canadian Edition, it is hoped that your understanding and appreciation of economics will increase and that you will be better equipped to respond intelligently to real-world economic issues that you read about and hear about every day. After all, many economic decisions made by business and political leaders have far-reaching implications for your personal life. Furthermore, a firm grasp of the principles of economics is invaluable to those of you who are pursuing careers in either economics or business. Second, and possibly of more immediate and practical concern to you, this Study Guide has been designed to prepare you for your examinations—to help you maximize your grade from this class given your limited studying time. If you work through each chapter of the Study Guide in its entirety after you have studied the chapter in the textbook, you will enter your tests with confidence and will score accordingly. This Study Guide can be viewed as a close and helpful companion—a much appreciated private tutor.

It should be kept in mind that this Study Guide is not a substitute for the textbook. Instead, it is a supplement. You should work through each chapter in the Study Guide only after you have *studied* the assigned chapter in the textbook as outlined above. In this way the Study Guide can avoid having to give you yet more stuff to "passively" read. After all, time is precious. This frees up an opportunity to concentrate on the task at hand—to learn economics by doing economics.

There is no *easy* way to learn anything. But some ways are *easier* than others. Most students who have problems with economics (which usually means with the exams), have problems because they are not prepared. Assuming you put forth the effort, then any lack of preparation usually stems from a lack of opportunities to apply the material, or being unable to determine what you need to know, or what is most important to know. Some people have trouble organizing what may appear as an overwhelming volume of material. That is, they may have trouble putting it all together. Still, others have trouble thinking "economically." There are many potential pitfalls students encounter in the study of economics that this Study Guide has been designed to help overcome. If the Study Guide is successful, you should find learning economics much easier and you should score much better on the exams. Hopefully, you will find that learning economics is relevant, interesting, rewarding and fun.

The format of each chapter of this book has been strategically designed to maximize your mastery of the material and therefore your ability to perform well on the exams—given your limited studying time. The specific sections of each chapter are outlined below.

I. CHAPTER AT A GLANCE

In this section you will find listed the most important points made in the chapter. These correspond to the list of objectives at the beginning of each chapter in the textbook. After each major point you will find reference (in parentheses) to the page number where you can find the discussion of this topic in the textbook. I have added some notes underneath each of these major points.

These notes in italics are intended to be brief and to the point—telling you what you need to know and how relatively important it is. For a review of the details simply reference the page number in the textbook that is provided. The notes are in italics so that you may better distinguish between my comments and the points made in the textbook. They are designed to accent the rest of the material (the major points found in the textbook)—as opposed to having to look at and read even more blocks of typed material that you will likely just end up highlighting and marking up anyway. This way it has already been done for you, and hopefully in a more visually engaging manner. (It sounds weird but it works!) However, you are encouraged to add to these notes where you think it would be helpful. In sum, this combination of highlights should help you *see* and therefore *think* about the chapter more clearly.

Moreover, this general overview of the chapter has been purposefully placed on one ot two sheets of paper. It might be helpful to think of this as a review sheet. This page (as well as all pages in this book) is perforated because you are encouraged to rip it out and stick it in your textbook or notebook for quick and easy reference. (Your are encouraged to frequently review this material—take it in small doses, one at a time). When preparing for an exam you will have each chapter on one or two review sheets. This should help you to organize the material better—enabling you to see it better and therefore enhancing your ability to put it all together.

II. MASTERY TEST

These are multiple choice questions designed as a check for you to see whether or not you have "mastered" the chapter material you have just read. For some cases, you may be required to actually do a bit more than just remember; you may be asked to do a calculation or to interpret a graph or table. Doing the multiple choice questions will help you to prepare for this type of question on exams. Even if you are not expecting multiple choice questions on an exam, the correcting and studying of these questions will help you to identify weak areas, learn the language of economics and increase your basic knowledge of the chapter before proceeding to the more challenging questions and problems that follow.

Once you have "mastered" the Mastery Test section, you will be prepared to attempt the next section— **Short Answer Exercises and Problems.**

III. SHORT ANSWER EXERCISES AND PROBLEMS

a. Short Answer Exercises

This section requires more participation on your part. This section enables you to begin learning economics by answering some relatively easy questions. Space is provided for you to write out the answers to these questions—use it! Don't just look at the answers. Having to write out the answers helps you to digest the material and to "imprint" what has been learned on your mind. It only takes a minute to write out the answers and it's well worth the time! Being able to successfully work at least most of these questions without peeking at the answers will not only help you to learn the material but will also build the confidence and background you need to tackle the more difficult problems that follow as well as analytical exam questions.

b. Problems

In this section you will get a chance to apply the skills and knowledge that you have been developing by reading the text, and doing the Study Guide to this point. As with the Short Answer Exercises above, don't look at the answers until you have attempted one on your own. Don't be overly concerned if you make mistakes. There is no better way to learn than by making mistakes and working toward not repeating them. The only serious mistake you can make is not trying to figure out the answers on your own.

IV. CHALLENGE PROBLEMS AND POTENTIAL ESSAY QUESTIONS

There are a variety of different types of questions in this section. They are meant to give you a variety of different kinds of opportunities to test your ability to apply the chapter material. This section will engage you in decision-making and critical thinking activities.

You will probably find this section more difficult than the previous ones. Work on these items with classmates. Bounce ideas off one another to solve the problem at hand. Again, when you are attempting these questions, make an effort to think about each one and to write something down before you look at the answers. A lot of learning will take place just by thinking about these questions. Don't be too concerned if your answers aren't quite as thorough as those provided. The purpose is to help you to discover those areas where you still need to improve. Don't forget to make use of the teacher-resource that you have been provided with. Most instructors truly enjoy working with serious-minded students.

a. Challenge Problems

These are not unlike the exercises and problems in the previous section but are designed to challenge you to apply what you have learned to some real-world situations. Hopefully, you will find them both fun to work and challenging at the same time. Successful completion of these problems will also increase your understanding of some of the more technical aspects of economics.

b. Potential Essay Questions

The questions in this section will give you an opportunity to practise putting your answers into eassay form. This will be especially helpful if you expect these types of questions on the exams. Some of these questions have been generated to stimulate thought or discussion about issues which do not necessarily have a right or a wrong answer. The "answer" one might provide depends on one's subjective value judgements or overall philosophy. These questions help illustrate where the science of economics ends and the "art" begins.

It won't take you that long to work through the Study Guide material for each chapter. Try to do so as soon as you have completed the chapter. The payoffs will be enormous!

I hope you find this Study Guide very helpful. I have tried to make it interesting, meaningful and challenging to work through. But regardless of the success of my undertaking, I also hope you come to appreciate the practical applications of economics, and find the study of economics both rewarding and interesting. After all, economics affects all of our lives in many important ways.

ACKNOWLEDGEMENTS

Over the years, many students have taken the trouble to help me, by their comments, to formulate better questions. I would like to thank them for all they have taught me.

My family has put up with my extended work hours while I worked on this project. I would like to thank each one of them individually for the many and varied things they did for me and for each other, so that I had worry-free time to concentrate on my work. Thank you to my children Tara, Andrena, Bridget, Stephen and Paul. And thank you to my loving husband Bob.

Special thanks go to Sabira Hussain at Times Mirror Professional Publishing who gave me much needed support every inch of the way.

It should be noted that this Study Guide is primarily the work of the original authors Richard Trieff, Benjamin Schlaes, and Douglas W. Copeland. Without their original work this Study Guide would not have been possible.

Susan Kamp

Contents

Chapter 1   Economics and Economic Reasoning

I. CHAPTER AT A GLANCE

Rip these two pages out for quick and easy reference.

1. **Five important things to learn in economics are: (6)**

   1) **Economic reasoning**

      is really benefit/cost analysis. If the benefits of something outweigh its costs then do it. If not, don't.

   2) **Economic terminology**

      Need to know what the terms and concepts mean (Study the "Testable Terms and Concepts" section of each chapter of this Study Guide!)

   3) **Economic insights**

      General statements about what causes what (Sometimes called economic theories, laws, models or principles.)

   4) **Economic institutions**

      Need to learn the structure or make-up of business, government and society and how they interact.

   5) **Economic policy options**

      There is more than one way to achieve an end or goal. Need to be aware of the different options and try to choose the "best."

2. **If the benefits of doing something exceed the costs, do it. If the costs of doing something exceed the benefits, don't do it. (8)**

   You really need to think in terms of the marginal, or "extra" benefits (MB) and marginal, or "extra" costs (MC) of a course of action.

   Rational
   Decision $\left\{ \begin{array}{l} \underline{\textit{If MB > MC}} \Rightarrow \underline{\textit{Do more of it}} \textit{ because "it's worth it."} \\ \underline{\textit{If MB < MC}} \Rightarrow \underline{\textit{Do less of it}} \textit{ because "it's not worth it."} \end{array} \right.$
   Making

   NOTE: The symbol "⇒" means "implies" or "logically follows"

3. **Opportunity cost is the basis of cost/benefit economic reasoning; it is the benefit of the best alternative foregone, or the cost of the best alternative to the activity you've chosen. In economic reasoning, that cost is less than the benefit of what you've chosen. (10)**

   *Opportunity cost ⇒ "What must be given up in order to get something else"
   Opportunity costs are often "hidden." Need to take into consideration <u>all</u> costs.*

4. **Remember this graph:**

The slope tells you the opportunity cost of good X in terms of good Y. In this particular graph you have to give up 2 Y to get 1 X when you're around point A. (12)

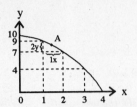

Production Possibilities Curve

Shows the tradeoff
(or opportunity cost)
between 2 things

5. The principal of increasing marginal opportunity cost: opportunity costs increase the more you concentrate on the activity. In order to get more of something, one must give up ever-increasing quantities of something else. (15)

Production Possibility Curve

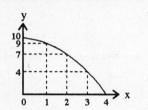

Production Possibility Table

x	y	opportunity cost of x (amount of y which must be foregone)	
0	10	⟩1	
1	9	⟩2	*Note* — As you get more of x you have to give up larger and larger amounts of y
2	7	⟩3	
3	4	⟩4	
4	0		

6. **Economic reality is controlled by three invisible forces: (18)**

What happens in a society can be seen as the reaction and interaction of these 3 forces.

1) **The invisible hand (economic forces);**

The market forces of demand, supply and prices, etc. . .

2) **The invisible handshake (social and historical forces); and**

The impact of generally accepted social morals and customs.

3) **The invisible foot (political forces).**

Political and legal forces effect decisions too.

7. **Microeconomic theory considers economic reasoning from the viewpoint of individuals and builds up; macroeconomics considers economic reasoning from the aggregate and builds down. (22)**

Microeconomics (micro) ⇒ concerned with some particular segment of the economy.

Macroeconomics (macro) ⇒ concerned with the entire economy.

8. **Positive economics is the study of what is, and how the economy works.**

> *Deals with "what is" (objective analysis)—Facts*

Normative economics is the study of how the economy should be, from society's standpoint.

> *Deals with "what ought to be" (subjective or philosophical analysis)—Opinion*

The art of economics is the application of the knowledge learned in positive economics to the achievement of the goals determined in normative economics.

> *In the art of economics, it is difficult to be objective but it is important to try. (24).*

> *The art of economics is sometimes referred to as "policy economics"*
> *—"good" policy tries to be objective, tries to weigh all the benefits and costs associated with all policy options and chooses that option in which the benefits outweigh the costs to <u>the greatest</u> degree.*

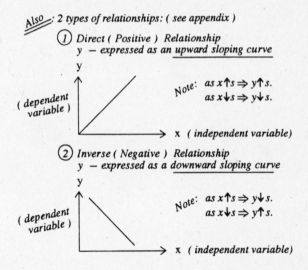

Also: 2 types of relationships: (see appendix)

① *Direct (Positive) Relationship*
y — expressed as an <u>upward sloping curve</u>

(*dependent variable*)   y

Note: *as x↑s ⇒ y↑s.*
as x↓s ⇒ y↓s.

x *(independent variable)*

② *Inverse (Negative) Relationship*
y — expressed as a <u>downward sloping curve</u>

(*dependent variable*)   y

Note: *as x↑s ⇒ y↓s.*
as x↓s ⇒ y↑s.

x *(independent variable)*

II. MASTERY TEST

1. The best way to describe economic institutions is that they are

   a) forces responsible for economic decision making.
   b) structures in society that significantly influence economic choices.
   c) together the invisible hand, the invisible foot, and the invisible handshake.
   d) a, b, and c.

2. Economic policy options are

   a) the opportunity costs associated with foregone choices.
   b) alternative possible outcomes from the invisible hand of the marketplace.
   c) comparisons of costs and benefits associated with several policy choices.
   d) possible actions or inactions by the government which influence the course of events.

3. Theories of behaviour are developed in the study of economics in order to
   a) improve reasoning by offering explanations and predictions of economic behaviour.
   b) intimidate, confuse, and confound introductory economics' students.
   c) illustrate the superiority of positive economics over normative economics.
   d) a and c.

4. Scarcity is an economic force in the sense that
   a) at any given time, the inputs society possesses are limited while the output desired is not.
   b) it is not an applicable concept outside the study of economics.
   c) the market mechanism is affected by scarcity but the political system is not constrained by economic rules concerning scarcity.
   d) in real life, choices are often made with no real sacrifice entailed.

Use the model below to respond to items #5 through #12. "B" - all public goods; "E" - all private goods.

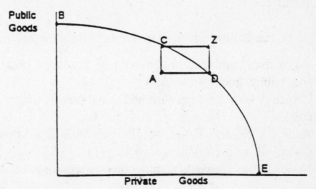

5. Efficiency in production is illustrated by combinations at

   a) B, A, E.   b) C, D.   c) Z.   d) B, C, D, E.

6. Increased production of public goods with no opportunity cost sacrifice of private goods occurs in the move from

   a) A to Z.   b) A to D.   c) A to C.   rd) D to C.

7. Inefficient production occurs at choice(s)

   a) A.   b) Z.   c) C and D   d) B and E.

---

8. Which statement about combination Z is not true?

   a) Choices C and Z generate an equal amount of public goods.
   b) Choices D and Z provide an equal amount of private goods.
   c) Society does not have sufficient resources to produce the combination at Z.
   d) Combination Z is not now, nor will ever be, a feasible choice.

9. Which statement about combination Z is true?

   a) At Z, input utilization is inefficient.
   b) Movement from alternatives C and D to Z can be realized without sacrifice of public or private goods.
   c) Movement from alternatives C and D to Z can be realized only if society is currently willing to give up private goods to get from C to Z or public goods to get from D to Z.
   d) More inputs or improved technology must be realized in order for Z to be reached.

10. Assuming the economy is currently operating at choice D, more public goods can be generated currently only if

   a) more inputs become available.   b) inputs become more productive.
   c) private goods are sacrificed.   d) a, b, and c.

11. Which of the following statements is an expression of normative economics?

   a) Choices D and Z are preferable to C because privately produced goods are preferable to government produced goods.
   b) Choice A is not desirable because existing resources are not fully employed.
   c) Choice A is desirable because it represents more efficient utilization of resources than either C or D.
   d) Choices C and D are more desirable than Z because it is not currently feasible for the economy to produce the combination of goods suggested by Z.
   e) b and c.

12. Which of the following is an expression of positive economics?

   a) If possible, combination Z should be produced because it represents more of both private and public goods than A, C, or D.
   b) Choice A is optimal because additional private and/or public goods can be produced without cost.
   c) A, B, C, D, and E are equally suitable, depending upon the judgment of society.
   d) Choice B is preferable to choice A.
   e) None of the above is a reflection of positive economics.

Refer to the graphs below to respond to items #13 through #16. Food production is measured on the vertical axes and non food output is measured on the horizontal axes. Which model best depicts the stated scenario?

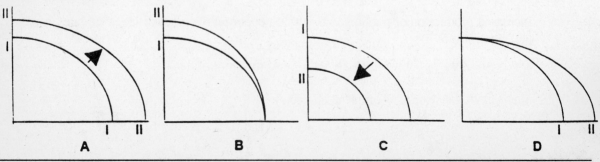

A   B   C   D

13. An innovation in integrated pest management promises to improve agricultural production significantly.

    a) A   b) B   c) C   d) D   e) None of the above.

14. A breakthrough in superconductivity research brings about innovations in rail transportation and shipping costs plummet.

    a) A   b) B   c) C   d) D   e) None of the above.

15. Worldwide drought results in substantial reduction of production of important agricultural commodities including corn, wheat, soybeans and cotton.

    a) A   b) B   c) C   d) D   e) None of the above.

16. A slowdown in real capital placement causes increased unemployment in food and non food sectors of the economy.

    a) A   b) B   c) C   d) D   e) None of the above.

Refer to the table below in order to respond to items #17 through #20. The table shows selected efficient production possibilities of an economy producing only computer software and textile products.

Goods/Choices	A	B	C	D	E	F
Textiles (tons)	0	75	150	225	300	375
Software (bushels)	100,000	95,000	85,000	65,000	40,000	0

17. The cost of getting an additional 75 units of textiles

    a) is constant for any change in combination of textiles and software.
    b) is 30,000 bushels of software.
    c) increases at the margin.
    d) decreases as more textiles are produced.
    e) is 300 tons of textiles.

18. The total cost of producing 150 units of textiles (at choice C) is
    a) 85,000 bushels of software.
    b) 10,000 bushels of software.
    c) 15,000 bushels of software.
    d) 225 tons of textiles.
    e) c and d.

19. Moving from choice E to choice D results in

    a) decreasing marginal opportunity costs.
    b) a gain of 25,000 bushels of software.
    c) total cost of 150 tons of textiles.
    d) marginal cost of 75 tons of textiles.
    e) All of the above.

20. Producing a combination of 250 tons of textiles and 65,000 bushels of software requires

    a) an expanded resource base or improvements in production technology.
    b) sacrificing textiles in order to move along the production possibilities curve to the desired point.
    c) reducing unemployment of resources to move from the interior of the model to the curve.
    d) sacrificing software in order to move along the production possibilities curve to the desired point.

21. Making decisions based on the expected results of future incremental changes, rather than on past experience, is referred to as

    a) positive economics.
    b) normative economics.
    c) marginalism.
    d) the art of economics.

22. The process of moving from economic outcomes resulting from marketplace forces to outcomes which may be more socially desirable is referred to as

    a) positive economics.
    b) normative economics.
    c) marginalism.
    d) the art of economics.

23. Identifying the outcomes of economic forces working on the behaviour of rational, self-interested marketplace participants is referred to as

    a) positive economics.
    b) normative economics.
    c) marginalism.
    d) the art of economics.

24. If as the result of laws passed restricting the advertisement of tobacco products there are fewer new tobacco users, the influence of _____ is evident.

    a) The Invisible Hand
    b) The Invisible Foot
    c) The Invisible Handshake

25. Although tobacco use is not restricted at his workplace or at his home, Jonathon has reduced his purchases and use of tobacco products because of harassment by anti smoking coworkers and the disapproval of his children. This illustrates the influence of _____ on economic behaviour.

    a) The Invisible Hand
    b) The Invisible Foot
    c) The Invisible Handshake

III. SHORT ANSWER EXERCISES AND PROBLEMS

a. Short Answer Exercises

1. What name is given to the institutional structure through which individuals in society coordinate their economic wants?

2. What term is used to describe the study of how human beings coordinate their wants?

3. What does the phrase "economic coordination" have to do with the effort to satisfy all of our wants for goods and services?

4. After engaging in physical exertion on a hot day, you need to refresh yourself with liquid refreshment. Use the table below to determine the proper response to the following questions?

	bottle #1	bottle #2	bottle #3	bottle #4
Total benefit	$2.00	$3.50	$4.50	$5.00
Marginal benefit				
Total cost	$1.00	$2.00	$3.00	$4.00
Marginal cost				

a) Complete the cells for marginal benefit and marginal cost.

b) How many bottles will a rational drinker consume? Why?

c) Why does the marginal benefit decrease while the marginal cost remains constant?

5. What term is used to describe getting the most output from available inputs?

6. What is the production possibilities model and for what is it used?

1. Assume you are planning for a party and have allocated $100 towards the purchase of beverage (pop) and food (pizza). The pop of choice goes for $5 per case while the pizza is $10 per pie. Complete the table and graph below to identify the combinations possible and then respond to the following questions.

Choice	Pop (cases)	Pizza (pies)
A	20	
B	16	
C	12	
D	8	
E	4	
F	0	

Choice	Pop (cases)	Pizza (pies)
A		0
B		2
C		4
D		6
E		8
F		10

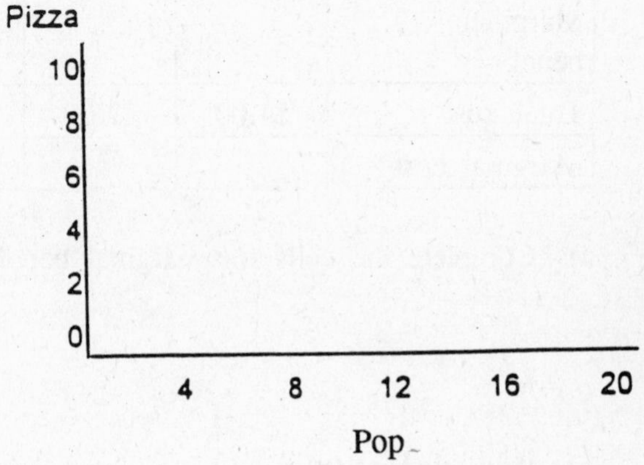

Pizza

```
10
 8
 6
 4
 2
 0 ┼────┬────┬────┬────┬────
      4    8   12   16   20
                          Pop
```

a) At combination D, how much pop is foregone by choosing 6 pizzas?

b) How much additional pop is given up by moving from choice D to choice E?

c) What happens to the opportunity costs at the margin for pizza by moving from choice A to choice B? . . . from choice B to choice C? . . . from choice D to choice E? . . . from choice E to choice F?

d) Label point X on the graph the combination of 8 cases of pop and 8 pizzas. Label point Y the combination of 5 pizzas and 5 cases of pop. Given the budget available, assess combination X and combination Y.

2. Two types of agricultural commodities are produced in Canada: corn and everything else. Let wheat represent everything else. Given the information in the table and production possibilities model below, respond to the following questions.

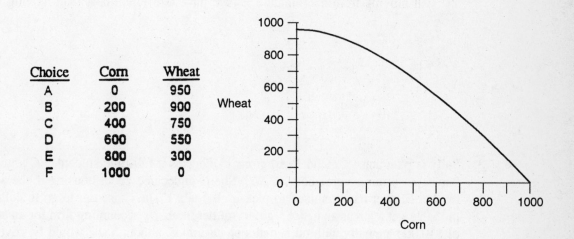

Choice	Corn	Wheat
A	0	950
B	200	900
C	400	750
D	600	550
E	800	300
F	1000	0

a) If the country is currently at combination B, what is the opportunity cost of producing an additional 400 units of corn (moving from B to D)?

b) What is the opportunity cost of moving from exclusive production of corn to producing 550 units of wheat?

c) Label the combination of 750 units of wheat and 600 units of corn "Z". What must happen to make Z possible?

d) Identify the opportunity cost of producing more corn in the following table.

From...To	Corn Gained	Wheat Lost
A ... B		
B ... C		
C ... D		
D ... E		
E ... F		

e) How would you describe the marginal opportunity cost of producing more corn? Why will moving from combination E to F have a different cost than moving from A to B?

3. Sally is planning to attend *Prestigious College* as a full-time student. *PC*'s tuition, fees and books per semester are about $2,500. She is undecided about housing if she attends college but her Mother has promised to pick up the tab. If she chose not to go to college she could probably get a job as an office "gofer" at her mother's accounting firm for an anticipated pay of $10,000 annually with no benefits or insurance, although she would be covered under her mother's private family policy.

Her friend Leah is torn between going to *Drawtech* business school to study computer drafting or starting work full time at a local blueprint design firm for whom Leah worked part time while she was in high school. The firm has offered her a $24,000 annual salary to start, plus a $10,000 benefits' package. Tuition, fees and books at *Drawtech* are $2,000 a semester. She will live at home whether she works or attends school. Her folks have promised to provide her with room and board until she is 21.

Leah's twin brother Leo is considering an offer to work construction. He has been promised training as a heavy equipment operator. Although the job does not offer much for benefits, business is good and overtime work is available so Leo expects to make close to $30,000 for the next year. He has also been offered a full athletic scholarship to *Lakeland University*. Tuition, fees, books, room and board at *LU* are $10,000 per year. As they have for his sister, Leo's folks have promised to provide room and board until he is 21.

a) Which one of the three faces the highest opportunity cost of pursuing higher education next year? What is it?

b) For whom is the opportunity cost of attending college the cheapest? What is it?

c) For whom is the opportunity cost of attending college between the cheapest and most expensive? What is it?

IV. CHALLENGE PROBLEMS AND POTENTIAL ESSAY QUESTIONS

a. Challenge Problems

1. For each of the following items, determine whether the concern is an interest of microeconomics or macroeconomics.

   a) The unemployment rate in the nation.

   b) The North American automobile industry's share of total sales of cars in the nation.

   c) The price of computers.

   d) The federal government's spending and taxation policies.

   e) The national inflation rate.

   f) The economic factors that determine the combination of goods and services produced in an economy.

   g) The forces present in the fashion industry which determine the price of clothes.

2. We know that economic reality is controlled by three invisible forces. How might these forces come into play for a good like whiskey?

3. Suppose you are the manager of a warehouse. You have been experiencing problems with employees stealing merchandise from the warehouse. You do not presently have any security system monitoring employees. However, studies in the industry show that having security guards on the warehouse floor is one of the most effective ways to reduce theft. Suppose that extensive research of your warehouse estimates that the benefit of reduced losses due to theft each year associated with the presence of security guards is as indicated in the following table. The problem for you to solve is to determine the most economical number of security guards to employ. Assume that the annual salary of each security guard is $24,000. (Hint: What is the marginal benefit and the marginal cost of each security guard?)

Number of Security Guards	Annual Losses Due to Theft
0	$185,000
1	$135,000
2	$ 95,000
3	$ 75,000
4	$ 65,000

b. **Potential Essay Questions**

1. What can a nation do to increase its rate of economic growth over time (to increase its production possibilities)—to provide for a larger-sized economic pie and therefore a higher standard of living for its people?

2. Respond to the following statement: "Theories are of no use to me because they are not very practical. All I need is the facts because they speak for themselves."

3. Canada is one of the wealthiest nations on earth, yet our fundamental economic problem is scarity. How can this be?

4. Does economics help teach us how to approach problems, or does it give us a set of answers to problems?

V. ANSWERS

II. Mastery Test

1. d	6. c	11. a	16. c	21. c
2. d	7. a	12. e	17. c	22. d
3. a	8. c	13. b	18. c	23. a
4. a	9. d	14. a	19. e	24. b
5. d	10. d	15. e	20. a	25. c

III. **Short Answer Exercises and Problems**

  a. **Short Answer Questions**

   1. the marketplace

   2. economics

   3. Resources must be allocated so as to provide for as many of the apparently limitless volume of goods and services that we would like to have.

   4. a)

	bottle #1	bottle #2	bottle #3	bottle #4
Marginal benefit	$2.00	$1.50	$1.00	$0.50
Marginal cost	$1.00	$1.00	$1.00	$1.00

  b) 3 bottles. The rational consumer will purchase beverages as long as the marginal benefit is greater than or equal to marginal cost.

  c) As additional drinks are consumed the consumer will desire the next drink less than he/she desired the previous drink. In this example each bottle is priced identically, which is typically the case for an individual.

   5. efficiency

   6. The production possibilities model is an abstraction from reality used to illustrate basic economic concepts such as scarcity, opportunity costs, increasing costs, efficiency, and the need to make choices, among other important ideas that the model is used to express.

  b. **Problems**

   1. a) 12 cases   b) 4 cases   c) 4 cases. . . The opportunity cost is constant.
       d) Combination Y will result in $25 of the budget not being spent. Combination X requires an expenditure of $120 which is beyond the budgeted amount.

   2. a) 350 units of wheat   b) 400 units of corn

       c) There must be an expansion in the resource base or improvements in technology which will allow an expansion of production of both commodities simultaneously.

       d)

From...To	Corn Gained	Wheat Lost
A ... B	200	50
B ... C	200	150
C ... D	200	200
D ... E	200	250
E ... F	200	300

e) The opportunity cost of producing additional units of corn increases at the margin. All resources are not equally productive for growing corn and all other agricultural commodities. For example, differences in growing seasons, soil conditions, farmer expertise, and other factors mean that as more corn is produced, the next (marginal) allotment of ground devoted to producing corn may not generate the same yields as the previous addition to corn ground. More and more land will be needed to generate equal additional returns of corn which means that more and more other agricultural goods will be sacrificed as production moves to land less suitable for corn and more suitable for wheat and other commodities.

3. a) Leah, $34,000.

   b) Sally, $15,000. If Sally chooses to go to PC she must pay $5,000 per year ($2,500 per semester) in tuition, etc. which she would otherwise get to keep. She will also forego her opportunity to earn $10,000 as an office "gofer."

   c) Leo, $20,000. If Leo goes to LU he will receive a scholarship to pay his tuition and fees of $10,000. If he chooses not to go, he will forego this benefit. If he works instead, he will earn $30,000, but will not get the scholarship.

IV. Challenge Problems and Potential Essay Questions

a. Challenge Problems

1. a) macroeconomics
   b) microeconomics
   c) microeconomics
   d) macroeconomics
   e) macroeconomics
   f) macroeconomics
   g) microeconomics

2. The invisible hand (economic forces) of demand and supply effect the price of whiskey and the amount bought and sold. The invisible handshake (social, religious and historical forces) determines when, whom and under what circumstances it is consumed if it is even consumed at all—notice that in some cultures (e.g., Moslem nations) very few people drink at all. The invisible foot (political forces) effect the conditions under which whiskey is bought, sold and consumed, etc. . . .(e.g., legal drinking age requirements, package and liquor-by-the drink sales are prohibited during certain times of the day or when voting booths are open). There is interaction between these forces as well. For example, a "sin tax" is *legally* imposed on whiskey because of the undesirable *social* side effects associated with the consumption of alcoholic beverages increasing its price in the *market*.

3. When undertaking benefit/cost analysis it is important to think on the margin. That is, to think in terms of the marginal (extra) benefits and the marginal (extra) costs. For as long as the marginal benefits exceed the marginal costs then continue to undertake that activity—in this case hiring security guards. (If the marginal costs exceed the marginal benefits then do less of it). Therefore, the most rational or economical number of security guards for the warehouse to employ is 2. The first 2 security guards reduce theft losses (marginal benefits) more than it costs you as a manager to employ them (marginal costs). You should not hire the third security guard because theft losses are reduced by $20,000 while the amount you would have to pay that security guard is $24,000—the marginal benefit of the third security guard is less than the marginal cost. For the same reason it's not worth employing the fourth security guard either. See the following table.

Number of Security Guards	Total Cost of Security Guards	Marginal Cost of each additioal Security Guard (Salary)	Annual Losses Due to Theft	Marginal Benefit of each Security Guard (Reduced Losses from Theft)
0	$0	—	$185,000	—
1	$24,000	$24,000	$135,000	$50,000
2	$48,000	$24,000	$ 95,000	$40,000
3	$72,000	$24,000	$ 75,000	$20,000
4	$96,000	$24,000	$ 65,000	$10,000

b. **Potential Essay Questions**

The following answers are annotated—they only indicate the general idea behind the answer.

1. Any nation (whether developed or underdeveloped) would have to increase its production possibilities. This could be accomplished by: a) increasing private capital accumulation—creating a greater incentive for privately owned businesses to invest in productive-enhancing capital (plant and equipment), thereby increasing the productivity of workers; b) increasing social capital accumulation-governmentally provided plant and equipment often called infrastructure (e.g., roads, bridges, deams, schools, airports, communication systems, etc. . .) which would also increase the productivity of workers; c) increasing the productivity of workers themselves (sometimes called investment in human capital) through greater nutritional, educational and skill level attainment, and, d) increasing technology (know-how).

2. Theories are practical because they are generalizations based on real world observations or facts. They enable us to predict and to explain real world economic behaviour. Because they are generalizatons they enable us to avoid unnecessary details or facts. The drawback, however, is that because they are generalizations, at times there will be exceptions to the prediction we would generally expect to observe.

Facts, on the other hand, do not always speak for themselves. One can often be overwhelmed by a large set of data or facts. Not until one systematically arranges, interprets and generalizes upon facts tying them together, and distilling out a theory (general statement) related to those facts, do they take on any real meaning. In short, theory and facts are inseparable in the scientific process because theory gives meaning to facts and facts check the validity of theory.

3. Canada is still faced with scarity because we are unable to have as much as we would like to have. Our resources (as vast as they are) are still scarce relative to the amount of goods and services we would like to have (indeed, our wants are unlimited).

4. Economics is a methodology, or an approach to how we think about the world. It does not come to us equipped with a whole set of solutions to complex real-world problems. However, it may help shed some light on the complexities of real-world issues helping us to find solutions.

Chapter 2   Supply and Demand

I. CHAPTER AT A GLANCE

Rip these two pages out for quick and easy reference.

1. The <u>law of demand</u> states that the quantity of a good demanded is <u>inversely related</u> to the goods' price. When price goes up, quantity should go down. (35)

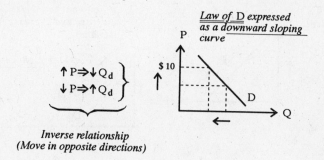

2. The law of demand is based upon individuals' ability to substitute. (38)

    As the P of beef ↑s we buy more chicken

3. <u>To derive a demand curve from a demand table</u> you plot each point on the demand table on a graph and connect the points. (39)

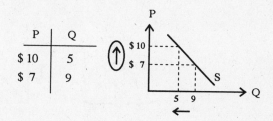

4. **Changes in quantity demanded are shown by movements along a demand curve. Shifts in demand are shown by a shift of the entire demand curve. (41)**

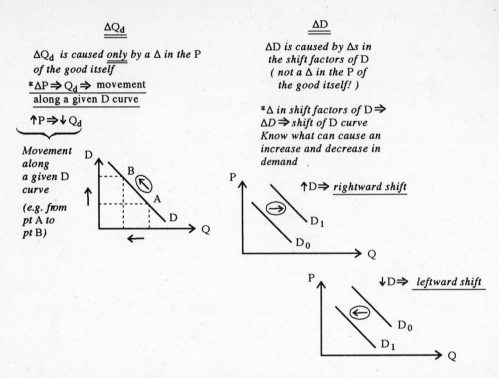

$\underline{\underline{\Delta Q_d}}$

ΔQ_d *is caused* only *by a* Δ *in the P of the good itself*

*$\Delta P \Rightarrow Q_d \Rightarrow$ movement along a given D curve

$\uparrow P \Rightarrow \downarrow Q_d$

Movement along a given D curve

(e.g. from pt A to pt B)

$\underline{\underline{\Delta D}}$

ΔD *is caused by* Δs *in the shift factors of D (not a* Δ *in the P of the good itself!)*

*Δ in shift factors of D $\Rightarrow$ $\Delta D \Rightarrow$ shift of D curve Know what can cause an increase and decrease in demand

$\uparrow D \Rightarrow$ *rightward shift*

$\downarrow D \Rightarrow$ *leftward shift*

*Don't get this confused on the exam!

5. **The** <u>law of supply</u> **states that the quantity supplied of a good is directly related to the goods' price. (43)**

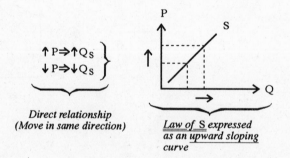

$\uparrow P \Rightarrow \uparrow Q_s$
$\downarrow P \Rightarrow \downarrow Q_s$

Direct relationship (Move in same direction)

<u>Law of</u> S *expressed as an* <u>upward sloping</u> *curve*

6. **To derive a supply curve from a supply table, you plot each point on the supply table on a graph and connect the points. (45)**

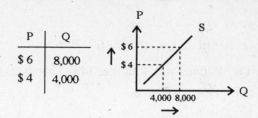

P	Q
$ 6	8,000
$ 4	4,000

7. **Just as with demand, it is important to distinguish between a shift in supply (a shift of the entire supply curve) and a movement along a supply curve (a change in the quantity supplied due to a change in price). (47)**

$\underline{\underline{\Delta Q_S}}$

ΔQ_S *is caused* <u>only</u> *by a* Δ *in the P of the good itself*

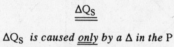

*$\Delta P \Rightarrow \Delta Q_S \Rightarrow$ <u>*Movement along the S curve*</u>

$\uparrow P \Rightarrow \uparrow Q_S$

Movement along a given S curve (e.g. from pt A to pt B)

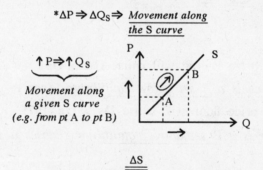

$\underline{\underline{\Delta S}}$

Δ *is caused by* Δs *in the shift factors of* S
(<u>*not*</u> *a* Δ *in the P of the good itself!*)

*Δ in shift factors of S $\Rightarrow \Delta s \Rightarrow$ *shift of S curve*
Know what can cause an increase and decrease in supply

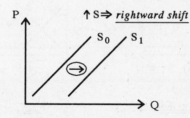

$\uparrow S \Rightarrow$ *rightward shift*

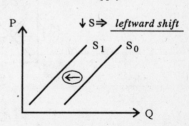

$\downarrow S \Rightarrow$ *leftward shift*

8. **The three dynamic laws of supply and demand are:**

1. If Qd > Qs ⇒ P increases (because of shortage)
    Qs > Qd ⇒ P decreases (because of surplus)

2. The larger is Qs − Qd, the faster P falls.
    The larger is Qd − Qs, the faster P rises.

3. If Qd = Qs, P does not change. (48) (because the market is in equilibrium)
    ① *If Qd > Qs ⇒ shortage ⇒ P will ↑*
    ② *If Qs > Qd ⇒ surplus ⇒ P will ↑*
    ③ *If Qd = Qs ⇒ equilibrium ⇒ no tendency for P to Δ (because there is neither a surplus nor a shortage)*

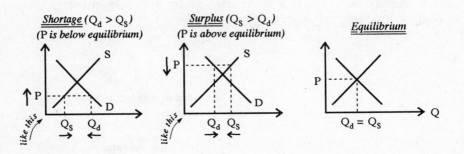

9. **An effective price ceiling will cause Qd > Qs.**

   P ceiling is a P set below equilibrium. (causes a shortage)

   An effective price floor will cause Qs > Qd. (57)

   P floor is a P set above equilibrium (causes a surplus)

ALSO NOTE:

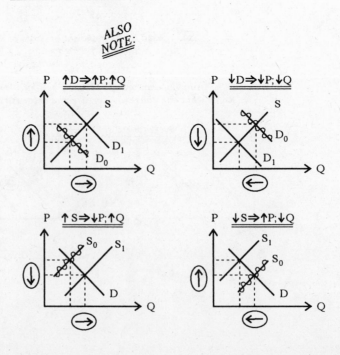

II. MASTERY TEST

1. Which of the following statements about the law of demand is false?

   a) Price and quantity demanded are inversely related.
   b) An increase in price results in a decrease in quantity demanded.
   c) A decrease in price results in a decrease in demand.
   d) The shift factors of demand are held constant.

2. Which of the following does not cause a change in quantity demanded?

   a) an increase in income   b) a decrease in price
   c) an increase in price   d) b and c

3. Which of the following is not an example of a change in demand?

   a) A decline in national income causes fewer sports cars to be purchased.
   b) The demand for steak increases as the outdoor grilling season begins.
   c) Higher price for beer results in less beer consumption.
   d) Lower production costs for soybeans causes increased production and purchases of soybeans.
   e) c and d

4. The law of supply states that as price increases

   a) sellers are motivated to produce more.
   b) supply increases.
   c) quantity supplied increases.
   d) supply decreases.
   e) a and c.

5. Which of the following is a shift factor of supply?

   a) a change in price
   b) a reduction in production costs
   c) higher family incomes
   d) government-imposed price ceilings
   e) a and b.

6. If demand for tennis rackets increases, which of the following is **not** likely to happen?

   a) Price increases.   b) Quantity supplied increases.
   c) Quantity demanded increases.   d) Supply decreases.

7. Which of the following indicates a change in supply?

   a) lower production costs result in increased production.
   b) movement along a particular supply curve
   c) higher prices result in increased production
   d) quantity supplied decreases as price decreases
   e) a and c

8. If demand for tennis rackets increases which of the following is likely to happen?

   a) The price of rackets increases.
   b) Quantity purchased increases.
   c) The racket demand curve shifts to the right.
   d) Quantity sold decreases.
   e) a, b, and c.

9. The demand for hot dog buns decreases today if

   a) Higher bun prices are expected at the end of the week..
   b) The price of hot dogs increases.
   c) New research proves hot dogs are a healthy food.
   d) Ketchup and mustard prices decline.
   e) a and b.

10. An increase in supply occurs when

   a) demand increases.
   b) price increases.
   c) production costs decrease.
   d) more buyers enter the market.
   e) c and d

11. If the supply of wheat increases

   a) the supply curve shifts to the right.
   b) the market price of wheat increases.
   c) the market quantity demanded of wheat increases.
   d) demand increases.
   e) a and c

12. If labour costs in the auto industry increase

   a) the demand for cars increases.
   b) the price of cars increases.
   c) fewer cars are bought and sold.
   d) quantity demanded for cars decreases.
   e) b, c, and d

13. An increase in taxes on Canadian whiskey results in

   a) higher price for Canadian whiskey.
   b) lower price for Canadian whiskey.
   c) lower price for Kentucky whiskey.
   d) decrease in demand for Canadian whiskey.
   e) c and d.

14. If between 1985 and 1995 the average price of hi-fi VCR's increases from $300 to $450 while the average price of high quality western boots increases from $100 to $200, then

   a) the relative price of boots increased compared to VCR's.
   b) the relative price of VCR's increased compared to boots.
   c) the relative prices of both goods increased.
   d) the relative prices of boots and VCR's did not change.

15. A government established price floor results in excess supply if

   a) the floor price is above equilibrium.
   b) quantity demanded is greater than quantity supplied.
   c) the price floor is below the equilibrium price.
   d) the floor price is equal to equilibrium price.
   e) a and b.

16. An increase in the market price and quantity of cotton occurs when there is a(n)

   a) increase in demand for cotton textiles.
   b) increase in the supply of cotton.
   c) decrease in the supply of cotton.
   d) increase in the demand and supply of cotton.
   e) a and d

17. An increase in the market price and decrease in market quantity of chocolate bars is expected when

   a) foreign sugar producers are restricted from selling in the domestic sugar market.
   b) foreign candy makers expand chocolate sales in the domestic market.
   c) domestic made chocolate becomes popular abroad leading to increased foreign purchases.
   d) health and fitness trends cause reduced domestic consumption of chocolate.
   e) a and b.

18. The market price of radial tires increases when

   a) demand for radial tires increases.
   b) labour costs in the tire industry increase.
   c) the price of rubber decreases at the same time that demand for automobiles decreases.
   d) a and b
   e) a, b, and c

19. The market quantity for beer most likely increases when

   a) beer demand increases and beer supply increases simultaneously.
   b) beer demand decreases and beer supply decreases simultaneously.
   c) beer demand increases and beer supply decreases simultaneously.
   d) beer demand decreases and beer supply increases simultaneously.
   e) a, c, and d

20. If demand for and supply of ice cream makers increases at the same time, what will happen in the market for ice cream makers?

   a) Price increases.
   b) Quantity increases.
   c) Price increases and quantity decreases.
   d) Price increases and quantity decreases.

Refer to the following table to respond to items #21 through #25.

Price	Quantity demanded	Quantity supplied
$3.00	5345	12175
2.75	5519	10695
2.50	5775	10005
2.25	6125	9662
2.00	7089	9443
1.75	9952	8768

21. Excess quantity supplied occurs at a price of

    a) $3.00
    b) $2.50
    c) $2.25
    d) $2.00
    e) a, b, c, and d

22. Excess quantity demanded will result from a government imposed price floor at

    a) $3.50
    b) $3.00
    c) $2.00
    d) $1.50
    e) a, b, c, and d

23. Equilibrium price is

    a) $2.25
    b) greater than $2.25
    c) less than $2.25
    d) less than $1.75
    e) c and d

24. Equilibrium quantity is

    a) 7089
    b) 9952
    c) more than 7089
    d) less than 8768
    e) c and d

25. At which price would a price ceiling create a shortage?

    a) $5.00
    b) $2.50
    c) $2.00
    d) $1.50
    e) None of the preceding

III. SHORT ANSWER EXERCISES AND PROBLEMS

a. **Short Answer Exercises**

1. What is the "law of demand"?

2. What is the "law of supply"?

3. Evaluate the scenarios that follow by selecting the appropriate phrase listed below.

   Decrease in supply   Decrease in quantity supplied
   Increase in supply   Increase in quantity supplied

   a) Rising hog prices encourage Manitoba pork producers to raise more pigs. (the market for hogs)

   b) Higher feed costs force cattle producers to reduce their livestock herds. (the market for cattle)

   c) Improvement in technology reduces the cost of producing high-speed computer chips. (market for personal computers)

   d) The tax on beer production increases $1.00 per six pack. (market for beer)

   e) Low wages discourage educators from seeking employment in elementary schools. (market for elementary school educators)

f) Growing negative attitude towards public education discourages qualified people from seeking employment as public school teachers. (market for public school educators)

4. Evaluate the scenarios that follow by selecting the appropriate phrase listed below.

Increase in demand   Increase in quantity demanded
Decrease in demand   Decrease in quantity demanded

a) Because of below zero temperature and very little snowfall during winter, snowmobiling does not attract much interest. (market for snowmobiles)

b) Plummeting air-fare prices cause a boom in airline ticket purchases. (market for airline tickets)

c) Because an increase in gasoline taxes are scheduled to kick in next week, drivers are filling up this week. (market for gasoline this week)

d) Poor growing conditions reduce the wheat crop causing the price of wheat to increase. (market for bread)

e) An outcome of the expanded popularity of compact disks is that an increased number of new auto buyers order CD players in their new cars. (market for car CD players)

5. Evaluate the scenarios that follow in terms of what happens to price and quantity in the marketplace. Identify whether the scenario can be described as a shift factor of demand or as a shift factor of supply. Then determine whether appropriate curve shifts in or out. Determine if price increases or decreases and if quantity increases or decreases.

a) New air pollution restrictions imposed on power lawnmowers increases their production costs. (market for lawnmowers)

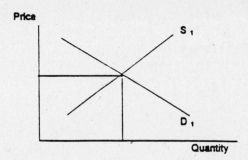

b) The World Cup soccer games are held in Canada which increases the popularity of the sport and the number of leagues, teams and participants. (market for soccer balls)

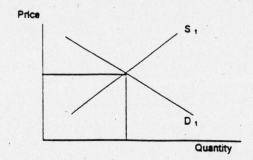

c) OPEC cuts its oil production by 25% causing oil prices to rise. (market for gasoline)

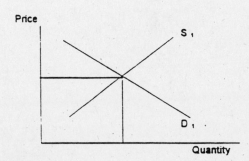

d) A $100-per-unit tax will be imposed next month on VCRs (market for VCRs in Canada this month)

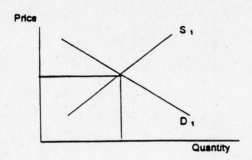

6. Assume the price of gasoline has increased 25% during the last five years. In that same time period assume the average price of all other goods and services has increased by 50%. Use the concept of relative price to explain how the price of gasoline has changed compared to the average price of all other goods.

b. **Problems**

1. Use the demand and supply data in the table below to plot demand and supply curves in the graph to the right of the table.

Price	Q$_d$	Q$_s$
$500	100	500
$400	200	400
$300	300	300
$200	400	200
$100	500	100

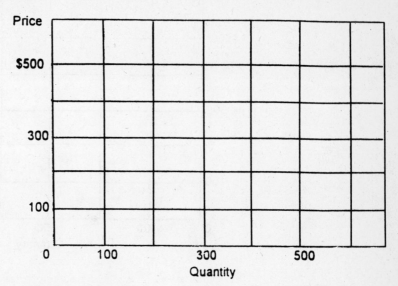

a) What are equilibrium price and quantity?

b) At a price of $200 what is the quantity demanded? . . . the quantity supplied?

c) What does one of the "dynamic laws" predict will happen at the $200 price?

d) At what price will an excess supply occur? What will happen to price?

2. Reproduce the demand and supply curves you derived in #1 above in the graph below.

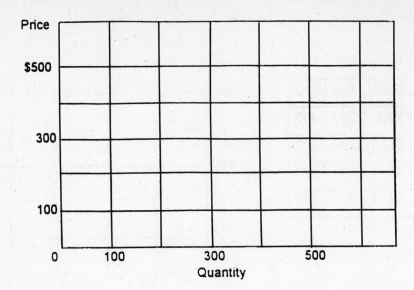

a) Pretend the graph above represents the market for mid level quality cassette decks. Say the price of compact disk players increases substantially because that market becomes dominated by a few sellers. How does that event affect the market for cassette players? Illustrate the impact on your model.

b) What happens to the demand for cassette decks?

c) What happens to quantity supplied?

d) What happens to market price and quantity?

3. Again, reproduce the demand and supply curves you derived in #1 above in the graph below.

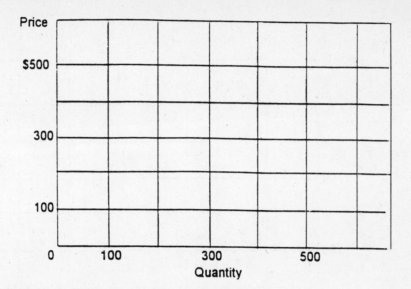

a) Assume a tax of $50 is levied by government on the production of cassette decks. Illustrate the impact of the tax by shifting the appropriate curve on the model.

b) What happens to supply?

c) What happens to quantity demanded?

d) What happens to market price and market quantity?

4. Reproduce the demand and supply curves you derived in #1 above in the graph below. Label the demand curve D_1 and the supply curve S_1. Add the demand curve from #2 above and label it D_2. Add the supply curve from #3 above and label it S_2.

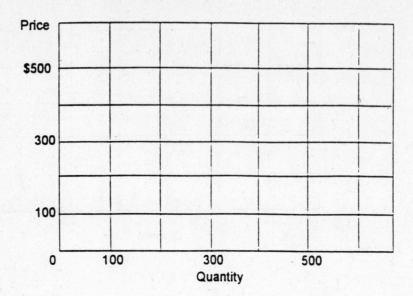

a) Compare the intital equilibrium price and quantity (D_1, S_1) with the final equilibrium price and quantity (D_2, S_2).

b) Why is the final price greater than the original price?

c) Given an increase in demand with a decrease in supply, will the outcome for quantity always be as you modeled it?

IV. CHALLENGE PROBLEMS AND POTENTIAL ESSAY QUESTIONS

a. Challenge Problems

1. Correct the following statements, if needed, so that there is correct usage of the terms "demand," "quantity demanded," "supply," and "quantity supplied."

   a) As the price of pizza increases, consumers demand less pizza.

   b) Whenever the price of bicycles increases, the supply of bicycles increases.

   c) The price of electricity is cheaper in the northwestern part of Canada and therefore the demand for electricity is greater in the northwest.

   d) An increase in incomes of car buyers will increase the quantity demanded for cars.

   e) An increase in the quantity demanded of lobsters means consumers are willing and able to buy more lobsters at any price—whatever the current price is.

   f) A decrease in the supply of frog legs means suppliers will provide fewer frog—whatever the current price is.

Use demand and supply curves to analyze each of the following problems. Always start by drawing demand and supply curves for the item under investigation. Recall that "price" (or P) is placed on the vertical (or Y) axis and the "quantity" (or Q) is placed on the horizontal (or X) axis. Indicate the initial market equilibrium price and quantity on your graph (found at the point of intersection between the original demand and supply curves). Then proceed by figuring out whether demand or supply (or possibly both) will be affected by the information provided in the problem (only deal with the information given! . . .especially on an exam!). Will it increase or decrease the curve(s)? Express the change in demand and/or supply graphically and then find the new equilibrium price and quantity (found at the new point of intersection between the new relevant demand and/or supply curves). Finally, compare the old equilibrium price and quantity with the new price and quantity bought and sold. In this way you are able to use demand and supply analysis to predict what will happen to the equilibrium price and quantity in a market given some information (you will be required to do some of this on the exam.) It can be fun! Go for it!

2. What impact will each of the following events have on the market for surfboards in Southern California:

   a) Southern California experiences unusually high temperatures, sending an unusually large number of people to its beaches.

   b) Large sharks are reported feeding near the beaches of Southern California.

   c) Due to the large profits earned by surfboard producers there is a significant increase in the number of producers of surfboards.

   d) There is a significant increase in the price of epoxy paint used to coat surfboards.

3. Suppose there has been a recent outcry by local citizens about the high cost of rental occupied housing culminating in a large demonstration outside City Hall. The mayor and a majority of the city council members pledged that something will be done about the problem. As a result, the city government imposes rent controls—a limit on how high rent may be set by landlords. These rent controls effect virtually all rental occupied housing in the city. While shopping at the local mall, you are chosen at random to be interviewed by TV 5's "Action news" team. You are asked: "What is your assessment of the rent controls recently legislated by our city government?" Respond using demand and supply analysis.

4. The law of supply asserts that an increase in price will increase the quantity supplied, and a decrease in price will decrease the quantity supplied. Yet, during the last decade or so, the prices of electronics products (such as VCRs, personal computers and calculators) have fallen (VCRs alone have fallen from about $800 to $300), while during the same period of time the quantity sold has increased substantially. Is the observed lower price and greater quantity supplied (and purchased) in the electronics market an exception to the law of supply, or have there been some changes in demand and supply which could account for this? (Hint: there has been a simultaneous increase in both production technology and the number of buyers willing and able to purchase these products.)

b. **Potential Essay Questions**

1. We are all aware of the rising cost of medical care. How can the fact that we are living longer and the fact that our incomes as consumers of medical care have been rising help account for the rising price we must pay for health care?

2. As our nation becomes more environmentally conscious we will likely pass more laws requiring manufacturers to install costly anti-pollution devices to reduce the amount of air and water pollution associated with their production processes. What effect might this have on the prices we must pay for those goods produced in these industries?

3. Many University campuses sell parking permits to their students allowing them to park on campus in designated areas. Although most students complain about the relatively high cost of these parking permits, what annoys many students even more is that after having paid for their permits, vacant parking spaces in the designated lots are very difficult to find during much of the day. Many end up having to park off campus anyway, where permits are not required. Assuming the University is unable to build new parking facilities on campus due to insufficient funds, what recommendation might you make to remedy the problem of students with permits being unable to find places to park on campus?

V. ANSWERS

II. Mastery Test

1. c	6. d	11. e	16. a	21. e
2. a	7. a	12. e	17. a	22. d
3. c	8. e	13. a	18. d	23. c
4. e	9. b	14. a	19. a	24. c
5. b	10. c	15. a	20. b	25. d

III. Short Answer Exercises and Problems

a. **Short Answer Exercises**

1. Price and quantity demanded are inversely related, ceteris paribus. That is, demand expresses the willingness and ability of a buyer or buyers to purchase a specific good or service at various prices in a set time period, holding shift factors constant.

2. Price and quantity supplied are directly related, ceteris paribus. Supply expresses the willingness and ability of a seller or sellers to provide a given good or service at various prices in a set time period, holding shift factors constant.

3. a) quantity supplied increases.
   b) supply decreases.
   c) supply increases.
   d) supply decreases.
   e) quantity supplied decreases.
   f) supply decreases.

4. a) demand decreases
   b) quantity demanded increases
   c) demand increases
   d) quantity demanded decreases
   e) demand increases

5. a) Shift factor of supply: Supply decreases, price increases.
   b) Shift factor of demand. Demand increases, price increases, quantity demanded increases.
   c) Shift factor of supply. Supply decreases, price increases, quantity demanded decreases.
   d) Shift factor of supply. Supply decreases, price increases, quantity demanded decreases.

6. The price of gasoline has declined relative to the price of other goods. While the absolute price of gasoline has increased, the price of other goods has increased even more. This makes the relative price of gasoline lower than the price of other goods.

b. **Problems**

1.

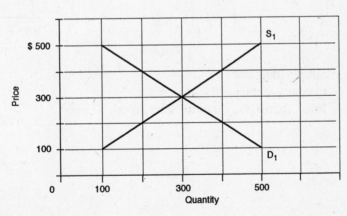

   a) $300 and 300 units
   b) Quantity demanded is 400 and quantity supplied is 200.
   c) At $200 there is excess demand and price will increase until equilibrium is restored.
   d) Excess supply occurs at any price greater than $300. Price tends to decrease when excess supply occurs.

2. a)

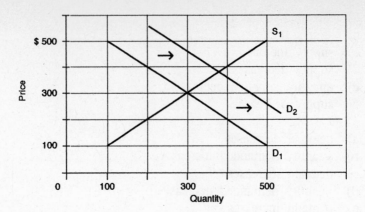

b) Demand increases
c) Quantity supplied increases
d) Price increases, quantity increases.

3. a)

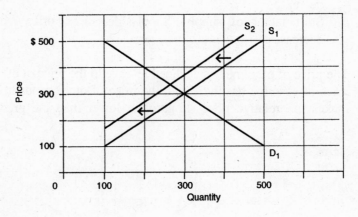

b) Supply decreases
c) Quantity demanded decreases
d) Price increases, quantity decreases

4.

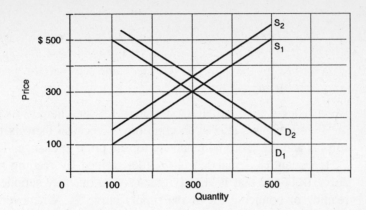

a) The final equilibrium price is higher than the original equilibrium price and the final equilibrium output may be higher, lower, or the same as the original equilibrium output.

b) An increase in demand (#1) increases market price. A decrease in supply (#2) increases market price. An increase in demand with a decrease in supply increases market price.

c) Depending on the relative strengths of the demand and supply shifts, final equilibrium quantity could be greater than, lesser than, or equal to the initial equilibrium quantity.

IV. **Challenge Problems and Potential Essay Questions**

a. **Challenge Problems**

1. a) As the price of pizza increases, the *quantity demanded* of pizza decreases.

   Note that a change in the price of an item will cause a change in the quantity demanded; not demand! A change in something else other than the price may cause a change in demand—such as a change in one of the shift factors of demand discussed in the book.

   b) Whenever the price of bicycles increases, the *quantity supplied* of bicycles increases.

   Note that a change in the price will cause a change in the quantity supplied; not supply! A change in something else other than the price may cause a change in supply—such as a change in one of the shift factors of supply discussed in the book.

   c) The price of electricity is cheaper in the northwestern part of the United States and therefore the Iquantity demanded of electricity is greater in the northwest.

   d) an increase in incomes of car buyers will increase the *demand* for cars.

   Notice that a change in a shift factor of demand, such as income, will change demand; not the quantity demanded!

   e) An increase in the *demand* for lobsters means consumers are willing and able to buy more lobsters at any price—whatever the current price is.

   Notice that in order for there to be an increase in the quantity demanded there would have to be a decrease in the price. Moreover, recall that an increase in demand is reflected as a rightward shift of the demand curve. Upon viewing a graph where the demand curve has shifted to the right you will see that more will be purchased at any given price.

f) This is a correct usage of the term "supply."

> *Note that a decrease in supply is reflected graphically as a leftward shift of the curve. Upon viewing a graph where the supply curve has shifted to the left you will see that less will be provided in the market at any given price.*

2. a) Always begin at an initial equilibrium price and quantity such as P_1 and Q_1 shown in the Figure below. This is an equilibrium because there is neither a shortage nor a surplus and therefore no tendency for the price to change. That is, when the price is P_1 the quantity demanded is Q_1 (determined by reading off the original demand curve D'1) and that is exactly equal to the quantity supplied of Q_1 (determined by reading or bouncing off of the supply curve S). Whenever the quantity demanded equals the quantity supplied ($Q_d = Q_s$), there is neither a shortage nor a surplus and therefore no tendency for the price to change—the market is in equilibrium.

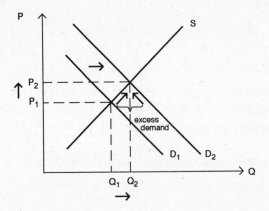

The hot weather will increase the demand for surfboards. This means consumers are willing and able to buy more surfboards at any price—whatever the current price is. An increase in demand is reflected as a rightward shift of the demand curve such as from D_1 to D_2. This increase in demand will create a temporary shortage. That is, there is excess demand (a shortage) illustrated by the horizontal distance by which the new demand curve D, lies to the right of the supply curve S *at the original price of P_1*.

This excess demand, or shortage at the original price of P_1 will be temporary because whenever a shortage exists there is an inherent tendency within all markets for the price to be competitively bid up by buyers. As the price rises, we know from the law of demand that the quantity demanded will fall (movement up along the new relevant demand curve D_2). Also, as the price rises, we know from the law of supply that the quantity supplied will rise (movement up along the supply curve S). When the price reaches P_2, there is no longer any excess demand (shortage) and therefore no longer any tendency for the price to rise.

Given the new demand curve D_2 and the supply curve S the new equilibrium price and quantity eventually becomes P_2 and Q_2. This is the new market equilibrium price and quantity because at P_2 there is neither a surplus (excess supply) nor a shortage (excess demand) and hence no tendency for the price to change.

In sum, an increase in demand will result in a higher equilibrium price and a greater equilibrium quantity.

When dealing with a change in D or S curves, just remember to go from the initial point of intersection between the curves to the new point of intersection. The initial point of intersection will give you the initial equilibrium P and Q and the new point of intersection will give you the new equilibrium P and Q. Then recall that if the price went up, it was a response to a temporary shortage (excess demand). If the equilibrium price went down, then it was a response to a temporary surplus (excess supply).

b) This would cause a decrease in the demand for surfboards—for sure! A decrease in demand means consumers are willing and able to purchase less at any current price and is reflected graphically as a leftward shift such as from D_1 to D_2 shown in the figure below.

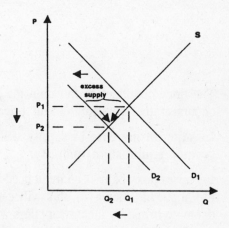

This decrease in demand creates a temporary surplus (or excess dupply) shown by the horizontal distance by which the supply curve lies beyond the new demand curve *at the original price of P_1*. Whenever a surplus (excess supply) exists there is an inherent tendency within all markets for the price to be competitively bid down by sellers (in order to rid themselves of their excess inventories, or excess production). As the price decreases the quantity demanded rises (movement down along the new relevant demand curve D_2) and the quantity supplied falls (movement down along the supply curve.) This process continues until the surplus is eliminated. The new equilibrium price and quantity eventually become P_2 and Q_2.

In sum, a decrease in demand will result in a lower equilibrium price and a smaller equilibrium quantity.

c) Because there are more producers there will be an increase in supply. You may recall that the market curve is simply the horizontal summation of all individual producer's supply curves. Well, an increase in the number of producers creates a greater quantity supplied at any price. A greater quantity supplied at any price means there is an increase in supply. This is reflected as a rightward shift such as from S_1 to S_2 shown in the figure on the next page. The excess supply at the original price (P_1) will cause the price to fall. *(Remember, whenever there is excess supply, or a surplus, the price will fall.)*

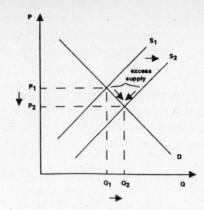

The price continues to fall until the excess supply (surplus) no longer exists. That occurs at the new equilibrium price and quantity P_2 and Q_2.

In sum, an increase in supply will result in a lower equilibrium price and a greater equilibrium quantity.

d) Because epoxy paint is an input used in the production of surfboards and the price of this input has increased, this will cause a decrease in the supply of surfboards. A decrease in supply means suppliers will make less available at any given price. This is reflected as a leftward shift of the supply curve such as from S_1 to S_2 shown in the figure below. A temporary shortage (excess demand) will exist at the original price causing the price to rise in the market. *(Remember, whenever there is excess demand, or a shortage, the price will rise.)* The new equilibrium becomes P_2 and Q_2.

In sum, a decrease in supply will result in a higher equilibrium price and a smaller equilibrium quantity.

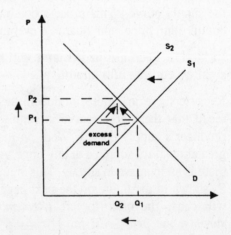

3. You are not the least bit bothered by the fact that possibly millions of viewers may be watching you on the evening news because you are crazy about economics and love to discuss economic matters whenever possible. You quickly recall that rent controls are simply an example of a price ceiling. Moreover, you recall that a price ceiling is a government-imposed limit on how high a price may be set. If it is to have any impact at all, a price ceiling is set below the price which would otherwise prevail in the market (called the equilibrium price). (A price ceiling is set below equilibrium; a price floor, or support, is set above equilibrium—it may help to think of this as an upside-down house.) Because the price ceiling is set below the equilibrium, or market-clearing level, it will create a shortage (excess demand) every time—and the shortage will persist for as long as the price ceiling is in existence. You also have a visual image of a price ceiling, and its consequences firmly in mind, similar to that illustrated in the figure below. You're ready! You respond:

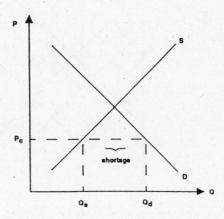

"Rent controls may be beneficial to those who are able to find a place to rent—at least for awhile. However, rent controls will create a shortage of rental units. At the relatively lower rental rates the quantity of rental occupied housing people wish to rent (*the quantity demanded*) will exceed the quantity of rental occupied housing landlords will put up for rent (*the quantity supplied*). That is, there will be a shortage of rental-occupied housing in our city because of the rent-controls. It will simply make it more difficult for many people to find places to rent in the first place."

You add:

"Moreover, over time because of population growth the demand for rental housing will increase. At the same time, many landlords will likely not keep their rental units in good shape because of the relatively low rents they must accept. Indeed, low rents received by landlords will likely result in a decrease in rental-occupied housing made available over time *(decrease in supply)*. These combined effects *(increase in demand and decrease in supply)* will create an even more acute shortage of rental-occupied housing over time."

The reporter barks: "You must be a landlord!" And you're abruptly cut off. Oh well. . .

4. What has happened in the electronics market is not an exception to the law of supply. There has been an increase in production technology which has increased supply. At the same time there has been an increase in the demand for these goods as more people have become interested in buying them. (There likely have been other changes as well.) However, the increase in supply (which has a tendency to reduce price) must have been greater than the increase in the demand (which has a tendency to increase price) in order for the equilibrium price to have fallen. Note also that an increase in demand and supply both have a tendency to increase the amount bought and sold. Therefore, the new equilibrium price is lower while the equilibrium quantity is greater.

All this is illustrated in the figure below. We started with the demand and supply curves D_1 and S_1. The new demand and supply curves are D_2 and S_2. Notice the lower price and greater quantity.

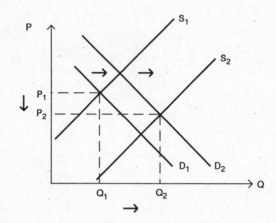

b. **Potential Essay Questions**

The following answers are annotated—they only indicate the general idea behind the answer.

1. This creates greater demand and therefore a higher price.

2. This will increase the costs of production in these industries. That decreases the supply of the affected products, increasing their prices and decreasing their equilibrium quantities.

3. The shortage of parking spaces implies that permit prices are below equilibrium. The price of a permit should be increased. At least with the purchase of a permit you could be reasonably certain that a space would be available.

Chapter 3   The Economic Organization of Society

I. CHAPTER AT A GLANCE

Rip this page out for quick and easy reference.

1. **The three main questions an economist must ask: (62)**

    a) *What to produce.*

    Try to produce that combo which most satisfies society.

    b) *How to produce it.*

    Try to be efficient.

    c) *For whom to produce it.*

    Who gets what and how much?

    *Exactly how they're answered depends on the relative influences of the three invisible forces.

2. a) **Capitalism** **is an economic system based on private property and the market. It gives private property rights to individuals, and relies on market forces to coordinate economic activity. (63)**

    Capitalism characterized by:

    (I) Mainly private ownership over resources
    (II) Market system answers the what? how? and for whom? questions

    Socialism **is an economic system that tries to organize society in the same way as do most families, all people should contribute what they can, and get what they need. (64)**

    Socialism—characterized by:

    (I) Government control over resources
    (II) Government answers the what? how? and for whom? questions

    **All real world economies have elements of both capitalism and socialism.

3. a) **Capitalism's answers to the central economic questions: (66)**

    1. *What to produce: what businesses believe people want, and is profitable.*

    2. *How to produce: businesses decide how to produce efficiently, guided by their desire to make a profit.*

    3. *For whom to produce: distribution according to individuals' ability to pay and/or inherited wealth.*

    b) **Soviet-style socialism's answers to the three questions: (66)**

    1. *What to produce: what central planners believe is socially beneficial.*

    2. *How to produce: central planners decide, based on what they think is good for the country.*

    3. *For whom to produce: central planners distribute goods based on what they determine are individuals' needs.*

4. a) Economic systems evolve because the institutions of the new system offer a better life for at least some and usually a large majority of the individuals in a society. (68)

    All economic systems are constantly evolving

   b) Feudalism evolved into mercantilism because markets and the development of money allowed trade to expand, which undermined the traditional base of feudalism. Tradition that can be bought and sold is no longer tradition it's just another commodity. (69)

    Feudalism ⇒ rule of the invisible handshake
    Mercantilism ⇒ rule of the invisible foot

   c) Mercantilism evolved into capitalism because the Industrial Revolution undermined the craft-guided mercantilist method of production. Machines produced goods cheaper and faster, making industrialists rich. They used their economic power to change the political support for mercantilism. (71)

    Capitalism ⇒ rule of the invisible hand

5. Markets coordinate economic activity by turning self-interest into social good (at least that's the idea). Competition directs individuals pursuing profit to do what society needs to have done. (71)

    Unbridled, pure or laisses-faire capitalism led to many abuses. This created support for at least some socialism.

    *We now have "Welfare Capitalism"—a mix of capitalism and socialism

6. Socialism was an attempt to bring out people's social conscience, rather than their self-interest. Many of the countries that attempted to introduce socialism have recently reverted to capitalism. (75)

    Some "appropriate" mix of socialism and capitalism is what all societies are searching for.

II. MASTERY TEST

1. Which of the following is not an example of an economic system?

   a) democracy   b) mercantilism   c) socialism   d) capitalism

2. Capitalism is characterized by

   a) private property rights.
   b) democracy.
   c) equal distribution of income.
   d) autocracy.
   e) a and b

3. Socialism is an economic system that answers economic questions

   a) by tradition.
   b) with state subsidies of private firms.
   c) by government planning.
   d) without involving government.
   e) b and c

4. In socialist societies, central planners decide

   a) resource allocation.   b) production techniques.
   c) income distributrion.   d) a, b, and c

5. In what respect does communism differ from pure communism?

   a) Pure communism makes some use of markets.
   b) Communism has never actually existed.
   c) Pure communism does not require government.
   d) Communism makes use of democratic political institutions.
   e) c and d

6. In feudal society, economic decisons were primarily influenced by

   a) *The Invisible Handshake.*   b) *The Invisible Hand.*
   c) *The Invisible Foot.*   d) merchants.

7. Central economic questions in feudal society were handled mostly by

   a) tradition.   b) planning.
   c) markets.   d) welfare capitalism.

8. Under mercantilism, the effect merchants had on central economic questions was

   a) unimportant
   b) important but subservient to political authority.
   c) important in answering what and how but not for whom.
   d) to undermine the authority of monarchs and to empower local political officials.
   e) b, c, and d

9. Under capitalism, economic coordination is provided for by

    a) *The Invisible Handshake.*   b) *The Invisible Foot.*
    c) *The Invisible Hand.*   d) government.

10. *The Wealth of Nations* describes how economic coordination is accomplished by

    a) markets.
    b) central planners.
    c) state socialism.
    d) welfare capitalism.
    e) a and d

11. Karl Marx argued that the transition to the ideal society would follow stages in the order:

    a) socialism, capitalism, socialism.
    b) capitalism, welfare capitalism, socialism.
    c) feudalism, capitalism, socialism.
    d) feudalism, state socialism, pure communism.
    e) feudalism, mercantilism, state socialism, pure communism.

12. Economic decision making under welfare capitalism is not influenced by

    a) capitalists.
    b) government.
    c) the proletariat.
    d) pressure groups
    e) none of the above is accurate.

13. Joseph Stalin's contribution to answering central economic questions in a socialist society was

    a) his model for pure communism.
    b) the initiation of worker democracy in factories.
    c) centralized planning.
    d) allowing markets to develop for agricultural goods.

14. The current trend in Eastern Europe for answering central questions is

    a) toward increased use of markets.
    b) away from marketplace decision making.
    c) the expansion of state socialism.
    d) experiments with pure communism
    e) b, c, and d

15. According to the textbook, the **best** way to describe the current state of affairs in the world economy is

    a) capitalism has triumphed over socialism.
    b) welfare capitalism is the final stage of economic development.
    c) neo mercantilism is the economic wave of the future.
    d) markets offer the best hope for countries in transition from socialism.
    e) none of the above.

16. During the 1700's and 1800's western society increasingly was characterized by

    a) industrial revolution.
    b) capitalism.
    c) democracy.
    d) socialism.
    e) a, b, and c

17. The revolution Marx predicted did not come about largely because

    a) people prefer a rising standard of living to political democracy.
    b) of the development of welfare capitalism.
    c) people prefer state socialism to communism.
    d) first World War I and then World War II disrupted the movement towards proletariat unity.

18. Which of the following is not a characteristic of mercantilism?

    a) *The Invisible Foot*
    b) Political forces control economic decision making
    c) Limited competition and monopoly protection
    d) Reduction of markets and suppression of trading activity.
    e) c and d

19. Relying upon the *Invisible Hand* for economic decision making does not preclude a role for government in the economic decision making because

    a) government is needed to protect property rights.
    b) pollution must be restricted in order to prevent environmental problems.
    c) income redistribution must take place to avoid impoverishing a segment of the population.
    d) a, b, and c
    e) None of the above is necessary.

20. In order for a market economy to function it is necessary that _____ be established and protected.

    a) private property rights.
    b) democracy.
    c) welfare capitalism.
    d) a and b
    e) a, b, and c

III. SHORT ANSWER EXERCISES AND PROBLEMS

a. Short Answer Exercises

   1. What does NIMBY stand for? What does it mean?

2. What is the difference between an autocracy and a democracy? Does the difference have anything to do with economic systems?

3. How does welfare capitalism differ from plain, old fashioned capitalism?

4. What is the difference between communism and pure communism?

IV. CHALLENGE PROBLEMS AND POTENTIAL ESSAY QUESTIONS

a. Challenge Problems

1. How does capitalism (a market-oriented economy) answer the fundamental economic questions of "what to produce," "how to produce it," and "for whom to produce?" How efficient is the market-oriented economy?

In the first chapter we looked at (among other things) the fact that the three invisible forces of the market (the invisible hand), society (the invisible handshake) and politics (the invisible foot) interact to determine what actually takes place in an economy (page 18). We also examined the differences in positive and normative economic analysis (page 24) and the difference between "what is" versus "what ought to be." Moreover, we examined benefit/cost analysis—rational decision making (page 6).

In Chapter Two considerable effort was exerted on your part in learning how market forces function (positive economics). In this chapter, the normative elements of "what ought to be" as expressed by society and politics (governments) have been more thoroughly introduced and we have seen that the market forces of capitalism are not always allowed to play themselves out. In other words, the invisible handshake (social forces) and the invisible foot (political forces) also play a role in any economy in determining what gets produced, how things are produced and who gets them. Keep these dynamic forces in mind when answering the remaining questions.

2. We know that all real-world economies in the Western world are characterized as "Welfare Capitalist" states. These are economies in which market forces dominate but where government exerts a significant influence over what is produced, how goods are produced and for whom they're produced. What has prompted these economies to move away from "pure capitalism" to "welfare capitalism"? That is, what problems exist within economies where market forces alone are allowed to dominate that have caused citizens within these countries to pursue government involvement and the adoption of at least some degree of "socialism" within their economies?

3. There has always been much political debate between "conservatives" and "liberals" in this country, as well as in other countries, over what constitutes the "appropriate" role for government to play in correcting the problems of a market-oriented, capitalist economy.

Why is this controversy not likely to ever go away?

4. What can help explain why some European countries like Norway, Sweden, Germany and France have opted for more governmental influence over economic affairs than has Canada?

b. **Potential Essay Questions**

1. What were Karl Marx's arguments for the eventual downfall of capitalism and the birth of socialism? In what ways was he correct and in what ways was he incorrect?

2. Winston Churchill once said about democracy: ''. . . its the worst form of government . . . except for all others.'' Could a similar statement be made about modern capitalism?

3. In what ways is the Canadian economy characterized as a ''Welfare State.''

4. What are the likely consequences of government-determined prices such as those determined in a Soviet-style economy?

V. ANSWERS

II. **Mastery Test**

1. a	6. a	11. c	16. e
2. a	7. a	12. e	17. b
3. c	8. b	13. c	18. d
4. d	9. c	14. a	19. d
5. c	10. a	15. e	20. a

III. **Short Answer Exercises and Problems**

a. **Short Answer Exercises**

1. NIMBY stands for ''not in my back yard.'' It refers to the reluctance of citizens to have their neighborhood and communities be the locale for dumps, toxic waste facilities, and other resting places for the effluent of an industrial economy. While we all enjoy the fruits of the modern economy, we tend not to want to live near the peels and pits.

2. A democracy is rule by an enfranchised electorate in society, generally a broad based one. An autocracy is ruled by a special group in society, generally a narrowly defined one. Capitalism characterizes the economies of autocracies and democracies while socialism is primarily associated with autocratic rule.

3. Welfare capitalism requires that government play a role in modifying and amelliorating the undesirable traits of old fashioned capitalism.

4. Communism requires governance (In Marx's terms, ''the dictatorship of the proletariat). Pure communism alleges that humanity will transcend the need for governing bodies.

IV. Challenge Problems and Potential Essay Questions

a. Challenge Problems

1. "What to produce" is determined by consumer demand. If consumers want more of a product then demand rises, the equilibrium quantity rises (they get more of the product) and more of our nation's resources are devoted to the product. The opposite is also true. Capitalism is very different in this regard.

   "How to produce it" is determined by competitive forces in the market. When competition prevails it ensures that the most efficient, least-cost method of production is used to make the product available at the cheapest possible price.

   "For whom is it being produced" is determined by the disbribution of income. Because it takes money to buy products then those with more money get more products.

   The capitalist system is very efficient in fulfilling demand based on dollar votes cast in the marketplace. It is more efficient than any other economic system. But it is not perfectly efficient. Nevertheless, whether it is "fair" (or "just") is debatable.

2. There is no debate over the existence of some problems or "market failures" associated with *pure* capitalism. However, reasonable people do disagree over the *extent* to which these probems exist, and therefore the *extent* to which government involvement is appropriate in attempting to correct for these problems. Commonly cited problems include:

   a) *The growth of monopoly power.* (demise of competition), wherever it exists, results in less being produced (and therefore fewer jobs) at higher prices, as well as a socially undesirable redistribution of income.

   b) *A misallocation of a nation's scarce resources results in some products being overproduced while others are underproduced.* Overproduced (underproduced) products are those which have undesirable (desirable) social side-effects associated with their production and/or consumption. If the private plus social costs exceed the private plus social benefits then it's overproduced. For example, products which give rise to pollution are overproduced if we do not take into account the social costs.

   c) *A lack of public goods and services.* Some goods and services are either not produced at all, or are "grossly" underproduced by private industry.

   d) *An inequitable ("unfair") distribution of income.* The free enterprise system can give rise to a concentration of wealth and income into the hands of a relatively few.

   e) *Macroeconomic instability.* The presence of the business cycle gives rise to socially and politically unacceptable high rates of inflation during the expansionary phases and high rates of unemployment and low rates of economic growth during the recessionary phases of the business cycle.

3. Although there is no debate over the existence of market failures there is much debate over the *extent* to which they exist. Controversy often begins with equally reasonable and well intentioned people assessing the extent of the problem differently. (For example, consider the controversy surrounding the extent of O-Zone damage.) If a consensus is reached, then the same equally reasonable, equally well intentioned people will likely measure the benefits and costs associated with government involvement differently. This gives rise to debate concerning the appropriate extent of government involvement.

4. Most nations have been less reluctant to use government to address market failures. But remember, what happens in all societies can be seen as a reaction to and interaction among the invisible hand (economic forces), the invisible foot (political forces), and the invisible handshake (social and historical forces). Although the invisible hand operates the same everywhere, the other invisible forces are unique to each nation.

b. **Potential Essay Questions**

The following answers are annotated—they only indicate the general idea behind the answer.

1. Karl Marx argued that capitalism would "sow the seeds of its own destruction." The capitalists would gain increasing control over the means of production through the growth of monopolies. They would create a contrived cutback in production—an artificial scarcity to drive their prices and profits up still further. Along with redistributing income and wealth into the hands of the capitalists this would also create some unemployment which would help depress wages and therefore the capitalists' labour costs. But, eventually this "army of the unemployed" (the proletariat) would rise up and overthrow the capitalists from power and create a socialist state.

   Karl Marx was correct in pointing out and predicting the serious abuses of unbridled capitalism. He was incorrect in the overthrowing of the capitalist state because capitalist governments stepped in and reduced or abolished some of the more severe abuses before things got out of hand.

2. Yes. although there exist some problems within modern capitalist states, which have been alleviated to some degree by governmental intervention, these problems are dwarfed in comparison to the problems found in Soviet-style socialist economies.

3. Because of its attempts at alleviating the problems associated with pure capitalism.

4. Government determined prices will likely result in shortages of some products and surpluses of others. This is because the market forces of demand and supply are always operating but not allowed to prevail when prices are set by government instead.

Chapter 4   Canadian Economic Institutions

I. CHAPTER AT A GLANCE

Rip this page out for quick and easy reference.

1. **For a bird's-eye view of the Canadian economy see Exhibit 2 on page 82 of the textbook. (80)**

   *Be able to draw and explain Exhibit 2.

   3 Basic economic institutions

   1) *Business*
      a) *S (supply) goods in goods market*
      b) *D (demand) factors in factors market*
      c) *Pay taxes and receive benefits from gov't.*

   2) *Households:*

      a) *S factors*
      b) *D goods*
      c) *Pay taxes and receive benefits from gov't.*

   3) *Government*

      a) *D goods*
      b) *D factors*
      c) *Collect taxes and provide services*

2. **Although businesses decide what to produce, they are guided by consumer sovereignty. (84)**

   Businesses produce what consumers demand.

3. a) **The five largest industries in Canada are: (85)**

      1. *Services*
      2. *Manufacturing*
      3. *Finance, insurance, and real estate*
      4. *Trade*
      5. *Government*

      Knowing which industries are growing lets us know where the jobs are.

   b) **A useful way to learn about the economy is to trace the path of a product from raw material to final product. (85)**

      *Distribution costs account for a large % of total costs.

4. <u>**The advantages and disadvantages of the three forms of business**</u> **are shown in the table on page 89. (89)**

   1) *Sole Proprietorship*
   2) *Partnership*
   3) *Corporation*

5. **Although, in principle, ultimate power resides with the people and households (consumer sovereignty), in practice the representatives of the people—firms and government—are sometimes removed from the people and, in short run, are only indirectly monitored by the people. (96)**

    1) Do we control business and gov't, or do they control us?

    2) The distribution of income (rich or poor) determines For whom?

    3) The invisible handshake effects what business and gov'ts do, or don't do.

6. a) **Two general roles of government are: (94)**

    1. as a referee.

    Sets the rules governing relations between households and government.

    2. as an actor.

    Collects taxes and spends money.

  b) **Seven specific roles of government are: (96)**

    1. Providing a stable structure within which markets can operate.

    What the government rules ought to be debatable.

    2. Promoting workable, effective competition.

    Know the different consequences associated with competition vs. monopoly power.

    3. Correcting for external effects of individuals' decisions.

    Know the distinction between <u>positive</u> vs. <u>negative</u> externalities and how gov't tries to correct for them.

    4. Providing public goods that the market doesn't adequately supply.

    Gov't provides these by collecting taxes from everyone to try to eliminate the free-rider problem.

    5. Ensuring economic stability and growth.

    Gov't tries to ensure: 1) Full employment
                                  2) Low inflation
                                    3) Economic growth ($\uparrow$s standard of living)

    6. Providing acceptably fair distribution of society's production among its individuals.

    To redistribute money and therefore goods the gov't uses taxes (and other methods)

    *Know the difference between progressive, regressive, and proportional taxes.

    7. Encouraging merit and discouraging demerit goods or activities.

    Should government decide what is "good" or "bad" for us?

    —government may:

    1) <u>subsidize merit</u> (socially desirable goods)
    2) <u>tax demerit</u> goods

    **#1–#5 are economic roles (less controversial)
       #6 and #7 are political roles

II. MASTERY TEST

1. The type of business with the largest percentage of private sector employment is

   a) manufacturing.
   b) finance, insurance, and real estate.
   c) services.
   d) wholesale and retail trade.

2. In terms of receipts, which business form is the largest?

   a) sole proprietorship
   b) partnership
   c) corporation
   d) entrepreneurship

3. The highest rate of incidence of low income occurs in which kind of family?

   a) single with no children.
   b) male lone-parent.
   c) married couple.
   d) female lone-parent.

4. A post-industrial society is one in which

   a) services supplant manufacturing as the primary economic activity
   b) the public sector supplants the private sector as the primary source of economic activity.
   c) a country imports manufactured goods and exports services.
   d) retailers and wholesalers operate between primary producers and consumers.

5. The fastest growing sector for employment is

   a) agriculture.
   b) manufacturing.
   c) construction.
   d) service.

6. The form of business enterprise in which the ownership interest(s) has unlimited liability for business debt is a

   a) sole proprietorship.
   b) partnership.
   c) corporation.
   d) cooperative
   e) a and b

7. The form of business enterprise in which the firm has a legal identity separate from its owner(s) is a

   a) sole proprietorship.
   b) partnership.
   c) corporation.
   d) cooperative.

8. The form of business enterprise in which the business decision making is separate from ownership of the business is

   a) sole proprietorship.
   b) partnership.
   c) corporation.
   d) cooperative.
   e) a, b, c and d

9. Which of the following statements about consumer sovereignty is accurate?

   a) Labour unions reduce the leverage households have over business.
   b) Households dictate to business and government.
   c) Government and business influence household consumption decisions.
   d) Households are the ultimate source of economic power.
   e) c and d

10. Which of the following are considered demerit goods?

   a) nuclear weapons
   b) pesticides
   c) marijuana
   d) cholesterol
   e) a, b, and c

11. Which of the following statements best describes a government budget deficit?

   a) Our government makes expenditures and transfers in excess of tax revenues coming into government.
   b) The total amount of our government's current and past borrowing.
   c) The portion of tax revenues which is used to finance our government's current interest obligation.
   d) Our government buys more goods and services made abroad than it sells abroad (in dollar terms).
   e) a and b

12. The government's economic role includes

   a) correcting for externalities.
   b) providing public goods.
   c) redistribution income.
   d) encouraging merit goods.
   e) a and b.

13. A negative externality occurs when

   a) pollution resulting from marketplace activity imposes third party costs.
   b) the private marketplace fails to provide a service demanded by households.
   c) monopoly power occurs in a market, increasing price to buyers.
   d) crime resulting from illegal drug markets increases the costs of public safety.
   e) b and d

14. A positive externailty occurs when

   a) the honey producer's bees pollinate apple orchards.
   b) the fire department receives expanded funding to purchase better equipment.
   c) the liquor tax is increased to fund the community's orchestra.
   d) a monopoly firm's prices and output become subject to government regulation.

15. Which of the following statements accurately describes a regressive income tax?

    a) Income is redistributed from the rich to the poor.
    b) The tax rate on higher levels of income decreases.
    c) The tax obligation of a higher level of income is greater than for a lower level of income.
    d) The tax rate on higher levels of income increases.
    e) c and d

16. Which of the following statements accurately describes a progressive income tax?

    a) Income is redistributed from the rich to the poor.
    b) The tax rate on higher levels of income decreases.
    c) The tax obligation of a higher level of income is greater than for a lower level of income.
    d) The tax rate on higher levels of income increases.
    e) c and d

17. Assume a state sales tax is at 5.25% on all nonfood and non medical purchases, but that the tax absorbs a larger portion of lower income household earnings than higher income household earnings. How would you describe the sales tax?

    a) Progressive   b) Regressive   c) Proportional

18. Assume the Medicare payroll tax is 1.45% on all earned income up to a ceiling of $200,000, after which there is no Medicare tax on additional income. How could this tax be described?

    a) It is progressive up to the ceiling because a flat tax generates a larger tax burden for higher income people than for lower income people.
    b) It is proportional up to the ceiling because households at all income levels are subject to the same rate of taxation on income earned.
    c) It is a regressive tax up to the ceiling because a constant tax rate means that regardless of the income level, each household has the same tax liability, which is more burdensome for lower income people than higher income people.
    d) It is a proportional tax at income levels greater than the ceiling because the effective tax rate is the same for all households.
    e) b and d

19. The bookkeeping identity expressed in a company's balance sheet is

    a) Net Worth = Net Worth.
    b) Net Worth = Sales − Cost of Goods Sold.
    c) Gross Profit = Sales − Cost of Goods Sold.
    d) Assets = Liabilities + Net Worth.

20. A firm's income statement differs from its balance sheet in that

    a) the former is a flow concept while the latter is a stock concept.
    b) the former identifies net income while the latter identifies stockholders' equity.
    c) the former considers assets and liabilities while the latter considers revenues and costs.
    d) a and b
    e) a, b, and c

21. The form of business in which ownership is least likely to be associated with entrepreneurship is

   a) corporation.
   b) partnership.
   c) proprietorship.
   d) b and c
   e) a, b, and c

22. The construction industry consists mainly of _____ firms with _____ employees.

   a) large firms; more than 500
   b) small firms; between 100 and 500
   c) small firms; fewer than 100
   d) medium sized firms; no more than 700

23. Stockholders, the owners of a corporation, can sell their shares of ownership to

   a) the corporation which wants to buy back its own stock.
   b) fellow stockholders in the company in the over-the-counter market.
   c) strangers through the services of a broker in an organized stock exchange.
   d) b and c
   e) a, b, and c

24. The federal government generates its financial support primarily through

   a) individual income taxes.   b) the GST.
   c) corporate income taxes.   d) excise taxes on alcohol, gas, tobacco, etc.

25. Approximately how much of federal government expenditure is allocated to financing the interest charges on government debt?

   a) 42%   b) 15%
   c) 24%   d) 35%

III. SHORT ANSWER EXERCISES AND PROBLEMS

a. Short Answer Exercises

   1. Provide the appropriate term from the following for each definition below.

   | free rider | ideology | vested interests | profit |
   | household | stock | monopoly power | business |

   a) a private producing unit in the economy

b) revenues less costs

c) certificate of firm ownership

d) people living together and making joint decisions

e) values held so deeply that they are not questioned

f) self-serving groups influencing public policy

g) control over prices and new entry of firms in a marketplace

h) one who receives a benefit without paying for it because others have paid

2. Identify the three levels of business activity.

3. Each of the following questions refers to the three forms of business organizations: sole proprietorship, partnership, corporation.

    a) Which form of business organization(s) is (are) characterized by limited liability?

    b) Which form of business organization allows for the greatest control over managing the business?

    c) Which form of business has the greatest opportunity for raising financial capital?

    d) In which form of business organization(s) are the owners not necessarily required to take an active role in management decisions?

    e) In which form of business organization(s) are the rights of ownership and the responsibilities of management clearly separated?

    f) The sale of stock is limited to which form of business?

4. Define "federal system of government."

5. Differentiate between government deficit and government debt.

6. List five economic roles of government.

7. Provide the appropriate term from the following for the described approach to taxation:
progressive   regressive   proportional

    a) The rate of taxation stays constant at all levels of income.

    b) The rate of taxation increases as the level of income increases.

    c) The effective tax rate declines as the level of income increases.

8. Identify the two largest categories of national government expenditure and express the percentage share of total spending for each.

9. Identify the two largest categories of national government revenue and express the percentage share of total revenue for each.

10. Identify the three tax categories from which provincial and local governments get much of their income.

11. What is the purpose of special purpose and general purpose transfers?

b. **Problems**

1. Refer to the following balance sheet for Hypothetical Company and complete the table.

HYPOTHETICAL COMPANY

Assets		Liabilities And Stockholders' Equity	
Current assets	$4,009,900	Current liabilities	$1,585,000
Property, plant, and equipment	850,000	Long-term liabilities	225,000
		Stockholders equity	(?)
Total assets	(?)	Total liabilities and stockholders' equity	(?)

2. Refer to the following income sheet for Hypothetical Company and complete the table.

HYPOTHETICAL COMPANY

Sales	$2,350,000
Cost of goods sold	1,342,000
Gross profit	(?)
Operating expenses	$135,000
Fixed interest payment	125,000
Income before federal income taxes	(?)
Federal income taxes	$ 99,000
Net income	(?)

3. Because of the noxious fumes emanating from hog confinement systems, government, as result of compromise between special interest groups, establishes a maximum of 100 odour units (ou's) per county. Hog producers have to purchase odour pollution rights. In ABC county the following bids have been made.

Bidder	Bid	Units bid for
Big Pig Co.	$50,000	50
Canadian Hog Farms Inc.	18,000	30
National Hot Dog Cooperative	30,000	20
Smith Family Farms Inc.	10,000	20
Bill Jones (farmer)	5,000	10
Sally Black (farmer)	5,000	5
Harry & Mary Brown (farmers)	8,000	4

a) Which hog producers will win bids and what are their respective ou's purchased?

b) How much income is generated for government by the bidding procedure?

c) What could the government do with the bid income to further placate residents in the hog production areas?

d) Can a neighborhood association do anything legally to reduce the alloted odour to below 100 units per county?

IV. CHALLENGE PROBLEMS AND POTENTIAL ESSAY QUESTIONS

a. Challenge Problems

1. "Consumer sovereignty" is sometimes interpreted as " the consumer is King." What is meant by "consumer sovereignty" when it comes to the role that households play in determining what gets produced? How sovereign is the consumer?

2. For each of the following determine which role government is exercising.

   a) Government enforces legal and binding contracts.

   b) Government bans the use of a particular pesticide which has been determined to significantly increase the chances of those exposed to it getting cancer.

   c) Government deregulates an industry making it easier for entrepreneurs to enter into that business activity.

   d) Government raises tax rates on upper-income individuals because it has been politically determined that they are not paying their "fair" share.

   e) Government builds a new interstate highway system.

   f) Government increases the federal budget deficit because it is argued this will help to reduce unemployment and provide for greater rates of economic growth.

   g) Government subsidizes the "arts" (e.g., symphony orchestras).

b. Potential Essay Questions

1. How could the government accomplish a significant reduction in its budget deficit? How politically popular do you think this would be?

2. Why has the government become involved in the various ways that it has in our economy?

3. Why do some households make more money than do other? How does this affect the "what is produced" and the "for whom" central economic questions?

4. Why do corporations account for the largest share of total output produced (receipts received) in most modern industrialized economies?

V. ANSWERS

II. Mastery Test

1. c	6. e	11. a	16. e	21. a
2. b	7. c	12. e	17. b	22. c
3. d	8. c	13. a	18. b	23. e
4. a	9. e	14. a	19. d	24. a
5. d	10. c	15. b	20. d	25. c

III. Short Answer Exercises and Problems

a. Short Answer Exercises

1. a) business
   b) profit
   c) stock
   d) household
   e) ideology
   f) vested interests
   g) monopoly power
   h) free rider

2. a) manufacturing   b) retail   c) wholesale

3. a) corporation   b) sole proprietorship
   c) corporation   d) partnerships and the corporation
   e) corporation   f) corporation

4. a system of government that includes multiple governing levels with the central (or national) government being pre-eminent

5. A government deficit arises when a government has expenditures and other outflows over a budgetary period (usually a year) which exceed government revenues which makes it necessary for the government to borrow the difference. Government debt refers to the accumulated outstanding borrowing of government.

6. to provide a stable institutional framework, to provide public goods
   to promote effective, workable competition, to ensure economic stability and growth
   to correct for externalities

7. a) proportional tax   b) progressive tax   c) regressive tax

8. Transfers to persons—34%; Interest payments—24%

9. Direct taxes from persons—58%; indirect taxes—23%

10. Property taxes, consumption taxes and provincial income taxes.

11. To provide for comparable levels of public service at comparable levels of taxation.

b. Problems

1. total assets = $4,859,900; stockholders' equity = $3,049,900, total liabilities and stockholders' equity = $4,859,900

2. gross profit = $1,008,000; income before taxes = $748,000; net income = $649,000

3. a) Browns' - 4 ou's; National Hot Dog - 20 ou's; Big Pig - 50 ou's; Black - 5 ou's; Canadian Hog - 21 ou's

Bidder	Bid	Units bid for
Big Pig Co.	$50,000	50
Canadian Hog Farms Inc.	12,600	(21 @ 600 ea.)
National Hot Dog Cooperative	30,000	20
Sally Black (farmer)	5,000	5
Harry & Mary Brown (farmers)	8,000	4

b) $105,600

c) Government could use revenues to provide property tax reduction to neighborhoods negatively impacted by odour; government could finance research to reduce hog production odours.

d) Neighborhood associations, developers, realtors could make bids for odour units or purchase granted odour units in order to take the amount of odour below the 100 unit maximum in a county.

IV. Challenge Problems and Potentiall Essay Questions

a. Challenge Problems

1. Businesses produce that which can be produced profitably. The profitability of an item is determined in large part by the demand for the item (dollar votes cast in the market). The greater the demand, the greater the profit potential and the greater the amount produced by businesses. That is, "the consumer is King" in that consumer demand largely determines what gets produced and how much of it gets produced. Nevertheless, there is still some controversy over the extent to which businesses respond to demand versus their role in creating demand through the use of sophisticated marketing techniques.

2. a) Providing a stable institutional framework.

3. b) Correcting for an externality (a negative externality in this case).

4. c) Promoting effective and workable competition.

5. d) Providing for a fair distribution of society's income.

6. e) Providing for public goods.

7. f) Ensuring economic stability and growth.

8. g) Determining demerit and merit goods or activities.

b. Potential Essay Questions

The following answers are annotated—they only indicate the general idea behind the answer.

1. Either by raising taxes or reducing spending. Exactly where taxes should be raised and spending cut is debatable. But, a look at where the revenues are currently being collected and where the money is being spent (95) may be enlightening. Speeches about raising taxes and/or reducing spending usually get applause but when implemented become quite controversial. The "not in my back yard" syndrome usually sets in.

2. Because of the real or perceived problems or abuses associated with the free market system. Reasonable people can disagree as to whether the government has intervened too much or not enough.

3. The distribution of income is largely determined by control over factors of production (resources)—especially labour because most income is in the form of wages and salaries. The more valuable your labour services the greater your income. Moreover, the greater your income, the more dollar votes you have to cast in the marketplace in favour of what you want to have produced affecting the "what is produced" question. Furthermore, "for whom are goods and services produced?" Those who have the money to buy them. The more money you have, the more goods and services you get.

4. Because of the large sums of funds (financial capital) which are required to operate and to compete in many cases. Corporations have an advantage of being able to raise funds more easily (e.g., by selling stock) than do the other forms of businesses. All things considered the advantages outweigh the disadvantages of the corporate form of business in many cases.

Chapter 5   An Introduction to the World Economy

I. CHAPTER AT A GLANCE

Rip this page out for quick and easy reference.

1. **The industrial countries of the world have a large industrial base and a per capita income of about $20,000 a year; the developing countries of the world include low- and median-income economies that have a per capita income of between $300 and $2,000 a year. (106)**

    There are also

    1) high income oil exporting countries
    (2) transitional economies
    (3) socialist economies

    *Know who and where all these countries are

2. **Some major producing areas for some important raw materials are: (106)**

    Aluminum—Guinea, Australia
    Cobalt—Zaire, Sambia, Russia
    Copper—Chile, U.S., Poland
    Iron—Russia, Brazil, Australia
    Zinc—Canada, Australia, Russia

    *Helps explain strategic roles some countries play in the world economy.

    *Geography also helps explain why countries have the comparative advantages they do.

3. **Two ways in which international trade differs from *intra*national (domestic) trade are:**

    1. **International trade involves potential barriers to trade; and**

        Free and open international trade along the lines of comparative advantage is mutually beneficial to all economies involved.

    2. **International trade involves multiple currencies. (108)**

        Foreign exchange markets exist to swap currencies.

4. **By looking at an exchange rate table, you can determine how much various goods will likely cost in different countries. (108)**

    Shows the relative value of other currencies in terms of the dollar and vice versa.

5. **Two important causes of a trade balance are: (112)**

    1. A country's competitiveness; and

    Reduced competitiveness ↑s a trade deficit due to:

    a) relatively lower productivity
    b) an ↑ in the value of the country's currency

    2. The relative state of a country's economy.

    A stronger economy means higher incomes, therefore more imports and a greater trade deficit.

6. **Five important international economic institutions are: (114)**

> 1. *The UN*
> 2. *The W.T.O.*
> 3. *The World Bank*
> 4. *The IMF; and*
> 5. *The EU*

> **They are designed to enhance negotiations (to avoid trade wars)*

> **Also know about global corporations*

7. a) **The European Union (EU) is an economic and political union of European countries that allow free trade among countries. It was created to provide larger marketplaces for member countries. (119)**

> *—EU has led to increased competition for member countries.*

> *—the EU is a larger, market than both the U.S. and Canada which may have helped create NAFTA.*

b) **Japan is a small, crowded, poorly endowed chain of island which has been enormously successful economically. (121)**

> **The difference between Canada and Japan should not be exaggerated.*

> *Japanese success can be traced to:*

> *(1) hard work*
> *(2) lots of savings*
> *(3) quality labor force*
> *(4) lots of government-business cooperation*
> *(5) lots of labor-management cooperation*

> **Think internationally because we live in a global economy!*

II. MASTERY TEST

1. A country that sells more abroad in value than it buys from abroad has a

   a) trade surplus.
   b) trade deficit.
   c) debt problem.
   d) balance of payments problem.
   e) b, c, and d

2. If Mexico has a comparative advantage over other countries in the production of automobile engines, then

   a) its opportunity cost of producing auto engines is lower than that of other countries.
   b) its opportunity cost of producing auto engines is higher than that of other countries.
   c) it will run a trade surplus.
   d) it will run a trade deficit.
   e) b and d

3. If two countries have identical opportunity costs for the production of basketball shoes

   a) neither has a comparative advantage making basketball shoes.
   b) a balance of trade exists.
   c) neither should produce basketball shoes.
   d) the country which has the lowest market price for basketball shoes has the comparative advantage.

4. Which of the following is not a characteristic of international trade?

   a) foreign exchange markets
   b) quotas and tariffs
   c) nontariff trade barriers
   d) common currency

5. Interest payment outflows occur when a nation

   a) receives foreign aid.
   b) reduces its savings.
   c) has a comparative advantage.
   d) is a debtor.
   e) a, b, and d

6. Which of the following best describes a tariff?

   a) a formal limit on the volume of a good entering a country from abroad
   b) standards established for goods sold domestically by foreign sellers
   c) an export fee
   d) a tax on imports

7. Export-led growth occurs when a country experiences increased output and income because of

   a) purchases of foreign domiciled assets by its citizens.
   b) increased sales of its goods and services abroad.
   c) interest inflows as a result of it being a creditor nation.
   d) the rising value of its currency relative to the other currencies in the world.
   e) a, b, and c

8. Japan's economy has been described as being

   a) capitalist.
   b) neo-mercantilist.
   c) high income.
   d) low saving.
   e) a, b, and c

9. Which of the following is an advantage associated with global corporations?

   a) multiple jurisdictions
   b) technological change
   c) increased domestic competition
   d) b and c
   e) a, b, and c

10. Which of the following is an accurate statement about the EEC?

   a) The number of members is declining.
   b) The collapse of central planning in Eastern Europe adversely affected the goals of the EEC.
   c) It was organized in reaction to the North American Free Trade Agreement.
   d) It aims for a unified currency by the start of the next century.
   e) b, c, and d

Respond to #11 and #12 on the basis of the information in the table below.

Canada		France	
Bushel of Beans	Litre of Beer	Bushel of Beans	Litre of Beer
$5/bu	$2/qt	100ff/bu	10ff/qt

11. Which of the following statements is true?

   a) Canada has a comparative advantage producing beans while neither country has a comparative advantage producing beer.
   b) The opportunity cost in France of a bushel of beans is 100ff.
   c) The exchange rate for one dollar is five francs.
   d) Beer is more expensive in Canada than it is in France.
   e) b and c

12. Which of the following statements is true?

   a) A litre of beer costs 10 bushels of beans in France.
   b) Beer is more expensive in France than in Canada.
   c) It benefits Canada to trade 3 litres of beer for one bushel of beans from France.
   d) It benefits France to trade 9 litres of beer for one bushel of beans from Canada.
   e) a, b, and c

13. Intranational trade is a transaction which is characterized by

a) the free movement of goods and services across international boundaries.
b) an exchange of currency prior to an exchange of goods.
c) a uniform standard of behaviour guiding the participants
d) nontariff trade barriers
e) a and b

14. A debtor nation is one which

a) has no comparative advantage.
b) is characterized by export-led growth.
c) buys more in value abroad than it sells.
d) runs government budget deficits.
e) a and c

15. If the currency exchange rate for a dollar is 110 yen and a Japanese camera is priced at 44,500 yen, then a Canadian buyer will pay

a) 44,500 yen.   b) $44.50.   c) $405.   d) 4,500 yen.

16. An example of a nontariff barrier to trade is

a) a price ceiling of 8ff per Canadian dollar imposed by France in currency exchange markets.
b) OPEC's decision to cut oil production by 10 percent.
c) France's refusal to allow the importation of machine cleaned poultry because of health concerns.
d) a nationalistic appeal in Canada to avoid the purchase of goods made abroad in order to maintain the country's national identity.
e) b, c, and d

17. When considering a country's balance of trade, it is important to recognize that *the state of the economy* is an important influence because

a) as a nation's income increases, it tends to increase its imports relative to its exports.
b) a trade deficit may lead to a reduction of output and income in an economy.
c) increased domestic competitiveness tends to result in a rising trade deficit.
d) a and b
e) a, b, and c

18. Which of the following statements is not an accurate representation of GATT?

a) It was inspired in part due to the trade wars that plagued the world during the Great Depression.
b) It is the acronym for the organization of the central bankers of the world's most powerful economies.
c) It was created to help developing countries find financing for long term capital projects.
d) It is the data gathering agency of the OECD.
e) b, c, and d.

19. The largest European economy is

   a) England.
   b) Germany.
   c) Russia.
   d) Sweden.

20. An important reason for the formation of the EEC was to

   a) improve economic coordination among member countries.
   b) reduce trade barriers among countries.
   c) improve trade relations with Canada.
   d) a and b
   e) a, b, and c.

21. Neo mercantilism refers to Japan Inc.'s

   a) emphasis on exports and discouragement of imports.
   b) close working relationship between business and government.
   c) refusal to allow unions to organize labour.
   d) a and b
   e) a, b, and c.

22. MITI is given credit for playing an important role in Japan's economic success. "MITI" refers to

   a) Japan's neo mercantilist policies.
   b) Japan's trade and industry ministry.
   c) the cooperative spirit and willingness to sacrifice of the Japanese people.
   d) the labour organizations in Japan which work so effectively with management and government.

23. Which of the following is not a basis for Japan's economic success?

   a) agriculture   b) lawyers   c) education   d) culture   e) a and b

24. Which of the following is a member of the group of seven but not the group of five?

   a) France   b) Britian   c) Italy   d) Germany   e) b and c

25. A country's *competitiveness*, its ability to produce goods as cheaply or more cheaply than its international competitors, depends upon

   a) its productivity.
   b) output per worker.
   c) its innovativeness.
   d) the relative value of its currency.
   e) a, b, c, and d

III. SHORT ANSWER EXERCISES AND PROBLEMS

a. Short Answer Exercises

1. List three forces other than comparative advantage that help determine what sorts of goods and services a country consumes.

2. Explain how being a debtor nation leads to a money outflow from the debtor economy to other economies?

3. What are the two determinants of a trade deficit?

4. How do consumers in any given country benefit from foreign trade?

5. If the currency of country A is becoming cheaper compared to the currency of country B, how is trade between countries A and B affected?

6. What is the meaning of *GATT*?

7. What are the names of the important economic institutions of the world identified by the initials . . .

   a) UN   c) OPEC

   b) IMF   d) OECD

8. What countries are included in the group of five?

9. What two additional countries, along with the five in #8, make up the group of seven?

10. List three advantages associated with the presence of global corporations in a nation's economy?

11. List three criticisms associated with the presence of global corporations in a nation's economy?

12. Give two reasons for the formation of the EEC.

13. Provide three reasons for the remarkable success of the Japanese economy.

14. Describe methods used by the Japanese government to encourage its citizens to save.

15. What is a more complete name for MITI? What is its function in the Japanese economy?

b. **Problems**

1. The table below lists hypothetical values of select international currencies, in terms of the Canadian currency. Use the table to respond to the questions that follow.

(a)	(b)	(c)
CURRENCY	IN DOLLAR TERMS	PER CANADIAN DOLLAR
British Pound	$1.55	
German Mark	$0.63	
Japanese Yen	$0.01	
French Franc	$0.18	
Mexican Peso	$0.29	

a) How much foreign currency would it take to buy a dollar? Complete column "c" to determine the price of the dollar in terms of other currencies.

b) What is the franc price of a mark?

c) What is the mark price of a pound?

d) How many British pounds will a German BMW cost if it is priced at $60,000?

e) Assume the yen becomes cheaper and it now takes twice as many to buy a Canadian dollar. How many yen will it take to buy a set of golf clubs priced at $750?

2. Use the following table to respond to the comparative advantage questions about the opportunity costs of production which follow.

a	b	c	d
COUNTRY	WIDGET PRICE	WADGET PRICE	WADGET COST
A	$25	$50	
B	50ff	100ff	
C	25m	75m	
D	5£	20£	

a) In column "d", determine the opportunity cost of producting a wadget in terms of widgets for countries A through D.

b) Between countries C and D, which has the comparative advantage in making wadgets?

c) Which country in the table has the best comparative advantage producing wadgets?

d) Which country in the table has the best comparative advantage producing widgets? What is its opportunity cost for producing a widget?

IV. CHALLENGE PROBLEMS AND POTENTIAL ESSAY QUESTIONS

a. Challenge Problems

1. a. Canada imports many products from Norway and Norway imports many products from Canada (which represents Canadian exports to Norway). Let's consider the importation of Norwegian salmon by Canadians and Norwegian importation of Canadian taco sauce. Suppose the price of Norwegian salmon in Norway is 50 Kroner per pound and the price of Canadian taco sauce in Canada is 3 dollars per jar. What is the price per jar of Canadian taco sauce in Norway? What is the price per pound of Norwegian salmon in Canada? Assume the Canadian dollar will buy 9 Kroner.

b. We know that a major determinant of a country's competitiveness is the value of its currency. Although we have taken a look at the trade between just Canada and Norway, and with respect to only salmon and taco sauce, the same general principles apply to the trade Canada undertakes with all nations and with respect to virtually all products traded. What effect does an increase in the value of the dollar in international exchange rate markets have on Canadian imports and exports (assuming nothing else is changing)? Will a higher value of the dollar create a greater trade deficit or movement in the direction of a trade surplus? Why?

2. Assume Canada can produce wheat at the cost of $3 per bushel and tomatoes for $6 per bushel. In Mexico, wheat can be produced at 12 pesos per bushel and tomatoes at 3 pesos per bushel.

   a. In Canada, what is the opportunity cost of producing additional units of wheat? Tomatoes?

   b. In Mexico, what is the opportunity cost of producing additional units of wheat? Tomatoes?

   c. Which country has a comparative advantage in the production of wheat? Tomatoes? Why?

b. **Potential Essay Questions**

   1. What is meant by export-led growth?

   2. Large trade deficits often inspire politicians to call for trade restrictions prohibiting imports. However, most economists oppose such restrictions because of the negative effects they may create. What are some of the problems associated with trade restrictions?

   3. What are the pros and cons of global corporations from society's perspective?

II. Mastery Test

1. a	6. d	11. d	16. c	21. d
2. a	7. b	12. d	17. d	22. b
3. a	8. e	13. c	18. e	23. e
4. d	9. d	14. c	19. b	24. c
5. d	10. d	15. c	20. d	25. e

III. Short Answer Exercises and Problems

a. **Short Answer Exercises**

   1. Religion, history, tradition, relative domestic prices

   2. Debt paper issued domestically to finance current expenditures generally requires the borrower to make interest payments and ultimately principal payment to the lender. If a foreign citizen or institution is the lender, then the finance payments exit the domestic economy.

   3. a) Canadian competitiveness and the relative value of the dollar; and b) the state of the domestic economy compared to that of other countries.

   4. Domestic consumers benefit from an expanded diversity of goods, lower prices due to increased domestic competition, and the greater likelihood of product innovation and technological advancement also stimulated by increased domestic competition.

   5. Citizens of B buy more of A's goods and services; since A's currency is becoming cheaper, its products are becoming cheaper! A's citizens buy fewer of B's goods and services because B's currency is expensive making it more expensive to buy B's goods.

   6. The General Agreement on Trade and Tariff

7. a) United Nations
    b) International Monetary Fund
    c) Organization of Petroleum Exporting Countries
    d) Organization of Economic Cooperation and Development

8. U.S., Japan, Germany, France, Britain

9. Italy and Canada

10. job creation, competition and lower prices, new technologies, reduction of international tensions

11. excessive political influence in high income countries, political domination in low income countries, less accountability for firm actions due to the multiplicity of jurisdictions

12. improve markets for European companies, and to improve the competitiveness of European business and industry versus North American business and industry.

13. cultural tradition of unified effort, high rate of saving, government encouragement and sponsorship of export industries

14. skimpy national pension system puts pressure on the individual Japanese to save for his/her retirement, government policies keep domestic consumer prices high and credit expensive, demanding educational system promotes hard work ethic and willingness to sacrifice.

15. Ministry of International Trade and Industry; provides assistance in coordinating the production efforts of Japan's private sector.

b. **Problems**

1. a)

(a) CURRENCY	(b) IN DOLLAR TERMS	(c) PER CANADIAN DOLLAR
British Pound	$1.55	0.645£
German Mark	$0.63	1.59m
Japanese Yen	$0.01	100Y
French Franc	$0.18	5.55ff
Mexican Peso	$0.29	3.45p

b) approximately 3.5 ff for a mark
c) approximately 2.46m per pound
d) approximately 38,700 pounds
e) approximately 150,000 yen

2. a)

a	b	c	d
COUNTRY	WIDGET PRICE	WADGET PRICE	WADGET COST
A	$25	$50	2 widgets
B	50ff	100ff	2 widgets
C	25m	75m	3 widgets
D	5£	20£	4 widgets

b) "C" - it takes fewer widgets in "C" to make a wadget (fewer widgets are sacrificed to get a wadget)

c) "A" and "B" - the opportunity cost is 2 widgets sacrificed to get a wadget; less than for "C" and "D"

d) "D" - one-fourth wadget is sacrificed to gain a widget

IV. Challenge Problems and Potential Essay Questions

a. Challenge Problems

1. a) A Kroner will buy $0.1111—approximately 11 cents. Norwegian salmon will cost Canadians $5.56 per pound. Taco sauce will cost Norwegians 27 kroner.

   b) A higher value of the dollar (an appreciation of the dollar—a stronger dollar) in international exchange rate markets will increase Canadian imports (because the relative price of foreign made goods to Canadians decreases) and decrease Canadian exports (because the relative price of Canadian-made products to the rest of the world are more expensive). As imports rise and exports fall in Canada then Canada experiences movement in the direction of a trade deficit (the trade deficit will worsen if we started with one).

2. a) Recall that an opportunity cost is what must be given up in order to get something else. So, the opportunity cost of producing an additional bushel of wheat in Canada is 1/2 bushels of tomatoes. The opportunity cost of tomatoes in Canada is 2 bushels of wheat.

   b) In Mexico, the opportunity cost of producing an additional unit of wheat is 4 bushels of tomatoes, whereas the opportunity cost of tomatoes is 1/4 bushels of wheat.

   c) Canada has a comparative advantage in the production of wheat because its opportunity cost of producing wheat is lower than in Mexico (1/2 bushel of tomatoes in Canada as opposed to 4 bushels of tomatoes in Mexico). On the other hand, Mexico has a comparative advantage in the production of tomatoes because it has to give up less wheat (1/4 bushels) as compared to Canada (where 2 bushels have to be given up).

b. Potential Essay Questions

The following answers are annotated—they only indicate the general idea behind the answer.

1. When exports rise this creates more jobs and therefore more income on the part of the workers. Most of this additional income is spent generating more sales by businesses motivating them to produce more, creating even more jobs, higher income and still more spending. A country with export-led growth has a trade surplus which stimulates growth in income.

2. Generally, there are two problems. First, trade restrictions reduce competition. Less competition means consumers have to pay higher prices than if the foreign competition were allowed. Second, trade restrictions often bring retaliation from other countries (they impose stricter trade restrictions as well) which reduces that amount domestic firms are able to sell abroad.

3. The pros of global corporations include: they create jobs; bring new ideas and technologies to a country; provide competition for domestic companies; they may help promote better relations between countries. The cons include: a potential lack of accountability to any country because of multiple jurisdictions; a potential for their power to be exerted on a government's policies which may reslut in their own interests being served at the expense of the interests of that counrty's people in general.

Chapter 6 Individual Choice and Demand

I. CHAPTER AT A GLANCE

Rip this page out for quick and easy reference.

1. The principle of diminishing marginal utility states that after some point, the marginal utility received from each additional unit of a good decreases with each unit consumed. (134)

   Marginal $\Rightarrow$ "extra"

   Utility $\Rightarrow$ "satisfaction"

2. Principle of rational choice: spend your money on those goods that give you the most marginal utility per dollar. (136)

   If $\dfrac{MUx}{Px} > \dfrac{MUy}{Py}$, choose to consume an additional unit of good x.

   If $\dfrac{MUx}{Px} < \dfrac{MUy}{Py}$, choose to consume an additional unit of good y.

   If $\dfrac{MUx}{Px} = \dfrac{MUy}{Py}$, you're maximizing utility; you cannot increase your utility by adjusting your choices.

   Extra satisfaction per last dollar spent on x equals that for y

3. According to the principle of rational choice, if there is diminishing marginal utility and the price of a good goes up, we consume less of that good. Hence, the principle of rational choice leads to the law of demand. (139)

   If $\dfrac{MUx}{Px} = \dfrac{MUy}{Py}$ and then $\underline{Px{\uparrow}s}$,

   we get: $\dfrac{MUx}{Px} < \dfrac{MUy}{Py}$,

   and we buy more of y and $\underline{buy\ less\ of\ x}$.

4. A good is a substitute for another good if its consumption goes up when the price of the other good goes up. A good is a complement for another if its consumption goes down when the price of the other good goes up. (14)

   Substitutes: $\uparrow Px \Rightarrow \uparrow D$ for y

   Complements: $\uparrow Px \Rightarrow \downarrow D$ for y

5. Economists use their simple self-interest theory of choice because it cuts through many obfuscations, and in doing so often captures a part of reality that others miss. (144)

   Approaching problems by asking "What's in it for the people making the decision?" can be insightful.

6. a) **Price elasticity of demand is defined as a measure of the percentage change in the quantity demanded divided by the percent change in the price. (144)**

Is a measure of consumer responsiveness to a price change.

$Ed > 1 \Rightarrow$ *elastic (responsive)*

$Ed = 1 \Rightarrow$ *unitary elastic*

$Ed < 1 \Rightarrow$ *inelastic (unresponsive)*

b) **If demand is inelastic, a rise in price increases total revenue. If demand is elastic, a rise in price lowers total revenue. If demand is unitary elastic, a rise in price has no effect on revenue. (146)**

$Ed > 1: \uparrow (\downarrow) P \Rightarrow \downarrow (\uparrow) TR \}$ *Inverse relationship*

$ED = 1: \uparrow (\downarrow) P \Rightarrow no\ \Delta\ in\ TR$

$Ed < 1: \uparrow (\downarrow) P \Rightarrow \uparrow (\downarrow) TR \}$ *Direct Relationship*

7. **As a general rule, the more substitutes a good has, the more elastic is its demand. (149)**

Also:
① *Greater time under consideration*
② *More of a luxury (vs. necessity)*
③ *More specifically the good is defined*

II. MASTERY TEST

1. The principle of diminishing marginal utility states that:

    a) Additional consumption always leads to additional satisfaction.
    b) Additional consumption never leads to additional satisfaction.
    c) Additional consumption, after some point, leads to decreasing satisfaction with each additional unit consumed.
    d) Additional consumption, after some point leads to increasing satisfaction with each additional unit consumed.

2. The modern concept of using utility to measure the level of satisfaction one gets from consuming goods or services is:

    a) based on cardinal measures.
    b) based on ordinal measures.
    c) not very useful in studying satisfaction received from consuming goods or services.
    d) replaces the use of dollars and cents in economic analysis.

3. The additional utility one gets from one's consumption of a product is called:

    a) satisfaction plus.
    b) marginal utility.
    c) total utility.
    d) point utility.

4. The theory of rational choice shows how:

    a) consumption and price are related.
    b) advertising and spending are related.
    c) id, ego and superego are related.
    d) self-esteem and approval by our peers are related.

5. If $\dfrac{MU_x}{P_x} > \dfrac{MU_y}{P_y}$ choose to consume

    a) an additional unit of y.
    b) an additional unit of x.
    c) an additional unit of either.
    d) an additional unit of neither.

6. If a consumer is maximizing her marginal utility per dollar spent

    a) her total utility for each good is identical to its price.
    b) she is maximizing her satisfaction from market purchases.
    c) her total utility per dollar spent is the same for all goods.
    d) the marginal utility is the same for each item purchased.

7. The principle of diminishing marginal utility leads to the:

    a) law of supply.
    b) law of increasing consumption.
    c) law of demand.
    d) law of rational minimizing.

8. If the marginal utility for a dollar box of popcorn is 30 and the marginal utility for a dollar cup of pop is 10:

   a) the total utility for the popcorn and pop is 40.
   b) a gain of 20 utils net can be achieved by spending one less dollar on pop and one more dollar on popcorn.
   c) a gain of 20 utils net can be achieved by spending one more dollar on pop and one less dollar on popcorn.
   d) a gain of 30 utils net can be achieved by spending one less dollar on pop and one more dollar on popcorn.

9. When deciding to choose between an expensive high quality foreign sports car and a domestically produced inexpensive 2-door hatchback, the consumer should choose the one that

   a) is least expensive.
   b) has the highest marginal utility.
   c) consumes the least gasoline.
   d) has the highest marginal utility per dollar.

10. A consumer's information in regard to choosing between two goods is as follows:

Good	MU	Price
A	70	$10
B	75	$15

The consumer would gain:

   a) 2 utils by spending one less dollar on B and one more dollar on A.
   b) 5 utils by spending one less dollar on A and one more dollar on B.
   c) $5 by spending one less dollar on B and one more dollar on A.
   d) 15 utils by spending one less dollar on B and one more dollar on A.

11. Dennis is deciding where to spend his spring break. If he goes to Whistler, British Columbia, the trip will give him 8,000 utils of satisfaction and will cost him $500. If, instead, he travels to Banff, Alberta, the trip will give him 6,000 utils of pleasure and will cost him $400. Dennis will most likely do best:

   a) going to Whistler because his total pleasure will be greatest.
   b) going to Banff because its cheapest.
   c) going to Whistler because his pleasure per dollar will be greatest.
   d) going to Banff because his pleasure per dollar will be greatest.
   e) to stay home and save his money because neither trip is worth it.

12. | Units of Consumption | MU of C | MU of D | MU of S |
|---|---|---|---|
| 1 | 12 | 20 | 30 |
| 2 | 8 | 16 | 25 |
| 3 | 5 | 12 | 20 |
| 4 | 4 | 10 | 16 |

If good C costs $1 per unit, good D costs $4 per unit and good S costs $5 per unit, what combination of goods should a consumer with $17 to spend buy to maximize utility?

a) 1 unit of C, 1 unit of D, and 3 units of S
b) 3 units of C, 1 unit of D, and 2 units of S
c) 4 units of C, 2 units of D, and 3 units of S
d) 2 units of C, 3 units of D, and 2 units of S

13. Price elasticity of demand can be calculated by using the formula:

a) percentage change in price divided by percentage change in quantity demanded.
b) percentage change in quantity demanded divided by percentage change in price.
c) percentage change in price divided by percentage change in income.
d) absolute change in quantity demanded divided by absolute change in price.

14. Which of the following is an *incorrect* reason for the price elasticity of demand always being negative?

a) There is a negative relationship between price and quantity demanded.
b) When the price of a good changes, quantity demanded changes in the opposite direction.
c) The importance of the substitution effect.
d) The demand curve has a zero slope.

15. Price elasticity of demand measures:

a) the shift in demand curve when price changes.
b) the responsiveness of the quantity demanded to price changes.
c) the demand for a product holding prices constant.
d) the quantity demanded at a given price.

16. A 50 percent rebate coupon is made available to customer Smith, who has a price elasticity of demand of 2.0 for the product at its current price, and also to customer Johnson, who has a current price elasticity of demand for the product of .8. Which customer is most likely to redeem the coupon?

a) Johnson
b) Smith
c) Both Smith and Johnson
d) Neither person is likely to redeem the coupon.

17. What can we conclude from a fall in price from $10 to $8, and quantity demanded increases to 100?

a) Demand is elastic in this price range.
b) Demand is inelastic in this price range.
c) Demand is unitary in this price range.
d) Not enough information to conclude anything about elasticity of demand.

18. A fall in the price of CDs from $10 to $8 results in an increase in quantity demanded from 60 to 80 units. The CDs price elasticity of demand over this price range is _____ (use average method)

a) 2.45   b) 1.7
c) 1.3   d) 1.00

19. The price elasticity for vacation travel is 2.5 when there is a 30 percent increase in quantity demanded. What percent decrease in price is necessary to increase quantity demanded by 30 percent?

a) 10 percent   b) 12 percent
c) 25 percent   d) 50 percent

20. If the quantity demanded for blood pressure medication is the same for each possible price, the price elasticity of demand is:

a) perfectly inelastic.   b) perfectly elastic.
c) elastic.   d) unitary.

21. It can be shown, that as we move along a downward sloping linear demand curve:

a) the slope changes but elasticity may be constant.
b) the slope and elasticities change.
c) the slope and elasticity may be constant.
d) the slope is constant but elasticities change.

22. The demand curve for Trek bicycles should be:

a) sometimes more and sometimes less elastic than the demand curve for bicycles in general.
b) less elastic than the demand curve for bicycles in general.
c) as elastic as the demand curve for bicycles in general.
d) more elastic than the demand curve for bicycles in general.

23. A good's price elasticity of demand is greatly influenced by:

a) the number of producers in the market.
b) the availability of close substitutes.
c) the number of buyers in the market.
d) the cost of producing the good.

24. Demand will likely be more _____, given a longer time frame involved.

a) flat.   b) inelastic.
c) steep.   d) elastic.

25. When economists refer to income elasticity, they define it as:

a) percentage change in quantity demanded divided by percentage change in income.
b) percentage change in income divided by percentage change in quantity demanded.
c) change in income divided by change in quantity demanded.
d) change in quantity demanded divided by change in income.

III. SHORT ANSWER EXERCISES AND PROBLEMS

a. Short Answer Exercises

   1. What is meant by the term, price elasticity of demand?

   2. Why is the price elasticity of demand always negative?

   3. Discuss the difference between cardinal and ordinal measures. Which approach did economists initially use to measure utility? Which approach do you recommend? Why?

   4. Distinguish between total utility and marginal utility.

   5. What is the principle of diminishing marginal utility?

   6. What is the relationship between marginal utility and the price you are willing to pay?

   7. Given the following general statements, determine which good to choose:

   If $\dfrac{MU_x}{P_x} > \dfrac{MU_y}{P_y}$, consume more of _____.

   If $\dfrac{MU_x}{P_x} < \dfrac{MU_y}{P_y}$, consume more of _____.

   If $\dfrac{MU_x}{P_x} = \dfrac{MU_y}{P_y}$, consume more of _____.

8. What is the relationship between the marginal utility rule and the law of demand?

9. Discuss the income effect and the substitution effect.

10. What other forces besides price and marginal utility play a role in determining what people demand?

11. Define the following:

    a) Elasticity > 1

    b) Elasticity = 1

    c) Elasticity < 1

12. The number of substitutes a good has is affected by several factors. Discuss three major factors.

13. Describe elasticity of demand concepts other than price elasticity.

b. **Problems**

1. You are given the following data on the quantities demanded for men's socks in a small clothing store.

Price	Quantity Demanded	Total Revenue	Price Elasticity
$8.00	8		
7.00	10		
6.00	12		
5.00	14		
4.00	16		
3.00	18		—

a) Complete the above table.
b) At what price will the store maximize its revenues?
c) At what range of prices will elasticity be characterized as elastic? Unitary? Inelastic?
d) Prepare a graph on the grid shown below indicating the relationship between price and quantity demanded.
e) Note the elastic, unitary and inelastic ranges

Price

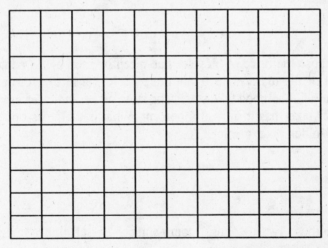

Quantity Demanded

2. The following table gives price and total utils of two goods, X and Y.

Quantity of X	Total utility of X	Quantity of Y	Total utility of Y
1	100	1	10
2	150	2	25
3	175	3	35
4	150	4	40
5	125	5	35

The price of X is $5 per unin and the price of Y is $1 per unit. As closely as possible, determine how much of X and Y you would buy with a budget of $19. Hint: The principles of rational choice and diminishing marginal utility should be used as a guide.

3. A family has provided you with the following information:

	Income per month	Quantity of hamburger demanded per month	Quantity of steak demanded per month
Period 1	$ 800	10 lbs.	3 lbs.
Period 2	1,000	7 lbs.	5 lbs.

Calculate the income elasticity for hamburger and steak for this family.

4. a) Suppose the price of bicycles has recently risen by 10 percent due to an increase in the cost of the lightweight frame materials. As a result, fewer new bikes are being sold in your neighborhood bike store. The store owner indicates to you that his repair business on older bikes has increased 4 percent. What is the cross-price elasticity of new bike sales and older bike repairs?

b) Are these two "goods" complements or substitutes?

5. The diamond/water paradox is: "Why is water, which is so useful and necessary, so cheap when diamonds which are so useless, and unnecessary, so expensive?" What is the economist's answer to this question?

6. Economists have developed terminology other than elastic and inelastic: perfectly elastic and perfectly inelastic. On the grid below, draw the following curves:

a) perfectly elastic demand and
b) perfectly inelastic demand.

Discuss the significance of each.

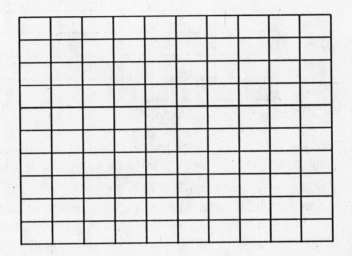

7. (Refer to Appendix A) You are faced with the choice of two activities: bicycling and swimming. After some consideration, you arrive at two levels of satisfaction (A and B) of various combinations of bicycling and swimming per month to which you are indifferent.

Level A Units of Bicycling (B) Swimming (S) per month		**Level B** Units of Bicycling (B) Swimming (S) per month	
(B)	(S)	(B)	(S)
80	0	100	0
20	10	40	10
5	20	20	20
2	30	10	30
1	40	5	40
0	50	0	50

a)   Use this information and the following grid to plot your indifference curves for bicycling and swimming for level A and level B of satisfaction. Label the curves Ai and Bi.

Bicycling

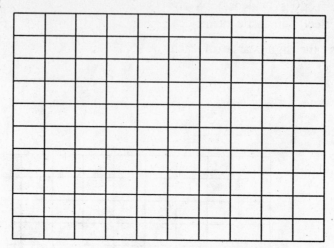

Swimming

b)   Suppose you have a monthly budget of $60 to spend on these activities and the price of bicycling is $1 per unit and the price of swimming is $4 per unit.

1.   Plot your budget line and label it BL$_1$.
2.   Given your indifference map and the above prices and income, what combination of bicycling and swimming will put you at your optimum point?
3.   Suppose the price of swimming drops to $2.22 per unit but the price of bicycling and your budget remain unchanged. Draw in the new budget line and label it BL2.
4.   After the change in part 3, which combination of bicycling and swimming will put you at an optimum point?

IV. CHALLENGE PROBLEMS AND POTENTIAL ESSAY QUESTIONS

a. Challenge Problems

1. Suppose you are interested in purchasing just bottles of wine and pounds of cheese for an upcoming party. Assume you have only $45 to spend, the price per bottle of wine is $5 and the price per pound of cheese is $10. You have estimated the utility (or satisfaction) from the consumption of wine and cheese at the party according to the following tables.

(Wine)		(Cheese)	
Quantity	Total Utility	Quantity	Total Utility
0	0	0	0
1	100	1	130
2	175	2	250
3	225	3	350
4	250	4	425
5	260	5	465

   a) How many bottles of wine and pounds of cheese should you purchase for the party? Why?

   b) Suppose the price of cheese per pound falls to $7.50. Now how many bottles of wine and pounds of cheese should you purchase for the party? Why?

   c) How is the observed change in the quantity demanded of cheese given the decrease in the price of cheese related to the law of demand?

2. In the 1970s and the early 1980s the gas mileage of automobiles rose substantially. In the 1990s it has stopped rising and has even fallen slightly. What is a likely explanation?

3. Suppose the price of almonds rises from $4.35 to $5.15 per pound and the quantity demanded falls from 800 to 735 pounds.

   a) What is the arc elasticity of demand for almonds in this price range?

   b) Are almonds elastic, unitary elastic, or inelastic in this price range?

   c) What is the interpretation of that price elasticity of demand—what does it mean?

   d) Suppose the price elasticity of demand coefficient calculated in part (a) above is the exact number representing consumer responsive to a price change for almonds. If there is a 10% decrease in the price of almonds, what would the percentage change in the quantity demanded be? If the price was to rise by 15%, what would the percentage change in the quantity demanded be?

   e) What happens to total revenue for almond sellers when the price rises from $4.35 to $5.15 per pound? How is this related to the price elasticity of demand for almonds?

   f) What could cause almonds to have this elasticity of demand calculated in part (a) above?

4. Suppose, in deciding what price to set for the video of Lion King, Disney decided to charge either $29.95 or $49.95. It estimated the demand to be quite elastic. What price did it choose and why?

b. Potential Essay Questions

1. Discuss the principle of diminishing marginal utility. How is this related to the principle of rational choice and the law of demand?

2. Explain why economists can believe there are many explanations of individual choice, but nonetheless focus on self-interest.

3. What can cause some products to exhibit an elastic demand while others have an inelastic demand?

4. Why are some businesses very interested in trying to determine which consumers have an elastic demand and which have an inelastic demand for the product being sold?

V. ANSWERS

II. Mastery Test

1. c	6. b	11. c	16. b	21. d
2. b	7. c	12. b	17. d	22. d
3. b	8. b	13. b	18. c	23. b
4. a	9. d	14. d	19. b	24. d
5. b	10. a	15. b	20. a	25. a

III. Short Answer Exercises and Problems

a. Short Answer Exercises

1. The responsiveness of the quantity demanded of a good to changes in its price. It is defined as the percentage change in quantity demanded divided by the percentage change in its price.

2. The law of demand states that quantity demanded is inversely related to the relative price. Increase in price leads to a decrease in the quantity demanded.

3. A cardinal measure is anything that can be measured by an actual number. An ordinal measure is a prioritizing or ranking of alternatives; no real attempt is made to establish an actual number value. Which approach would the student use? Hopefully, the ordinal approach because there is no rational device for measuring the amount of pleasure one receives from a good.

4. Total utility refers to the total satisfaction one gets from one's consumption of a product. Marginal utility refers to the satisfaction one gets from the consumption of an incremental or additional product above and beyond what one has consumed up to that point.

5. As individuals increase their consumption of a good per period of time, at some point consuming another unit of the product will not yield as much additional pleasure as did consuming the preceding unit.

6. Given the price of the good, the higher the marginal utility you receive from a good, the more you are willing to buy of that good. Similarly, given the price, the lower the marginal utility you receive from a good, the less you're willing to buy more of it.

7. $$\frac{MU_x}{P_x} > \frac{MU_{y.}}{P_y}$$ consume more of good <u>X</u>.

                  $$\frac{MU_x}{P_x} < \frac{MU_{y.}}{P_y}$$ consume more of good <u>Y</u>.

                  $$\frac{MU_x}{P_x} = \frac{MU_{y.}}{P_y}$$ consume more of neither.

8. When the price of a good goes up, the marginal utility per dollar we get from that good goes down. Therefore we lower our consumption of that good. The principle of rational choice shows us formally that following the law of demand is the rational thing to do.

9. The income effect points out that a consumer with a fixed money income will buy more of a product if there is a decline in its price. The substitution effect says that a lower price will make a product relatively more attractive and therefore increase the consumers willingness to substitute it for other products.

10. Changing tastes, technical innovations, cultural differences, and changes in income.

11. a) Elasticity > 1
            Percent change in quantity > percent change in price.
    b) Elasticity = 1
            Percent change in quantity = percent change in price.
    c) Elasticity < 1
            Percent change in quantity < percent change in price.

12. 1. The larger the time interval considered, the more elastic is the demand curve for the goods. There are more substitutes in the long run than in the short run. Alternatives can be located.
    2. The less a good is a necessity, the more elastic is its demand curve. Necessities tend to have fewer substitutes than do luxuries. Demand is highly inelastic.
    3. The more specifically a good is defined, the more elastic is its demand curve. If the definition of a good is specifically defined, such as an orange for breakfast, there are many substitutes that can be found such as bananas, grapefruit, peaches, etc. On the other hand, broadly defining a good, such as fresh fruit, leads to few substitutes.

13. 1. Cross elasticity of demand (the percent change in quantity demanded of one good divided by the percent change in the price of another good).
    2. Income elasticity of demand (the percent change in quantity demanded of a good divided by the percent change in income).

b. **Problems**

1. a)

Price	Quantity Demanded	Total Revenue	Price Elasticity
$8.00	8	$64	
			1.67
7.00	10	70	
			1.18
6.00	12	72	
			.85
5.00	14	70	
			.60
4.00	16	64	
			.41
3.00	18	54	

b) $6

c) Elastic: Above $6. Unitary: Approximately $6.
Inelastic: Below $6.

d)

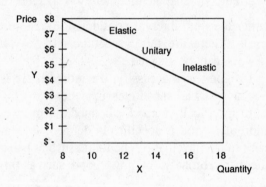

2.

Purchases		Budget
Good X	Good Y	$19
1		$\dfrac{-5}{15}$
2		$\dfrac{-5}{10}$
	1	$\dfrac{-1}{9}$
	2	$\dfrac{-1}{8}$
3		$\dfrac{-5}{3}$
	3	$\dfrac{-1}{2}$
	4	$\dfrac{-1}{\$0}$ Budget is totally spent

$$\frac{MU_x}{P_x} \frac{(25)}{(5)} = \frac{MU_y}{P_y} \frac{(5)}{(1)} = 5$$

at 3X and 4Y with all income ($19) spent

3. Hamburger: $\dfrac{3/8.5}{\$200/\$900} = -1.59$ Steak: $\dfrac{2/4}{\$200/\$900} = 2.25$

4. a) Cross price elasticity: .04/.10 = .4
   b) The goods are substitutes for each other.

5. In the US where water is plentiful, total utility is high, but its marginal utility is small because of the principle of diminishing marginal utility. Total utility from diamonds is relatively small (due to their scarcity) but their marginal utility is high (again due to their scarcity) so we are willing to pay a lot for them.

6. When the demand curve is flat, the elasticity is infinite. If one raises price, total revenue falls to zero. When the demand curve is perfectly vertical, the elasticity is zero. If one raises price, total revenue increases proportionately.

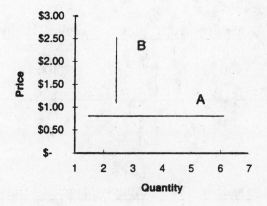

7. (a) (b-1,b-3)

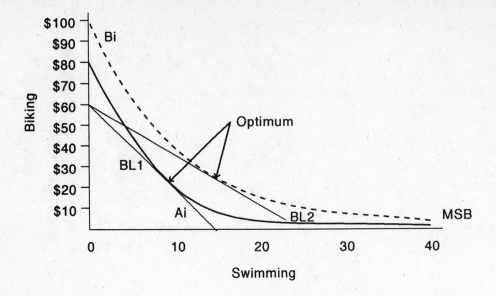

b-2 Approximately 20 biking and 10 swimming
b-4 Approximately 30 biking and 13 swimming

IV. Challenge Problems and Potential Essay Questions

a. Challenge Problems

1. a) You should purchase 3 bottles of wine and 3 pounds of cheese because the marginal utility ("extra satisfaction"—marginal means "extra"; utility means "satisfaction") in relation to the price for wine and cheese is equal at this quantity of wine and cheese purchased. $MU_w/P_w = MU_c/P_c$ at 3 bottles of wine and 3 pounds of cheese. See the table below. Also notice that no other combination of wine and cheese will yield as much total utility (575 utils) for $45.

(Wine)

Quantity	Total Utility	Marginal Utility	MUw/Pw
0	0	—	—
1	100	100	20
2	175	75	15
3	225	50	10
4	250	25	5
5	260	10	2

(Cheese)

Quantity	Total Utility	Marginal Utility	MUc/Pc
0	0	—	—
1	130	130	13
2	250	120	12
3	350	100	10
4	425	75	7.5
5	465	40	4

b) Now you should purchase 3 bottles of wine and 4 pounds of cheese because the marginal utility in relation to the price for wine and cheese is equal at this quantity of wine and cheese purchased. MUw/Pw = MUc/Pc at 3 bottles of wine and 4 pounds of cheese. See the table below. Also notice that no other combination of wine and cheese will yield as much total utility (650 utils) for $45.

(Wine)

Quantity	Total Utility	Marginal Utility	MUw/Pw
0	0	—	—
1	100	100	20
2	175	75	15
3	225	50	10
4	250	25	5
5	260	10	2

(Cheese)

Quantity	Total Utility	Marginal Utility	MUc/Pc
0	0	—	—
1	130	130	17.33
2	250	120	16
3	350	100	13.33
4	425	75	10
5	465	40	5.33

c) The law of demand states that the quantity demanded will rise as the price of the item falls. This was observed in our case of the falling price of cheese. The law of demand exists because of the principle of rational choice.

2. The relative price of gas has fallen. Because gas and cars are complementary goods, the decrease in the relative price of gas has increased the demand for relatively bigger cars, especially minivans, and engines with higher performance which consume more gas.

3. a) Ed = 0.5 (remember to drop the negative sign).

b) Consumers have an inelastic demand for almonds in this price range because the absolute value of the elasticity of demand coefficient is less than one.

c) Price inelasticity that means that consumers are relatively unresponsive to a price change.

d) One has to be careful in placing too much emphasis on the price elasticity of demand coefficient (number) because it is only an estimate of consumer responsiveness (the percentage change in the quantity demanded given some percentage change in the price). However, assuming this elasticity of demand coefficient is an exact number representing consumer responsiveness to a price change, then given that the Ed = 0.5, and the price falls by 10% then the quantity demanded will rise by 5%. [The trick is to multiply the Ed coefficient (0.5), or number, by the percentage change in the price (10) to get the percentage change in the quantity or demanded (5). But remember, the law of demand tells us that the quantity demanded moves in the opposite direction from the change in the price.] If the price was to rise by 15% then the quantity demanded would fall by 7.5% (0.5 × 15 = 7.5).

e) Total revenue (equal to P × Q) rises from $3,480 to $3,785.25. Whenever the elasticity of demand is inelastic then a price increase will increase total revenue (this is because the percentage increase in the price is greater than the percentage decrease in the quantity demanded). If the price was to fall (e.g. from $5.15 to $4.35) then total revenue would fall (e.g. from $3,785.25 to $3,480). So, there is a direct relationship between a change in the price and the change in total revenue for an inelastic good or service.

f) Because almonds have an inelastic demand then there must be few substitutes for them. See also p. 149 in the textbook.

4. It would choose the lower price, $29.95, because a lower price will increase total revenue when demand is elastic.

b. **Potential Essay Questions**

The following answers are annotated—they only indicate the general idea behind the answer.

1. The principle of diminishing marginal utility states that as more of a good, service or activity is consumed its marginal utility ("extra satisfaction") decreases, This is related to the principle of rational choice because we have to consider the marginal utility in relation to the price of the additional unit of a good, service or activity we are thinking about consuming. If $MUx/Px = MUy/Py$ then we have found the appropriate combination of "x" and "y" to consume because this indicates that the marginal utilities per dollar of the goods consumed are equal (the extra satisfaction per last dollar spent on the two goods are equal). Given our constraints (income and the prices of the items), no other combination will yield as much utility (satisfaction). However, if $MUx/Px > MUy/Py$ then we should consume more of "x" and less of "y" (because the extra satisfaction per last dollar spent on good "x" is greater than that for good "y") until the marginal utilities per dollar of the goods are equal. The opposite is also true. The same logic can be applied to more than two goods. All of this is related to the law of demand because if the price of good "x" decreases then this causes $MUx/Px > MUy/Py$ and we will consume more of good "x"—exactly what the law of demand predicts: we buy more of a good as the price falls.

2. Economists use their simple self-interest theory of choice because it cuts through many obfuscations, and in doing so often captures a part of reality that others miss. (See page 144.)

3. As a general rule, the more substitutes a good has, the more elastic is its demand. The number of substitutes is, in turn, affected by the time interval under consideration, whether the good is considered a necessity or a luxury, and the specificity to which the good is defined.

4. In order to maximize revenues firms will try to charge a higher price to those consumers which have a more inelastic demand (an increase in the price increases total revenue) and a lower price to those which have an elastic demand for the product.

Chapter 7   Supply, Production, and Costs: I

I. CHAPTER AT A GLANCE

Rip these two pages out for quick and easy reference.

1. When you supply a factor, you are forgoing its benefits for yourself. The opportunity cost of that foregone pleasure tends to increase the more you supply, which is why opportunity costs underlie the law of supply. (162)

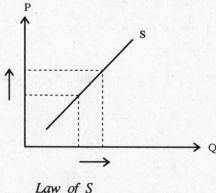

Law of S
states that as $P\uparrow s$, $Qs\uparrow s$

2. $Es = \dfrac{\text{Percent change in quantity}}{\text{Percent change in price}}$ (163)

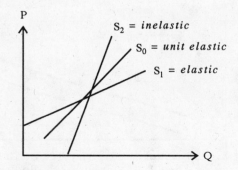

If $Es > 1 \Rightarrow$ *elastic*

$Es = 1 \Rightarrow$ *unit elastic*

$Es < 1 \Rightarrow$ *inelastic*

3. The long-run decision is a planning decision in which the firm has maximum flexibility. In the long run the firm can vary whatever inputs it wants. In the short run, some inputs are fixed. (166)

Long run $\Rightarrow$ *all inputs are variable* $\Rightarrow$ *all costs are variable costs.*

Short run $\Rightarrow$ *at least one input is fixed* $\Rightarrow$ *some fixed and some variable costs.*

4. a) The <u>law of diminishing marginal productivity</u> states that as more and more of a variable input is added to an existing fixed input, after some point the additional output one gets from the additonal input will fall. (168)

> *Sometimes called "flower pot law," its existence eventually causes costs of production to rise.*

> **<u>Study</u> all Exhibits in this chapter!*

   b) As more and more of a variable input is added to a fixed input, the law of diminishing marginal productivity causes marginal and average productivities to fall. As these fall, marginal and average costs rise. (173)

> *When productivity curves are falling, the corresponding cost curves are rising.*

> *Review Exhibit 6 on P. 175.*

5. a) Total cost curves relate total costs to output. Average costs measure total cost divided by the quantity produced. (170)

> *All costs are either fixed or variable and the sum of fixed and variable costs equals total cost TC = FC + VC*

> *Review Exhibit 4 on P. 172.*

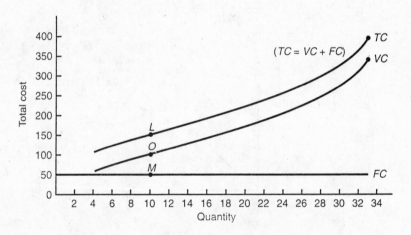

b) The marginal cost curve goes through the minimum point of the average total cost curve and average variable cost curve; each of these curves is U-shaped. The average fixed costs curve slopes down continuously. (172)

Review Exhibit 5 on P. 173.

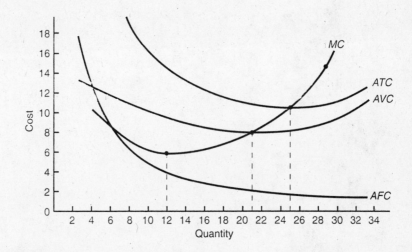

Know these diagrams and why the per unit cost curves are U-shaped: the law of diminishing marginal productivity.

6. When marginal cost exceeds average cost, average cost must be rising. When marginal cost is less than average cost, average cost must be falling. This relationship explains why the marginal cost curve always intersects the average cost curves at the minimum of the average cost curve. (174)

If MC > ATC, then ATC is rising.
If MC = ATC, then ATC is at its low point.
If MC < ATC, then ATC is falling.

*Also know how to calculate all 7 short-run cost figures! (FC, VC, TC, MC, AFC, AVC, and ATC)

II. MASTERY TEST

1. What is meant by the term **long run**?

   a) Certain inputs are fixed.
   b) All inputs are variable.
   c) A production period longer than one year.
   d) The market period.

2. The _____ is a period of time in which at least one input is fixed.

   a) production period.   b) market period.
   c) contracted period.   d) short run.

3. A variable input:

   a) varies with the output.
   b) remains unchanged.
   c) is strictly a short run consideration.
   d) is one that wears out with use.

4. Which input does not vary with output in the short run?

   a) Variable.   b) Fixed.
   c) Marginal.   d) Average.

5. How is marginal product calculated?

   a) The change in total product divided by change in total input.
   b) Total product divided by total input.
   c) The change in total product.
   d) Total product divided by the change in total output.

6. Average product may be described as:

   a) total product divided by the quantity of variable input used.
   b) increasing when marginal product is greater than average product.
   c) reaching a peak when marginal product and average product are equal.
   d) a, b, c.

7. Which costs do not vary with the level of output?

   a) Economic.
   b) Variable.
   c) Opportunity.
   d) Fixed.

8. What is the law of diminishing marginal returns?

   a) Total output from increases in variable inputs will eventually fall as more of the variable input is used with fixed inputs.
   b) Total output begins to fall as a result of a constant input of a variable resource.
   c) Additional output increases with additional inputs, and decreases with fewer inputs.
   d) Marginal product produced from increases in variable inputs will eventually fall as more of the variable input is used with the fixed inputs.

9. What costs are included in total costs?

a) Variable costs and fixed costs.
b) Average total costs plus marginal costs.
c) Average variable costs plus marginal costs.
d) Average fixed costs plus average marginal costs.

10. Marginal cost is best described as:

a) percentage change in variable cost.
b) percentage change in production costs divided by total output.
c) the change in total cost.
d) a, c.

11. When marginal product is rising, marginal costs are:

a) rising.   b) falling.
c) unitary.   d) inelastic.

12. When marginal product is falling, total cost and variable cost curves are:

a) falling.   b) equal.
c) rising.   d) elastic.

13. If labour costs $12 per hour, and marginal output is 6 units, what is the marginal cost of producing the next unit of output?

a) $72   b) $20
c) $2   d) $.50

14. A straight-line supply curve passing through the origin:

a) must be unit elastic.
b) has a constant elasticity, but need not be unit elastic.
c) is more elastic at the top than at the bottom.
d) is more elastic at the bottom than at the top.

15. Other things being equal, if deregulation of airline fares led to lower prices and higher revenues, it could be concluded that:

a) demand was elastic.
b) demand was inelastic.
c) supply was elastic.
d) supply was inelastic.

16. Elasticity of supply refers to:

a) percentage change in price resulting from a 3% change in quantity produced.
b) percentage change in quantity produced resulting from a percentage change in price.
c) percentage change in price produced resulting from a percentage change in quantity.
d) percentage change in price resulting from a change in quantity produced.

17. Calculate the average (arc) elasticity of supply from the following data:

Date	Price	Quantity
January 1	$ 90	400
January 31	$100	500

a) .222
b) .496
c) 2.22
d) 4.96

18. An elasticity of supply of .72 means that:

a) supply is elastic.
b) quantity supplied changes .72 units for each 1% change in price.
c) quantity supplied changes .72% for each 1% change in price.
d) price changes by .72% for each 1% change in quantity produced.

19. When a supply curve is perfectly horizontal, it is:

a) perfectly inelastic.
c) unit elastic.
b) perfectly elastic.
d) elastic.

20. The St. Laurence Manufacturing Company pays $1500 for inputs, and sells its product for $2500. Its value added is:

a) $1000
c) $2500
b) $1500
d) $4000

21. The relationship between any combination of input service and the maximum attainable output from that combination is the:

a) technology function.
b) learning curve.
c) production function.
d) cost/revenue function.

22. Big Steel Company increased its work force by almost 25% in 1995 but only increased output by 18%. What is the likely explanation?

a) the law of increasing utility.
b) the law of diminishing supply.
c) the law of diminishing demand.
d) the law of diminishing marginal returns.

23. Harry's Hamburger Heaven produces 500 burger sandwiches at a total cost of $350. Harry's average variable cost is 50¢ per unit. What is Harry's total fixed cost?

a) $150
c) 25¢
b) $300
d) $100

24. A curve that always appears downsloping is the:

a) marginal cost curve.
c) average variable cost curve.
b) average fixed cost curve.
d) production function curve.

25. The change in total cost divided by the change in output is the:

   a) marginal cost.
   b) average cost.
   c) variable cost.
   d) fixed cost.

26. Over that range of output in which the law of diminishing marginal productivity is experienced then:

   a) increasing returns are realized.
   b) this is the most likely range of output for a firm to produce.
   c) diminishing marginal productivity is being experienced and average productivity is negative.
   d) marginal productivity is rising and marginal costs of production are falling.
   e) there are too few units of a variable input being used with the fixed input(s).

27. Which of the following statements is true?

   a) Marginal product is the output per worker.
   b) Average product is the extra output associated with one additional unit of a variable factor of production.
   c) If a firm can produce 500 units of output with 5 workers, 540 units of output with 6 workers, then the average product of 6 workers is 90 units of output.
   d) If a firm can produce 500 units of output with 5 workers, 540 units of output with 6 workers, then the marginal product of the 6th worker is 90 units of output.
   e) Whenever average productivity is rising then average variable costs are rising.

28. Which of the following statements are true about a firm's costs of production?

   a) If a firm shuts down for a month then its total costs for the month will equal its fixed costs for the month.
   b) Average fixed costs equal average variable costs minus average total costs.
   c) Marginal costs equal the change in total costs divided by the change in variable costs.
   d) Average total cost equal total cost multiplied by the output level.
   e) Average fixed costs fall and then rise as output expands.

29. A firm is producing 100 units of output at a total cost of $800. The firm's average variable cost is $5 per unit. The firm's:

   a) marginal cost is $8.
   b) total variable cost is $300.
   c) average fixed cost is $3.
   d) average total cost is $500.
   e) total fixed cost is $755.

30. The only variable input used in the production of pickles in a small factory is labour. Currently 5 workers are employed; each works 40 hours per week and is paid $15 per hour. If fixed costs are $4,000 per week and total output is 4,000 jars of pickles per week, then:

   a) average fixed cost is $1.
   b) total costs are $7,000.
   c) total variable costs are $3,000.
   d) average costs are $1.75.
   e) All of the above.

III. SHORT ANSWER EXERCISES AND PROBLEMS

a. **Short Answer Exercises**

1. a) What is the law of supply?

    b) Why does the law of supply exist? Include in your answer a discussion of the opportunity cost.

2. What is meant by the term "price elasticity of supply"?

3. What is the difference between "short-run" and "long-run" in production planning?

4. Explain the law of diminishing marginal productivity.

5. List and discuss the various production costs discussed in the chapter.

6. What is the relationship between (a) the average variable cost curve and marginal cost curve and (b) the average product curve and marginal product curve?

7. Fill in the following with *constant, falling,* or *rising.*

   If MC > ATC then ATC is _____.

   If MC = ATC, then ATC is _____.

   If MC < ATC, then ATC is _____.

8. The author described an easy way to estimate the elasticity of any supply curve. What was suggested?

9. What is the function of a "production table"?

10. Explain why the average total cost curve is intersected at its lowest point by the marginal cost curve.

b. **Problems**

1. Helen's Stitchery produces a single product: "gimme" caps. The caps are produced using a fixed plant size, with 10 sewing machines and varying quantities of labour. Helen has noticed that as she hires additional workers, the total output of caps goes up for a while. She has also noticed, that at times the workers seem to get in each other's way and extra output begins to decline.

   a) Given the information below, calculate the marginal product of Helen's workers.
   b) Graph the total and marginal products.
   c) How many workers can Helen employ before diminishing marginal returns set in?

Workers	Output (Dozens of caps per day.)	Marginal Product
0	0	
1	8	
2	19	
3	32	
4	45	
5	60	
6	71	
7	75	
8	77	
9	77	
10	75	
11	65	

Graph of total product produced

Graph of marginal product produced

2. Complete the following table of cost figures and then graph the information on the graphs provided below. Assume total fixed costs are $4.

Output	Total Variable Costs	Total costs	Average Variable cost	Average total cost	Marginal cost
0	0	8.00			
1	4.00				
2				5.50	
3		13.00			
4					3.00
5			3.20		
6					5.00
7	27.00				

Dollars (total fixed and total variable costs)

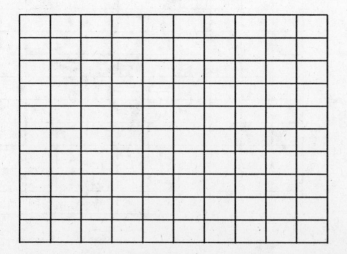

Dollars (average total, average variable and marginal costs)

3. Carefully study the below graph.

   a) Describe the relationship between MC and AC at their intersection.
   b) Does this relationship fit the patterns you have been studying in this chapter?
   c) What should the relationship be at the intersection?

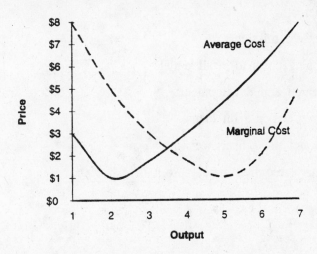

4. Calculate the price elasticity of supply using average prices and average quantities from the following hypothetical supply schedule for tea.

Quantity supplied per Week	Price per ounce (cents)	Price elasticity of supply
1,000	25	
700	20	
400	15	
100	10	
0	5	

IV. CHALLENGE PROBLEMS AND POTENTIAL ESSAY QUESTIONS

a. Challenge Problems

1. a). Suppose the price rises from $8 to $9 and the quantity supplied rises from 4,000 to 5,000 units. What is the price elasticity of supply coefficient, or number equal to? How would one interpret that number—what does it mean?

   b) What determines the degree of price elasticity of supply—the responsiveness of suppliers to a price change?

   c) What is the geometric trick for estimating the elasticity of supply introduced in this chapter of the textbook?

2. Determine whether each of the following cost items, or categories would most likely be a fixed cost (FC) or a variable cost (VC) item or category by placing a check in the appropriate column.

	FC	VC
Labour:	_____	_____
Raw materials:	_____	_____
Rent for building and land:	_____	_____
Advertising:	_____	_____
Sales commissions:	_____	_____
Shipping costs to retail outlets:	_____	_____
Research and development:	_____	_____
Interest expense on loans:	_____	_____
Fire and theft insurance:	_____	_____
Owner's required annual profit of $75,000:	_____	_____

3. Suppose you have just bought a car wash and you're going to rename it "The Personal Touch Car Wash." You have been provided with the following information found in the table below. This information is on a per hour basis. Suppose labour is your only variable input and your cost of labour per hour (the wage rate plus income taxes...) is $10 per worker. Fill in the missing information in the table and then answer the following questions.

Labour	Output (TP)	MP	AP	FC	VC	TC	MC*	AFC	AVC	ATC
0	0			$50						
1	4			$50						
2	12			$50						
3	17			$50						
4	20			$50						
5	21			$50						
6	19			$50						

*Because marginal cost is the extra cost of producing one additional unit of output, you will have to estimate the marginal cost for each of the additional units of output produced—except for the 21st. Just simply divide the change in total cost by the change in the output level.

a) With which worker(s) do we realize increasing returns? How do you know?

b) With which worker do we first realize the law of diminishing marginal productivity? How do you know?

c) With which worker(s) do we realize diminishing returns? How do you know?

d) Would you employ the sixth worker? Why or why not?

e) How are marginal productivity and marginal cost related?

f) How are average productivity and average variable cost related?

g) What is the relationship between the marginal productivity and average productivity of these workers?

h) What is the relationship between marginal cost and average variable cost? What is the relationship between marginal cost and average total cost?

4. Refer to the cost curves for a firm shown below when answering the following questions. Assume the firm is currently producing 100 units of output.

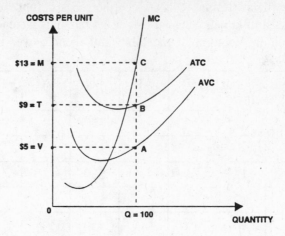

a) What is the number representing the marginal cost of producing the 100th unit of output? What geometric line segment represents that number?

b) What is ATC when output is 100? What geometric line segment represents that number?

c) What is AVC when output is 100? What geometric line segment represents that number?

d) What is AFC when output is 100? What geometric line segment represents that number?

e) What is TC when output is 100? What geometric area represents that number?

f) What is VC when output is 100? What geometric area represents that number?

g) What is FC when output is 100? What geometric area represents that number?

h) Why does the vertical distance between the AVC and ATC curves decrease as output expands?

b. Potential Essay Questions

1. Why do opportunity costs underlie the law of supply?

2. What are the similarities and differences between the price elasticity of demand and the price elasticity of supply?

3. a) What would happen to the AVC, ATC, and MC cost curves if fixed costs increased but variable costs remain unchanged.

   b) What would happen to AVC, ATC, and MC cost curves if variable costs increased but fixed costs remain unchanged?

4. What is your opportunity cost of studying one additional hour beyond that which you have already studied? Ooops? ... See you later?

V. ANSWERS

II. Mastery Test

1. b	6. d	11. b	16. b	21. c	26. b
2. d	7. d	12. c	17. c	22. d	27. c
3. a	8. d	13. c	18. c	23. d	28. a
4. b	9. a	14. a	19. b	24. b	29. c
5. c	10. d	15. a	20. a	25. a	30. e

III. Short Answer Exercises and Problems

a. Short Answer Exercises

1. a) The law of supply states there is a direct (positive) relationship between the price and the quantity supplied. That is, as the price rises (falls) the quantity supplied rises (falls).

   b) The law of supply exists because of increasing opportunity costs. In other words, the supply of goods is dependent upon individuals' willingness to supply the inputs they own. Higher prices have to be paid to input owners—like wages to workers—to compensate them for their opportunity costs (leisure). Therefore, costs per unit rise as more is produced. Hence, a higher price is required to produce a greater quantity supplied in the market.

2. It is the percent change in quantity supplied divided by the percent change in price. It is a measure of the responsiveness of quantities supplied to changes in price.

3. In the long-run a firm can choose among all possible production techniques; in the short run it is constrained in its choices.

4. As more and more of a variable input is added to a fixed input, the additional output the firm gets will eventually decrease.

5. Those costs that are spent (or committed) and cannot be changed in the period of time under consideration are **fixed costs**. There are no fixed costs in the long-run, because all inputs are variable and hence their costs are variable.

   Costs that change as output changes are **variable costs**. Examples would include materials used and labour hours.

   All costs are fixed or variable, so the sum of fixed and variable costs equals total cost. The general statement is: TC = FC + VC.

   Total cost divided by the quantity produced is the **average total cost**. The general statement is: ATC = TC/Q

   Total fixed cost divided by the quantity produced is the **average fixed cost**. The general statement is: AFC = FC/Q

   Variable cost divided by quantity produced is the **average variable cost**. The general statement is: AVC = VC/Q

   The change in total cost evoked by a change in quantity produced is the **marginal cost**. The general statement is: MC = ΔTC

6. The average cost curve and marginal cost curve are mirror images of the average product curve and the marginal product curve.

7. Rising
Constant
Falling

8. Extend the curve toward the X and Y axis of the graph. If the extended curve intersects the X axis, the supply curve is inelastic. If the extended curve intersects the Y axis, the supply curve is elastic. If the extended curve intersects the axis at the origin, the supply curve is unitary.

9. It shows the output resulting from various combinations of factors of production or inputs.

10. If marginal cost is less than average total cost, the average total cost must fall. When marginal cost is greater than average total cost, average cost must rise. Therefore, marginal cost intersects average total cost at its lowest point.

a. **Problems**

1. a)

Workers	Output (Dozens of caps per day.	Marginal Product
0	0	—
1	8	8
2	19	11
3	32	13
4	45	13
5	60	15
6	71	11
7	75	4
8	77	2
9	77	0
10	75	–2
11	65	–10

1. b)

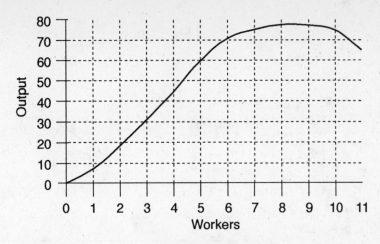

Marginal Output

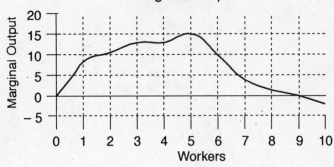

2.

Output	Total Var Cost	Total Cost	Avg Var Cost	Avg Total Cost	Marginal Cost
0	$0	$4	$	$	$
1	4	8	4	8	4
2	7	11	3.50	5.50	3
3	9	13	3	4.33	2
4	12	16	3	4	3
5	16	20	3.20	4	4
6	21	25	3.50	4.17	5
7	27	31	3.86	4.43	6

Total Fixed and Variable Costs

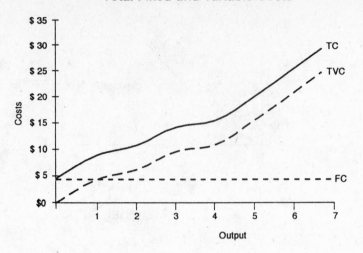

Average Total, Variable and Marginal Costs

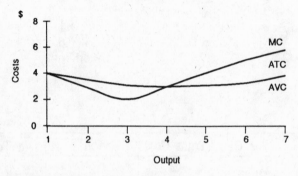

3. a) According to the graph, C intersects AC to the left of the minimum point of AC.
    b) It does not fit a normal pattern.
    c) MC should intersect with AC at AC's minimum point. As MC falls, AC falls. As MC rises, AC rises.

4.

Quantity supplied per Week	Price per ounce (cents)	Price elasticity of supply
1,000	25	1.59
700	20	1.91
400	15	3.00
100	10	3.00
0	5	

IV. Challenge Problems and Potential Essay Questions

a. Challenge Problems

1. a) Es = 2. [Note that the quantity increases by 25% (1,000/4,000 = 1/4 = 0.25 = 25%) when the price increases 12.5% (1/8 = 0.125 = 12.5%), and Es equals percent change in quantity divided by percent change in price (25% divided by 12.5% = 2)]. This means that in this price range, for every one percent increase (decrease) in the price there will occur approximately a two percent increase (decrease) in the quantity supplied. (Note the similarities between the calculations and the interpretations of the price elasticity of demand and supply).

    b) The most important determinant is the number of substitutes for the good (e.g., the number of other goods which could be produced by the producers). The ease of substitution depends on the amount of time under consideration. The shorter the time period under consideration, the fewer the possibilities of substitution (e.g., the fewer the number of other goods which the producers could produce), and the less elastic (more inelastic) the supply.

    c) If the supply curve intersects the horizontal axis then it's inelastic. If it intercepts the vertical axis then its elastic. If it goes through the origin, it's unitary elastic. (See graph on P. 164).

2. Variable costs are those costs which do vary with the output level (and *because* the output level changes). The only variable cost items, or categories are: labour, raw materials, sales commissions, and shipping costs. All other cost categories are fixed costs because the costs associated with these items or categories do not vary with the output level. That is, you would not expect these cost categories to change because the quantity produced changes.

3. See table below.

Labour	Output (TP)	MP	AP	FC	VC	TC	MC	AFC	AVC	ATC
0	0	—	—	$50	—	—	—	—	—	—
1	4	4	4	$50	$10	$60	$2.50	$12.50	$2.50	$15.00
2	12	8	6	$50	$20	$70	$1.25	$ 4.17	$1.67	$ 5.84
3	17	5	5.7	$50	$30	$80	$2.00	$ 2.94	$1.76	$ 4.70
4	20	3	5	$50	$40	$90	$3.33	$ 2.50	$2.00	$ 4.50
5	21	1	4.2	$50	$50	$100	$10	$ 2.38	$2.38	$ 4.76
6	19	−2	3.2	$50	$60	$110	—	$ 2.63	$3.16	$ 5.79

    a) Increasing returns are experienced through the first two workers because marginal productivity is increasing.

    b) The third worker because marginal productivity (MP) is first diminishing with this worker.

c) Diminishing returns are experienced beginning with the third worker and continues with each additional worker employed because marginal productivity continues to fall. This happens because of the law of diminishing marginal productivity.

d) No, because the sixth worker's marginal productivity (extra output–cars washed) is negative. This worker is just getting in the way–total output is falling. Therefore, it may be helpful for you to draw a line through that row in the table because we will never be experiencing any of the costs associated with the sixth worker.

e) Whenever marginal productivity is rising (falling), marginal cost is falling (rising).

f) Whenever average productivity is rising (falling), average variable cost is falling (rising).

g) Whenever marginal productivity is greater than (less than) average productivity, average productivity rises (falls).

h) Whenever marginal cost is less than (greater than) average variable or average total cost then average variable and average total cost is falling (rising).

4. a) MC for the 100th unit of output is equal to $13 (the extra cost of producing that 100th unit is $13), or line segment OM. (The line segment OM simply represents the distance or amount of $13).

b) ATC = $9, or line segment OT, when output is 100.

c) AVC = $5, or line segment OV, when output is 100.

d) AFC = $4. Note that AFC = ATC − AVC. The line segment representing AFC is line segment AB, which is also equal to line segment VT. Recall that, at a given output level, the vertical distance between the ATC and AVC curves equals AFC at that particular output level.

e) TC = $900. (Note that TC = ATC × Q = $9 × 100 = $900). The geometric area representing TC is area OTBQ. (Note that like any area, the area OTBQ is equal to a width multiplied by a length. Think of the width as line segment OT, representing ATC. Think of the length as line segment OQ, representing the output level, Q. OT multiplied by OQ equals area OTBQ.)

f) VC = $500 (VC = AVC × Q = $5 × 100 = $500), or area OVAQ (OVAQ = line segment OV multiplied by line segment OQ).

g) FC = $400 (FC = AFC × Q = $4 × 100 = $400; or, FC = TC − VC = $900 − $500 = $400). The area representing FC is area VTBA. (FC = TC − VC = OTBQ − OVAQ = VTBA).

Note that one can obtain all seven (7) short-run cost figures when only provided with the MC, AVC, and ATC curves! Remember how to do this. It will come in handy later.

h) Because the vertical distance between the ATC and AVC curves equals AFC, and AFC decreases as output increases, then the vertical distance between the ATC and AVC curves decreases as output increases.

b. Potential Essay Questions

The following answers are annotated—they only indicate the general idea behind the answer.

1. As additional units of output are produced, then ever larger amounts of inputs, like workers, will be required. In order to attract even more workers then even higher wages have to be paid. Some people have a high opportunity cost—pay they could receive elsewhere, or a high value of foregone leisure associated wth working more. Higher prices paid input owners (like wages) means that producing more output increases per unit costs of production. Moreover, decreasing marginal productivity increases per unit costs of production. Hence, higher prices are required to produce more output. That is, there is a direct (positive) relationship between the price of a good and the quantity supplied—the law of supply is observed.

2. They both measure the responsiveness to a price change. They both use the same equation and the interpretation of the elasticity coefficient, or number is the same—except, of course in one case we're talking about buying and the other, supplying. However, on the supply side there is no negative sign to contend with. Moreover, the main determinant of the elasticity of supply is the amount of time the producer has to respond to the price change. The greater the amount of time under consideration, the greater the output response, and therefore the greater the elasticity of supply (the more elastic).

3. a) The AVC and MC curves would remain unchanged because they are unaffected by any change in fixed costs. However, the ATC curve would shift up indicating an increase in average total costs. The ATC curve shifts up because AFC will have increased at every output level (recall that ATC = AVC + AFC, and the vertical distance between the AVC and ATC curves equals AFC).

   b) All three curves would shift up because TVC would increase causing AVC to increase as well as ATC. Redo question 3) in the previous section using VC = $15 per unit of the variable factor instead of $10.

4. The opportunity cost would be the value to you of the activity which you gave up; e.g., watching TV, partying.

Chapter 8   Supply, Production, and Costs: II

I. CHAPTER AT A GLANCE

Rip this page out for quick and easy reference.

1. Technical efficiency is efficiency that does not consider costs of inputs. The least-cost technically efficient process is the economically efficient process. (180)

    Firms try to be economically efficient because they want to minimize costs.

2. In the long run all inputs are variable, so only economies of scale can influence the shape of the long-run curve. (182) *See Exhibit 1.*

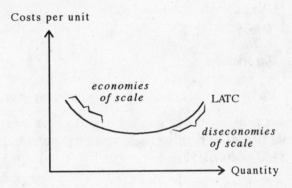

3. Diminishing marginal productivity refers to the decline in productivity caused by increasing units of a variable input being added to a given input. Diseconomies of scale refer to the decreases in productivity which are brought about because of increases of all inputs equally. (183)

    Diminishing marginal productivity refers to the short run (at least one input is fixed). In the long run all inputs can vary.

    If double all inputs and __per-unit__ costs fall (rise) then you have economies (diseconomies) of scale experienced.

4. The envelope relationship is the relationship explaining that, at the planned output level, short-run average total cost equals long-run average total cost, but at all other levels of output, short-run average total cost is higher than long-run average total cost. (184) *See Exhibit 3.*

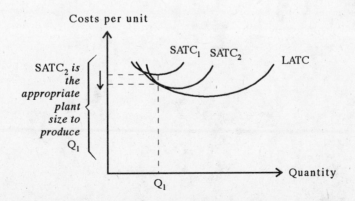

5. The difference between the expected price of a good and the expected average total cost of producing it—the good's opportunity cost—is the supplier's expected economic profit per unit. The opportunity cost must be below price for a good to be supplied. (185)

> *Potential economic profit motivates entrepreneurs to supply those goods demanded by consumers. The greater demand, the greater the price and profit potential, and the greater the quantity supplied.*

> **Distinguish accounting from economic profit!*

6. Some of the problems of using cost analysis in the real world include: (186)

   1. *Economies of scope;*
   2. *Learning by doing and technological change;*
   3. *Many dimensions;*
   4. *Unmeasured costs;*
   5. *Joint costs;*
   6. *Indivisible costs;*
   7. *Uncertainty;*
   8. *Asymmetries; and*
   9. *Multiple planning and adjustment periods with many different short runs.*

7. Marginal cost analysis can be applied to just about every decision facing you. For example, the marginal benefit of reading these marginal notes must exceed the marginal cost, or you shouldn't read them. (190)

> *(Marginal ⇒ "extra")*

> *Think on the margin! What's the extra benefit and cost of one additional unit?*

II. MASTERY TEST

1. Long-run average total costs can decrease due to:

   a) economies of scale.
   b) short-run average cost decreasing.
   c) long-run total costs decreasing.
   d) an increase in long-run marginal costs.

2. The long-run average total cost curve will start to rise beyond a certain point due to:

   a) economies of scale.
   b) diseconomies of scale.
   c) greater returns to scale.
   d) higher morale among employees due to increased production.

3. Which of the following is a major contributing factor to diseconomies of scale?

   a) Lack of access to modern technology.
   b) Inability to shift plant site and size.
   c) Increased monitoring costs.
   d) Government interference.

4. The long-run and the short-run are basically different in that:

   a) zero output in the long-run still incurs a cost.
   b) variable costs are higher in the short-run than they are in the long-run.
   c) All inputs are fixed in the long-run, and only certain inputs are fixed in the short-run.
   d) Some inputs are fixed and others variable in the short-run, while all inputs are flexible in the long-run.

5. The short-run average cost curve is at its minimum point and is equal to long-run average cost curve when:

   a) production is on the long-run average cost curve.
   b) production is at its short-run minimum point.
   c) both the short-run and long-run curves are negative.
   d) the long-run average cost curve is at its minimum.

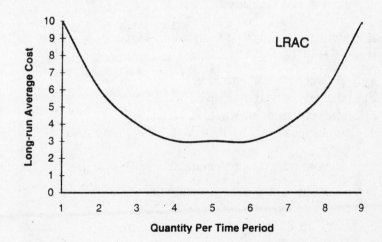

6. Refer to the figure in question 5. For any output up to 4, this company will experience:

   a) smaller returns to scale.
   b) constant returns to scale.
   c) diseconomies of scale.
   d) economies of scale

7. Refer to the figure in question 5. Constant returns to scale will occur at output levels of:

   a) 1 to 5. b) 4 to 6.
   c) 7 to 9. d) none of the above.

8. Refer to the figure in question 5. Between output levels of 6 and 9, the firm is in the range of:

   a) constant returns to scale.
   b) diseconomies of scale.
   c) economies of scale.
   d) increasing returns to scale.

9. Profit over and above covering explicit costs and implicit costs is:

   a) accounting profit.
   b) normal profit.
   c) implicit profit.
   d) economic profit.

10. The Greater Montreal Distributing Co. accounting profit was $30,000 last year. The owner has been offered a job with another company with an annual salary of $25,000. The total investment in the business is $70,000, and a 12% return could be earned in other investments. The economic profit is:

    a) $6,600. b) $66,400.
    c) −$3,400. d) −$8,400.

11. Economies of scope refers to:

    a) short-run marginal costs.
    b) long-run average costs.
    c) spreading indivisible set-up costs over multiple product lines.
    d) dimensional decisions.

12. If labour is assumed to be abundant in Mexico, the economically efficient method of producing shoes would be:

    a) relatively capital intensive.
    b) relatively labour intensive.
    c) relatively land intensive.
    d) the same as in Canada.

13. The economically rational entrepreneur brings together the factor inputs of production to:

    a) make the world a better place in which to live.
    b) provide jobs for workers.
    c) clean up the environment.
    d) earn a profit.

14. What is technical efficiency?

    a) Lowest cost production methods.
    b) As few inputs as possible are used to produce a given output.
    c) Extensive use of technology in production.
    d) Emphasis on research and development in the firm.

15. Using the method of production that produces a given level of output at the lowest possible cost is:

    a) economic efficiency.
    b) technical efficiency.
    c) increasing returns to scale.
    d) constant returns to scale.

16. If the total cost of producing 10,000 ball-point pens is $4,000 and the total cost of producing 20,000 ball-point pens is $6000, then the firm is experiencing:

    a) economies of scope.
    b) diseconomies of scale.
    c) economies of scale.
    d) diminishing marginal productivity.

17. Diminishing marginal productivity is associated with all but:

    a) increasing per-unit costs.
    b) short run.
    c) fixed costs.
    d) economies of scale.

18. North Bay Manufacturing Company experiences economies of scale over all its relevant levels of output. Its long-run average total cost curve will always:

    a) be horizontal
    b) slope downward
    c) slope upward
    d) be vertical.

19. A firm's minimum level of production refers to:

    a) levels of production that spreads set-up costs out far enough to produce profitably.
    b) its maximum level of production.
    c) typical level of production.
    d) economic level of production.

20. The U-shape of a firm's long-run average cost curve is usually associated with:

    a) short-run cost structure.
    b) indivisible set-up costs.
    c) marginal productivity.
    d) economies and diseconomies of scale.

21. Increased monitoring costs are usually associated with:

    a) diminishing marginal productivity.
    b) diseconomies of scale.
    c) indivisible set-up costs.
    d) increased specialization.

22. Bully Vending Machine Co. expanded production by doubling its factory size. Output increased from 100 units of output per day to 190 units per day. This most likely represents:

    a) diminishing marginal productivity.
    b) economies of scale.
    c) economies of scope.
    d) diseconomies of scale.

23. What is the "envelope relationship"?

    a) The short-run average total cost equals long-run average total cost at planned output level, but at all other points, short-run average total cost is lower than long-run average total cost.
    b) Short-run average total cost equals long-run average total cost, at planned production, but at all other points, short-run average total cost is higher than long-run average total cost.
    c) The long-run average total cost curve includes the minimum point on each short-run average total cost curve.
    d) Long-run average total cost equals short-run average total cost at every level of output.

24. A business owner makes 400 items by hand in 500 hours. She could have earned $20 an hour working for someone else. If the item sells for $50 each and the explicit costs total $12,000, then:

    a) total revenue equals $20,000.
    b) implicit costs equal $10,000.
    c) the accounting profits equal $8,000.
    d) the economic loss equals $2,000.
    e) All of the above.

25. You own 40 shares of X Company stock at a cost of $200 and 50 shares of Y Company stock at a cost $300. You can sell either the X or the Y Company stock for $500. Ignoring any tax consequences, an economist would suggest:

    a) sell the shares that cost $200.
    b) sell one-half of each, because the selling price is the same.
    c) sell the shares that cost $300.
    d) make your decision based on what you expect to happen to the price of the stock in the future.

26. Sally Student cashed in $1,000 of bonds paying 10% annual interest and used the money to purchase stock. She sold the stock after one year for $1,300. Her *economic* profit on these transactions was:

    a) $1,300.
    b) $300.
    c) $200.
    d) $1,000.

III. SHORT ANSWER EXERCISES AND PROBLEMS

a. Short Answer Exercises

1. What is meant by the term "technical efficiency" in producing outputs?

2. When a firm is pursuing "economic efficiency" what is it doing?

3. Discuss how diminishing marginal productivity influences the shape of the short-run cost curve.

4. How do economies of scale influence the shape of long-run cost curves?

5. If economies of scale are quite extensive in a particular industry, would you expect a large number of relatively small firms or a small number of relatively large firms operating within the industry?

6. In an underdeveloped country we might reject primitive labour intensive techniques in farming. Could this be economically efficient? Explain.

7. What role do entrepreneurs and profits play in a market created economy?

8. What is meant by the term "diseconomies of scale"? What are the major contributors to it?

9. Describe the envelope relationship between short-run cost curves and long-run cost curves.

10. Explain the central role of opportunity costs in all supply decisions.

11. What is meant by "economies of scope"?

12. Over and above quantity decisions, what other continuing questions must be considered in the real world?

13. Compare an accountant's and an economist's measurement of profit.

b. Problems

1. Assume you are able to accumulate the following long-term production and cost figures for a component Chryford Inc. is producing. Complete the graph below and indicate on the curve a) economies of scale, b) minimum level of production, and c) diseconomies of scale.

Quantity (thousands)	Long Run Average Cost
24	$116
26	107
28	102
30	100
34	100
36	102
38	103
39	105
40	108
42	112

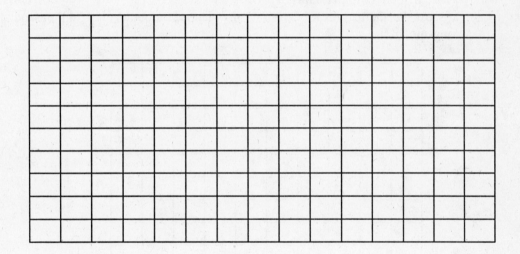

2. Chryford Inc. (see 1 above) fixed costs are currently $1,036 thousands and average variable costs are as follows:

Output (in thousands)	AVC	TC	ATC
24	$70		
26	67		
28	65		
30	69		
34	80		

a) Given this short-run period, complete the above table for total costs and average total costs.

b) Graph your results on Chryford's long-run average total cost graph you prepared for (1) above.

c) Given this short run situation, what level of production would Chryford get the lowest average total cost per unit?

d) Discuss the alternatives for Chryford of a planned output level of 34 thousand units on a long-run basis.

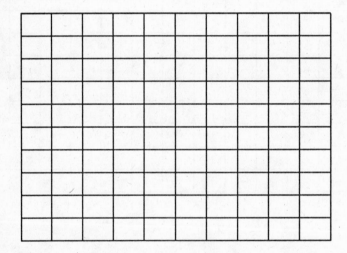

3. Tommy Salesman quit a promising career to go into business for himself. He purchased a retail frozen yogurt and sandwich store franchise (including the fixtures and equipment) for $50,000 from his savings, and started learning and operating the business. He felt that the business seemed pretty good, but he was having trouble paying the bills on a timely basis. At the end of his first year of operations, Tommy prepared the following brief income statement for the business and asked you for an opinion and advice.

Tommy's Frozen Yogurt
Income Statement
For the Year ended December 31, 1996

Total sales		$72,000
Operating costs:		
Food supplies	$22,000	
Store rent	18,000	
labour	20,000	
Utilities	6,000	
Insurance	1,500	
Total (accounting) costs		67,500
Profit		$ 4,500

Other useful information: During the year, Tommy purchased additional furniture and equipment for $8,000. Tommy withdrew $10,000 for personal living expenses.

In addition to the above information you learn that Tommy previously earned $40,000 to $50,000 per year as a salesman, and earned an average of 7% interest on his savings. You also learn that several similar businesses in the area have recently closed due to lack of public acceptance of the product. The equipment and the franchise has a current resale value at this time of $10,000.

a) As an economist, reanalyze the financial data taking into consideration the hidden costs.
b) What would you recommend Tommy do?

IV. CHALLENGE PROBLEMS AND POTENTIAL ESSAY QUESTIONS

a. Challenge Problems

1. Explain the following statement: "It is possible for a firm to be technically efficient and not economically efficient, but it is impossible for a firm to be economically efficient without being technically efficient."

2. What could help account for computer hardware manufacturers getting increasingly more involved with the development and production of computer software, or the airline passenger service businesses getting involved in air parcel and small package delivery service, or soft drink manufacturers buying up fast food restaurants (e.g. Pepsi-Cola company buying up Kentucky Fried Chicken and Pizza Hut—to name a few)?

3. Suppose you and a friend are thinking about opening a fast food vending service at a nearby resort during your summer break. This will entail serving pizzas out of a vendor's truck. This is an alternative to working a factory job where you could each earn $7,000 over the summer break. A fully equipped truck could be leased for $9,000. Insurance and other miscellaneous operating expenses total $1,000. Given your projected sales revenues of $33,000 you anticipate your variable costs to total $8,000. Together, you and your friend have just enough money to cover all of the summer's fixed and variable costs of the business in the bank. If you pull that money out of the bank then you will have to collectively forego $1,500 in interest income for the summer.

   a) What would be the accounting profit for your business?

   b) What would be the economic profit for your business?

4. Explain why, when long-run average costs are decreasing and economies of scale are experienced, it may be better for a firm to operate a larger plant with some excess capacity (not operating at that scale of operation's minimum average total costs) rather than a smaller plant which is operating at peak efficiency (at that plant sizes' minimum average total costs). (*Hint: You may want to graph a long-run average cost curve as an envelope of short-run average cost curves and use that graph as a visual aid in helping you answer this question.*)

b. Potential Essay Questions

1. What impact will "learning by doing" (sometimes called a learning curve phenomenon) have on the long-run average cost curve?

2. What is meant by economies and diseconomies of scale, and what causes them to be experienced? What impact does this have on the shape of the long-run average cost curve?

3. What's the difference between diminishing marginal productivity and diseconomies of scale?

4. Assume a painting firm is offered a contract (and no other contracts are being offered to the firm at this time) for $24,000 to paint the interior of a new office building. Labour and other variable costs are expected to be $18,000. The firm has all of the materials necessary to complete the job on hand in its inventory. Assume that the materials (primarily paint) originally cost the firm $7,000 but that price declines in paint have resulted in a current market value of $5,000. The market price for paint is not likely to change in the near future, so no gains are expected from holding the paint in inventory. Should the firm accept the contract? Why, or why not?

V. ANSWERS

II. Mastery Test

1. a	7. b	13. d	19. a	25. d
2. b	8. b	14. b	20. d	26. c
3. c	9. d	15. a	21. b	
4. d	10. c	16. c	22. d	
5. d	11. c	17. d	23. b	
6. d	12. b	18. b	24. e	

III. Short Answer Exercises

1. As few inputs as possible are used to produce a given output.

2. Given the available inputs and the prices, and after reviewing the available production technologies, the firm will try to choose the method of production that produces a given level of output at the lowest possible cost.

3. As more and more of a variable input is added to a fixed input, eventually marginal output begins to fall. As marginal output begins to fall, marginal cost begins to rise.

4. Certain production technologies require substantial indivisible set-up costs. By spreading these indivisible set-up costs over a large number units, the long-run average cost per unit is relatively low.

5. If economies of scale are quite extensive in an industry (i.e., larger and larger scales of operation result in lower and lower long-run average costs of production) one would expect a relatively few number of very large firms. This is because all firms will be trying to reduce their costs, to lower their prices, and to gain a greater share of the market. You have to get big or get out—or be driven out of business by your competitor's lower prices.

6. Yes. Using the latest technology in the combination of inputs employed may be a more costly production process than using more primitive techniques—especially when labour is cheap. What a firm wants to do is to use whatever combination of inputs that will minimize costs of production.

7. Profits are the reward to entrepreneurs for organizing, managing and coordinating the inputs of a firm. Whenever there is a profit potential, whenever possible, someone will produce that product. The profit potential is in turn determined by consumer demand. The greater the demand, the greater the profit potential, and the greater the nation's resources (inputs) devoted to satisfying that demand because it's profitable. (Hence, profits, and entrepreneurs scurrying about to earn those profits, help allocate our nation's scarce resources into the production of those goods and services most desired by society.)

8. Diseconomies of scale refer to the eventual rise in long-run average cost from a continued expansion of production. Major contributors include a) increased cost of monitoring the expanding firm, and b) reduction of morale and "team spirit" of employees.

9. Short-run AC curves are generally U shaped due to diminishing marginal returns. Long-run AC curves are also U shaped (with a broader U) due to initial economies of scale and then eventually diseconomies of scale. Because the long-run AC curve is made up of several short-run AC curves, the long-run AC curve is an "envelope" connecting the short-run AC curves.

10. The entrepreneur responsible for bringing together all the factors of production is doing so for potential personal gain. Alternative uses of capital and effort (opportunity costs) are considered. The economically rational entrepreneur will pick the alternative offering the best potential. This would be the supply decision with the least opportunity cost.

11. When making supply decisions, firms will consider other products currently in production. It is sometimes economically feasible to share certain production and sales inputs among several outputs, and thereby spread costs over several products.

12. Other questions include (but are not limited to) quality, sizing, inventory levels, marketing strategies, and packaging.

13. An accountant's measurement of profits is based on the equation:

$$\text{Accounting profits} = \text{Revenues} - \text{Costs}$$

Revenues are generally defined here as amounts earned from the actual sale of products or services to customers. Costs are the actual or historical costs of doing business.

An economist would prefer the following equation:

$$\text{Economic profits} = \text{Economic revenues} - \text{Economic costs}$$

Economic revenues are generally considered to include **all** the increases in the firm's resources, including earnings from customers plus any gains in the market value of holdings. Economic costs would include the *explicit* costs (historical costs) of doing business, plus estimated *implicit* costs (opportunity costs). The implicit costs, sometimes referred to as *unmeasured costs* are among the causes of business failures.

b. **Problems**

1.

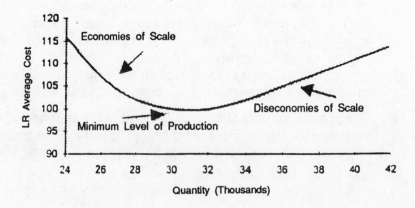

Long Run Average Cost (LRAC)

2.

	Average Total Cost	Total Cost
a)	$[(24 \times \$73) + \$1,036]/24 = \$116$	$2788
	$[(26 \times \$67) + \$1,036]/26 = \$107$	$2778
	$[(28 \times \$68) + \$1,036]/28 = \$105$	$2940
	$[(30 \times \$70) + \$1,036]/30 = \$105$	$3136
	$[(32 \times \$83) + \$1,036]/32 = \$115$	$3692

b)

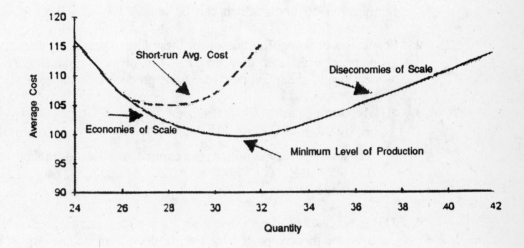

c) 28 thousand units with an average cost of $105 per unit.

d) The alternatives available to Chryford are a) maintain their current plant size and an average unit cost of $105. or b) they can expand the plant size, take advantage of economies of scale, and reduce the average cost to $100 per unit.

3. a) Analysis of financial data:

Revenues			$ 72,000
Explicit costs		$67,500	
Implicit costs:			
Foregone earnings	$40,000		
Foregone interest	3,500		
Decline in market value of investment	40,000+	83,500	
Total explicit and implicit costs			151,000
Economic loss for the year			$ 79,000*

*This is one possible answer. Depending on assumptions, other answers are possible.

**Remember, one only has to be correct in one business enterprise to be a success. Unfortunately, failure is very common and must be understood to achieve success.

b) Tough love advice to Tommy: Operate the business as a **hobby** if he likes the business and the long hours. The economic outlook is gloomy, unless he has some scheme to at least double the business and not increase any costs. Or, close it down, accept the loss, and try to get his sales job back. He might then start saving his money so that he can buy or start another business.

IV. Challenge Problems and Potential Essay Questions

a. Challenge Problems

1. To be technically efficient means you are producing an output level with the least amount of inputs—without using more inputs than necessary. But, there is more than one technically efficient combination of inputs (e.g. workers and machines) to produce any given output level. Economic efficiency, on the other hand, means that you are not only producing the desired output level by using one of those technically efficient combinations of inputs, but, in addition, you are using that one technically efficient combination of inputs which can be obtained at the cheapest total cost.

2. Economies of scope. Its cheaper for these firms to produce, market, or distribute these goods or services when they are already involved in producing the other. Indeed, this concept seems to explain best why firms produce multiple rather than single products.

3. a) Accounting profit = Total revenue − Explicit measurable costs = $33,000 − ($9,000 + $1,000 + $8,000) = $15,000 accounting profit.

   b) Economic profit = Implicit and explicit revenues − Implicit and explicit costs = $33,000 − ($7,000 + $7,000 + $9,000 + $1,000 + $8,000 + $1,500) = − $500; $500 economic loss.

4. This is best explained with the visual aid of a long-run average cost (LATC) curve. See the figure on the next page. Note that the downward sloping portion of the LATC curve indicates decreasing LATC and therefore economies of scale. Also, one needs to keep in mind that a LATC curve is really an envelope of short-run average total cost (SATC) curves, and that each SATC curve is associated with a larger scale of operation (or plant size) as the quantity increases. Finally, recall that a firm's objective is to find that scale of operation (or plant size) which minimizes LATC given the targeted output level it wishes to produce. This is shown as that scale of operation where its SATC curve is just tangent to the LATC curve at the targeted output level. Now suppose that a firm has determined that the profit maximizing quantity it should produce, given the market demand for its product, is Q_1—this is the targeted output level. To produce Q_1, the firm should use the plant size associated with $SATC_2$—this curve is just tangent to the LATC curve. No other plant size can produce Q_1 cheaper, even though this scale of operation is not operating at its minimum average costs (we are not at the low point on $SATC_2$). Notice that $SATC_1$ is a smaller plant size. It could produce Q_1 at its minimum average costs (at the low point on $SATC_1$). But, the per unit costs associated with this smaller plant size are higher (note that $SATC_1$ is greater than $SATC_2$). The idea, in the long run, is to minimize long run average costs (even if that means operating with a scale of operation which has some excess productive capacity—not operating at its $SATC$ curve's low point).

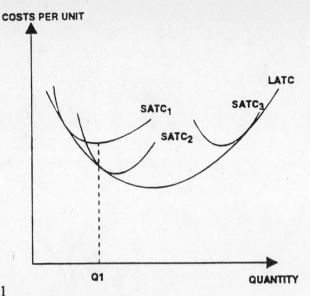

Fig. 8-1

b. Potential Essay Questions

The following answers are annotated—they only indicate the general idea behind the answer.

1. Whenever learning by doing (or technological change) occurs, the long-run cost curve shifts down since the same amount can be produced at a lower cost.

2. Economies (diseconomies) of scale mean that lower (higher) per unit costs are experienced in the long run when larger scales of operation are utilized. Economies of scale are experienced because a large enough output level can be sold that is beyond the minimum efficient level of production. That is, the indivisible setup costs can be spread out over that large output level which makes that output level profitable. Moreover, economies of scale are often experienced because of the greater specialization of management by departments—as opposed to the sole proprietor whom has to manage the accounting, finance, marketing, operation and production control...Diseconomies of scale are experienced because management loses control over the business—monitoring costs become very high and team spirit falls. Economies (diseconomies) of scale cause the long-run average cost curve to slope downward (upward).

3. Diminishing marginal productivity refers to the short run—a given scale of operation (plant size), and is the ultimate cause of the higher average (and marginal) costs in the short run. On the other hand, diseconomies of scale are a long-run phenomena. It refers to larger scales of operations and the resulting higher average costs.

4. First, note that the historical cost of the paint in inventory ($7,000) is a fixed cost, or sunk cost—a cost which cannot be altered by the current decision (in this case to either accept or reject the contract). In other words, the firm has experienced a $2,000 loss on its inventory whether it accepts or rejects the contract. Therefore, like any fixed or sunk cost it should be ignored in making any current decision. The relevant cost of the paint is its current market value—its opportunity cost—of $5,000. Add in the $18,000 of variable costs means the total cost to the firm is $23,000. Because the cost is less than the $24,000 in revenues, the firm should accept the contract and realize a $1,000 profit. Otherwise reasoned: the extra, or marginal, revenue (marginal benefit) from this job exceeds its marginal cost (which includes only the relevant opportunity cost). Therefore, its worth accepting.

Chapter 9   Perfect Competition

I. CHAPTER AT A GLANCE

Rip this page out for quick and easy reference.

1. **Seven conditions for a market to be perfectly competitive are: (194)**

    1. Both buyers and sellers are price takers.
    2. Large number of firms.
    3. No barriers to entry.
    4. Homogenous product.
    5. Instantaneous exit and entry.
    6. Complete information.
    7. Profit-maximizing entrepreneurial firms.

    Compare these with the non-competitive markets (next 2 chapters).

2. **If marginal revenue does not equal marginal cost, a firm obviously can increase profit by changing output. Therefore, profit is maximized when MC = MR = P. (199)**

    P = MR for a perfectly competitive firm.

    In general, if: MR > MC $\Rightarrow$ ↑Q
    MR = MC $\Rightarrow$ maximizing Profit
    MR < MC $\Rightarrow$ ↓Q

3. **Because the marginal cost curve tells us how much of a produced good a firm will supply at a given price, the marginal cost curve is the firm's supply curve. (199)**

    The competitive firm's short-run S curve is its MC curve above minimum AVC because at any P > min AVC a competitive firm will produce where P = MR = MC.

4. **The profit-maximizing output can be determined in a table (as in Exhibit 4 of the textbook) or in a graph (as in Exhibit 5 of the textbook). (201)**

    Just simply find that output level in which MR = MC. This is shown graphically where the 2 curves intersect (remember: the D curve facing the firm is also its MR curve)

5. **Since profits create incentives for new firms to enter, output will increase, and the price will fall until zero profits are being made. (205)**

    Over time if econ profits are earned $\Rightarrow$ ↑ # of Sellers $\Rightarrow$ ↑ mrkt S $\Rightarrow$ ↓ mrkt P $\Rightarrow$ ↓ D curve facing firms $\Rightarrow$ ↑ firms' profits until econ profits are competed away (zero econ profits—normal profit earned in long run).

6. **Supply and demand curves can be used to describe most real-world events. (210)**

    Changes in D & S explain changes in mrkt P & mrkt Q.

7. a) **The Pareto optimal criterion is that no person can be made better off without another being made worse off. (212)**

    Competitive mrkt achieves this.

b) **Three criticisms of the Pareto optimal criterion are: (212)**

1. *The Nirvana criticism.*
2. *The second-best criticism.*
3. *The normative criticism.*

II. MASTERY TEST

1. Johnson Products, a perfectly competitive firm, sells its output for $5 per unit. At 1,000 units of output, marginal cost is $4 and is increasing. Average variable cost is $3.50 and average total cost is $6. To maximize short-run profit, what should Johnson do?

   a) Increase output.
   b) Decrease output, but not shut down.
   c) Maintain its current rate of output.
   d) Shut down.

2. _____ is not a characteristic of perfect competition.

   a) Many small firms.
   b) Severe rivalry and price cutting among firms.
   c) Homogeneous product.
   d) Free entry and exit.

3. Bill's Mfg. Company, a perfectly competitive firm sells its output for $5 per unit. At 500 units of output its marginal cost is $5 and is decreasing. Average variable cost is $5.50 per unit, and average total cost is $6.50 per unit. What should Bill do to maximize profit?

   a) Increase output.
   b) Decrease output or shut down temporarily.
   c) Maintain current rate of output.
   d) Not enough information given to answer the question.

4. Atlantic Bottlers, a perfectly competitive firm, sells its output for $4 per unit. At 100 units of output it has an average total cost of $4. Marginal cost is below average total cost at that point. To maximize profit, what should Atlantic do?

   a) Increase output.
   b) Decrease output.
   c) Maintain its current rate of output.
   d) Not enough information given to answer the question.

5. The short-run supply curve for a perfectly competitive firm is:

   a) the upward-sloping part of its marginal cost curve lying above average total cost.
   b) the upward-sloping part of its marginal cost curve lying above average variable cost.
   c) the upward-sloping portion of its marginal cost curve.
   d) its marginal cost curve.

6. Uptown Manufacturing Co., a perfectly competitive firm, is operating at a point where marginal cost and product price are between average variable cost and average total cost. Uptown's accounting profit must be:

   a) positive.
   b) negative.
   c) zero.
   d) Not enough information given to answer the question.

7. In the long run in a competitive industry:

    a) economic profits will be zero.
    b) all factors may not earn their opportunity costs.
    c) some firms will be experiencing economic losses.
    d) only entrepreneurs will earn more than their opportunity costs.

8. If there is an increase in demand for wheat, assuming it is a perfectly competitive product, then:

    a) producers already in the market will for a time earn economic profits.
    b) new producers will be attracted to the market.
    c) price will rise more in the short run than in the long run, assuming the change in demand to be permanent.
    d) All of the above.

9. The perfect competitor faces a demand curve for the individual firm that is:

    a) horizontal at the going price.
    b) vertical at the going price.
    c) perfectly inelastic.
    d) negatively sloped.

10. In the perfect competition model:

    a) each seller is a price taker.
    b) all firms together can affect price.
    c) all firms produce a homogeneous product.
    d) All of the above.

11. In the perfect competition model, firms want to maximize:

    a) marginal profits.
    b) average profits.
    c) total profits.
    d) market share.

12. Downtown Mfg. Co., will maximize total profits at that output at which:

    a) MC = MR.
    b) MC > MR.
    c) P = AC
    d) P = MR

13. At Barbara's Bakery short-run break-even price:

    a) accounting profits equal economic profits.
    b) economic profits are negative.
    c) economic profits are zero.
    d) economic profits are positive.

14. Sunnyvale Farm's marginal cost of producing an additional bushel of corn:

    a) includes fixed costs.
    b) is the opportunity cost to society of producing one more bushel of corn.
    c) is found by reading Sunnyvale's average variable cost curve.
    d) includes only seed costs.

15. Gerard Debreu's proof of the Pareto optimal criterion allows economists to:

    a) use perfect competition as a benchmark.
    b) show deviations from perfect competition represent a welfare loss to society.
    c) show that many people do quite well in the competitive equilibrium in the form of consumers' and producers' surplus.
    d) All of the above.

16. Skylark Products marginal revenue for the last birdhouse it produced was $20 and its marginal cost was $18. Skylark should:

    a) increase production.
    b) decrease production.
    c) hold production constant.
    d) shut down.

17. Harry's Confections is able to sell sno-cones at the Calgary Stampede for $1.25 and plans to sell 5,000 of them. Harry's marginal cost of producing the last one is $1.28. What should Harry do?

    a) Sell more sno-cones.
    b) Sell fewer sno-cones.
    c) Analyze sales and costs more thoroughly.
    d) Shut down.

18. A perfectly competitive firm's supply curve is:

    a) the average total cost curve when price exceeds average variable cost.
    b) the marginal cost curve when price exceeds average variable cost.
    c) the marginal cost curve when price exceeds the average total cost.
    d) equal to the industry supply curve.

19. The main difference between an economist's calculation of profits and an accountant's calculation of profits is that economists include:

    a) total costs.
    b) normal costs.
    c) explicit costs.
    d) opportunity costs.

20. A relevant cost is one that:

    a) is fixed.
    b) is normal.
    c) matters to the decision at hand.
    d) is a sunk cost.

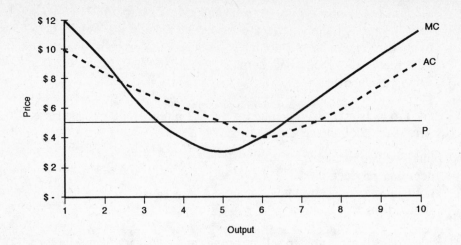

21. The above figure shows the price, average cost, and marginal cost curves of McBig Burgers in a perfectly competitive industry. It suggests that:

a) McBig is earning economic profits and there is incentive for new firms to enter the industry.
b) McBig is in long-run competitive equilibrium.
c) McBig is suffering economic losses, and there is incentive for it to leave the industry.
d) McBig is covering all its costs and there is no incentive for firms to enter or leave the industry.

22. A special tax of $1,500 is levied on cigarette sellers in all regions of the nation. Assuming that the cigarette sellers industry was in equilibrium prior to the initiation of the new tax, in the long run the tax will:

a) have no effect on the average selling price of cigarettes.
b) decrease the number of cigarette sellers.
c) increase the number of cigarette sellers.
d) have no effect on the number of cigarette sellers.

23. Assume that the price of tomatoes is currently 40¢ per pound and there are constant returns to scale. The minimum possible average cost of producing tomatoes in the long run is 30¢ per pound. Other things being equal, it follows that:

a) the price of tomatoes will be 40¢ in the long run.
b) the price of tomatoes will be somewhere between 30¢ and 40¢ in the long run.
c) the price of tomatoes will be 30¢ in the long run.
d) it is not possible to determine the price of tomatoes in the long run.

24. Assume the lap-top computer industry is a perfectly competitive industry of constant costs and is currently in equilibrium. New technology of producing lap-tops lowers the minimum possible average cost of production. In the long run:

a) there will be no effect on the price of lap-tops.
b) the price of lap-tops will decrease at first and then return to their initial level.
c) new firms are unlikely to enter the industry.
d) the price of lap-tops should decrease.

25. If the marginal costs to society are equal to the marginal benefits in a perfectly competitive society, then

   a) a perfectly competitive market equilibrium would be Pareto-optimal.
   b) the marginal benefits are greater than the marginal costs.
   c) the marginal costs to society are less than the marginal benefits.
   d) the total costs to society are equal to the total benefits.

Answer questions 26, 27 and 28 by referring to the diagram below. It represents a perfectly competitive firm.

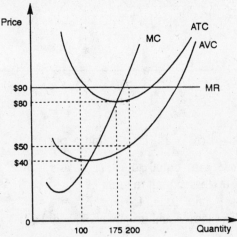

26. In the short run this firm

   a) is earning an economic profit equal to $2,000.
   b) should produce 100 units of output and charge a price of $40.
   c) is incurring total costs equal to $80.
   d) has total fixed costs equal to $40.
   e) should shut down because price is less than average variable cost.

27. In the long run

   a) this firm will go out of business.
   b) new firms will enter.
   c) some firms will leave the industry.
   d) output will be 200 and all firms will break even.

28. In the long run, this firm

   a) will produce 200 units output for a price of $80 per unit.
   b) will charge a price of $90 and make zero profit.
   c) will produce 175 units of output and charge a price of $80 per unit.
   d) will produce an output greater than 200 and price will rise above $90 per unit.

29. If you were willing to pay $3 for a can of pop, but only had to pay the going price of $1.00 you would be receiving

   a) producer surplus.
   b) welfare loss.
   c) marginal revenue.
   d) consumer surplus.

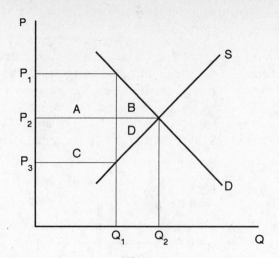

Refer to the above diagram.

30. If output is Q_1, and price is P_1 in this industry,

    a) there is a welfare gain equal to areas A and C.
    b) there is a welfare loss equal to area A.
    c) there is a welfare gain equal to area B.
    d) there is a welfare loss equal to areas B and D.

III. SHORT ANSWER EXERCISES AND PROBLEMS

a. Short Answer Exercises

1. In perfectly competitive markets, buyers and sellers are said to be price takers. Why?

2. List and describe some of the barriers to entry that would cause imperfect competition.

3. If losses are being incurred by a firm in perfect competition, then under what conditions should this firm shut down?

4. What is meant by homogeneous product in perfect competition?

5. Under perfect competition, what is the normal time delay for a firm to be able to enter or exit a market?

6. What is the sole assumed goal of firms in a perfectly competitive market?

7. What is the shape and nature of the demand curve for a firm in a perfect competition market?

8. Explain why producing an output at which marginal cost equals price maximizes total profit for a perfect competitor.

9. Why do perfectly competitive firms make zero profits in the long run?

10. What is the Pareto optimal criterion?

11. Sunnyvale Farms has a total average cost of $5 per bushel to produce a certain product. The product has a market price of $4 per bushel. What should they do in the short-run? The long-run? (Growing something else is not acceptable here.)

12. What are the pros and cons associated with a perfectly competitive market environment from society's perspective?

13. Beach Sand Co., a firm in a perfect competition market, is selling sand for $50 per load. At 100 loads, marginal cost is $40 and is increasing. Average variable cost is $35 and average total cost is $60 per load. To maximize short-run profit, what should Beach Sand do?

14. Define the term "consumer surplus."

15. What is meant by term "producer surplus"?

16. What is meant by social welfare loss when the output level in a market is below that which would be determined in a competitive market?

17. What will be the probable outcomes if there is an increase in demand for the product of a perfectly competitive industry?

b. Problems

The cost schedule for Atom Enterprises is shown below:

Q	TC	FC	VC	AVC	ATC	MC	P	P1	P2
0	$100	$100							
1	130	100							
2	150	100							
3	160	100							
4	172	100							
5	185	100							
6	210	100							
7	240	100							
8	280	100							
9	330	100							
10	390	100							

A. Complete the Atom Enterprises cost schedule

B. Graph ATC, AVC, and MC. What is the relationship between MC and AVC?

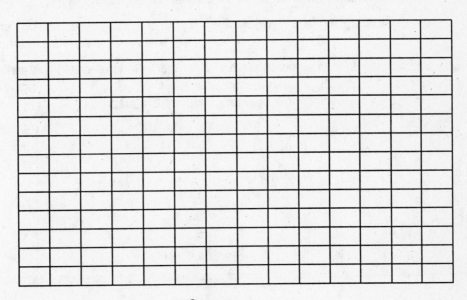

Output

C. Suppose the market price (P) is $30. How much will the firm produce in the short run? How much are the profits? Show them on the graph.

D. Suppose the market price (P₁)is $50. How much will the firm produce in the short run? How much are the profits? Show them on the graph.

E. Suppose the price is $10 (P₂). How much would the firm produce in the short run? How much would the profits be? Show them on the graph.

IV. CHALLENGE PROBLEMS AND POTENTIAL ESSAY QUESTIONS

a. Challenge Problems

1. Refer to the table below for a perfectly competitive firm when answering the following questions.

OUTPUT	PRICE	TOTAL COSTS
0	$100	$200
1	$100	$290
2	$100	$350
3	$100	$390
4	$100	$470
5	$100	$560
6	$100	$700
7	$100	$900

a) What is the profit-maximizing (loss-minimizing) quantity of output for this firm to produce? Why?

b) What is the profit (or loss) at this profit maximizing (loss-minimizing) output level?

c) Should this firm shut down or remain in operation? Why?

d) Assuming this is a representative firm in the industry or market, given the profits or losses incurred, what can be expected to happen over time in the market?

2. Answer the following questions based on the following graphs (a) and (b) shown below. Graph (a) represents a perfectly competitive market. Graph (b) is a graph for a representative perfectly competitive firm operating within that market.

a)

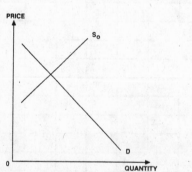

b)

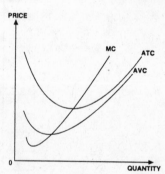

a) Illustrate the equilibrium price and quantity for the market in graph a) above. At this equilibrium price in the market, graphically illustrate in graph b) the demand curve for the firm.

b) What is the shape of the demand curve facing the perfectly competitive firm? Why? How is this related to the firm's marginal revenue of additional units produced and sold?

c) What is the profit-maximizing (or loss-minimizing) quantity for any firm to produce? Why? Illustrate in graph b) above the quantity which this firm should produce.

d) Is this firm earning an economic profit, zero economic profit (normal profit), or incurring an economic loss? Why? Graphically illustrate any profit or loss in graph b).

e) On graph b) indicate the area representing:

   I) Total revenue.

   II) Total cost.

   III) Variable cost.

   IV) Fixed cost.

f) Given the situation depicted in the figure above, what is expected to happen over time (in the long run) to the market supply curve, the market price and the market output level, as well as the demand curves facing firms, firm's profits or losses and their individual output levels? Why?

3. a) What is a normal profit equal to for an entrepreneur?

   b) What's the difference between accounting profit and economic profit? Does an economist consider the normal profit required for the entrepreneur to be a fixed or variable cost to the firm?

   c) Why are economists more interested in what the economic profits are in an industry or market than what the accounting profits may be?

4. Suppose a competitive firm experiences a sudden increase in its fixed costs. For example, suppose property taxes increase dramatically. What impact, if any, will this have on the firm's profit maximizing quantity to produce? What will happen to the firm's profit?

b. Potential Essay Questions

1. How can one determine whether an economic profit or loss is being experienced by any firm (not just a competitive firm)? If losses are incurred, then under what conditions should any firm shut down?

2. If economic profits are currently being earned by competitive firms, then what is expected to happen over time (in the long run)? What if zero economic profits are currently being earned? Economic losses?

3. Why is the competitive firm's short-run marginal cost (MC) curve above minimum average variable cost (AVC) the firm's short-run supply curve? How is this related to the market supply curve?

4. Why is the market supply curve more elastic than the individual marginal cost curves of firms which, when horizontally summed, make up the market supply curve?

5. What is the difference between accounting profit and economic profit?

V. ANSWERS

II. Mastery Test

1. a	6. d	11. c	16. a	21. a	26. a
2. b	7. a	12. a	17. b	22. b	27. b
3. d	8. d	13. c	18. b	23. c	28. c
4. a	9. a	14. b	19. d	24. d	29. d
5. b	10. d	15. d	20. c	25. a	30. d

III. Short Answer Exercises

1. In a perfectly competitive market, supply and demand determine the price; both firms and consumers take the market price as given. If individual firms attempt to set a price above the market determined price, consumers will purchase elsewhere. In addition, there is no incentive for a firm to reduce a price because in this market structure, firms can sell all the units they can produce at the market price.

2. a) Patent and copyright laws would prevent unrestricted production of certain goods.
   b) Minimum efficient scale of production would prevent smaller firms from entering a market.
   c) Zoning ordinances could limit the number of firms in a given area.
   d) Exclusive franchises granted by local communities for TV cable service and other utilities.
   e) Insufficient availability of resource inputs.
   f) Social restrictions due to cultural or ethnic differences.

3. If P < ATC then an economic loss is incurred. If a loss is incurred then the firm should shut down if P < AVC.

4. Each firm's output is indistinguishable from any other firm's output. Products are perfect substitutes for each other.

5. Firms have instantaneous knowledge of all market, technology and other factors as they happen. New firms are able to instantly enter or leave a market as desired. There are zero time delays.

6. Profit-maximization. Other goals such as gaining market share, restricting entry of competing firms, etc. are not considered.

7. The curve is horizontal and would be described as perfectly elastic. If the firm raised its price, its demand would fall to zero, and if it lowered its price, it would reduce its per unit profit.

8. Under perfect competition, P = MR. If MC < MR, there is incentive for the firm to expand production to take advantage of the difference. The firm will continue to increase output until MC = MR at which point it will have maximized profits.

9. If firms earn economic profits, new firms will enter the market to pursue those profits. As new firms enter the market, the additional supply will push the price downward to the cost of production, thereby eliminating those profits.

10. No one can be made better off without another being made worse off.

11. a) They should compare the market price with their AVC. If P > AVC, they should continue production in the short-run. If P < AVC, they should immediately shut down.

    b) If long-run outlook indicates that P < ATC is going to be a permanent situation, they should consider the following:

        1. Reduce costs, or
        2. if unable to reduce costs, leave the business.

12. Perfect competition results in a Pareto optimal position. Production occurs at the point of intersection between the competitive demand and supply curves. The supply curve represents the marginal cost to society of producing the good. The demand curve represents the marginal benefit to society of consuming the good. Because production occurs at the point of intersection between the two curves then the marginal benefit to society of the last unit consumed is just equal to the marginal cost to society of producing that last unit. Therefore, just the right amount is produced—not too much and not too little. (Remember, we want to keep doing something until the marginal benefit is just equal to the marginal cost.) (See pages 211–213).

13. Beach should try to increase output. Price is above marginal cost, and also above average variable cost.

14. It is the difference between what consumers would have been willing to pay and what they actually pay.

15. It is the difference between the price at which producers would have been willing to supply a good and the price they actually receive.

16. Assume a competitive market. If the demand curve represents the marginal benefits and the supply curve represents the marginal cost to society of producing and consuming additional units of output, then in equilibrium (the price and quantity associated with the point of intersection between the demand and supply curves) the marginal benefits equal the marginal costs to society of producing and consuming the last unit produced. When output is below equilibrium, the demand curve lies above the supply curve. Therefore, marginal benefits exceed marginal costs associated with the last unit produced and the product is being underproduced. Likewise, if the output level is above the competitive equilibrium, marginal costs exceed marginal benefits (because the supply curve lies above the demand curve) and the product is being overproduced.

17. The probable outcomes will include new firms being attracted to the industry, firms already in the industry will, for a time, earn pure economic profits, price will rise more the short run than in the long run, assuming the change in demand to be permanent.

b. **Problems**

A.

Q	TC	FC	VC	AVC	ATC	MC	P	P1	P2
0	$100	$100	$0	$0	$100	$0	$30	50	10
1	130	100	30	30	130	30	30	50	10
2	150	100	50	25	75	20	30	50	10
3	160	100	60	20	53.33	10	30	50	10
4	172	100	72	18	43	12	30	50	10
5	185	100	85	17	37	13	30	50	10
6	210	100	110	18.33	35	25	30	50	10
7	240	100	140	20	34.29	30	30	50	10
8	280	100	180	22.50	35	40	30	50	10
9	330	100	230	25.56	36.67	50	30	50	10
10	390	100	290	29	39	60	30	50	10

B.

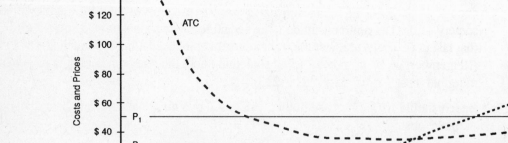

MC intersects AVC at its lowest point. This falls between 5 and 6 units.

C. The firm will produce between 6 and 7 units at a price of $30. At 6 units, the firm will show a loss of $5 per unit for a total loss of $30. At 7 units, the loss will be $4.29 per unit for a total loss of $30. (At 5 units the total loss would be $35, and at 8 units the total loss would be $40.)

D. The firm will produce between 8 and 9 units at a price of $50. The profit per unit at 8 units would be $15 for a total profit of $120. The profit per unit at 9 units would be $13.33+ for a total profit of $120.

E. At a price of $10, the firm cannot cover AVC so it should shut down and lose its fixed costs of $100.

IV. Challenge Problems and Potential Essay Questions

a. Challenge Problems

1. a) This firm should produce 5 units of output to maximize profits (or minimize losses) because that is the output level which comes closest to MR = MC (marginal revenue equal to marginal cost of production). Recall that P = MR (price per unit equals marginal revenue—the price per unit is the extra revenue per unit for the competitive firm).

   You need to keep firmly in mind that the highest profit (lowest loss) from producing output is always obtained at that output level in which MR = MC (or as close as you can come to that). At any output level in which MR > MC, the firm is adding more to its revenues than it is to its costs by producing that additional unit of output, and should therefore produce more output in order to continue to add to its total profit. If MR < MC the firm should produce less. See the table below.

OUTPUT	PRICE (MARGINAL REVENUE)	TOTAL COSTS	MARGINAL COST	PROFIT (Loss)
0	$100	$200	—	−$200
1	$100	$290	$90	−$190
2	$100	$350	$60	−$150
3	$100	$390	$40	−$90
4	$100	$470	$80	−$70
5	$100	$560	$90	−$60
6	$100	$700	$140	−$100
7	$100	$900	$200	−$200

   b) Loss = $60. (Profit = Total revenue − Total cost = $500 − $560 = −$60, or a loss of $60). See the table above.

c) The firm should remain in operation to minimize its losses because the losses from remaining in operation are less than total fixed costs. The best (or least worst) it can do is to remain in operation and lose $60 per time period (e.g. per day). Note that if the firm shuts down it will still have to pay its fixed costs (FC) of $200 per time period. [Note that you can determine fixed costs by looking at what total costs (TC) are when output is zero. This is because there are no variable costs (VC) when output is zero.] Shutting down would entail a greater loss ($200 versus $60 per time period). So remain in operation and lose less.

Otherwise stated, the firm should remain in operation because the price per unit (P = $100) is greater than average, or per unit, variable cost (AVC = $72). (Note that VC = TC − FC = $560 − $200 = $360. Also, AVC = VC/Q = $360/5 = $72.) In other words, the price is able to cover average variable costs and the firm will have $28 left over to apply toward average fixed costs (AFC). Indeed, the firm will have $140 (5 units of output multiplied by $28 per unit) in total to apply toward its total fixed costs. Because fixed costs (FC) total $200 and the firm is able to cover all of its variable costs (VC) and still have $140 left over to apply toward its total fixed costs, then the firm will be losing only $60 by remaining in operation—less than the $200 of fixed costs which have to be paid, and the firm would lose per time period, if it shut down.

There is yet a third way to look at why the firm should remain in operation even though it is losing money. And that is as long as total revenue exceeds total variable costs then remain in operation. Because total revenue (TR) equals $500, and total variable costs (VC) equal $360 (VC = TC − FC = $560 − $200 = $360; or, VC = AVC × Q = $72 × 5 = $360), then the firm should remain in operation. Total revenues are able to pay all variable costs and have $140 left over to apply toward the $200 of total fixed costs. Hence, the firm will be losing only $60 if it remains in operation—less than its total fixed costs of $200 if it were to shut down. (Remember, fixed costs have to be paid whether the firm is producing any output or not.)

In sum:

Remain in operation if:	*Shut down if:*
1. *Losses < FC*	1. *Losses > FC*
2. *P > AVC*	2. *P < AVC*
3. *TR > VC*	3. *TR < VC*

d) Because losses are incurred in this market, then over time, some firms will voluntarily leave or they will be driven out of the market through bankruptcy. The decreased number of sellers will decrease market supply (shift the market supply curve to the left) and increase market price. A higher price will increase the total revenue of those firms remaining in the market (TR = P × Q). Their costs may also fall. This could be due to the decreased demand for the inputs employed by these firms pushing input prices and therefore costs down. This means the losses of the remaining firms will decrease. In the long run (over time), the losses will continue to decline until they disappear—that is, until only a zero economic profit (a normal profit) is earned, the firms will just be "breaking even."

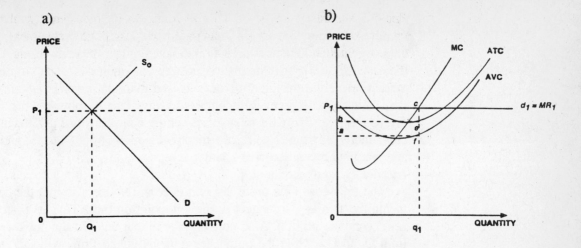

a)

b)

2. a) See the above figure. The equilibrium price and quantity for the market is P_1 and q_1. The demand curve for the firm is d1.

   b) The demand curve facing the firm is horizontal (perfectly elastic) at the market price. The firm has so many competitors that any attempt to charge a higher price results in no sales. Furthermore, there is no need to lower price in order to sell more. That is, the individual firm is so small in relation to the market that it can sell as much as it can produce at the market price. (For example, think about an individual farmer.) This constant price facing the firm means that the marginal revenue from any unit sold is equal to the price; and is constant. Hence, the demand and marginal revenue curves become one and the same.

   c) The profit-maximizing (loss-minimizing) quantity of output for any firm to produce (whether it is a competitive firm or not) exists at that output level in which MR = MC. MR = MC at point c in graph b) and therefore the firm should produce q_1. Note that at any output level below q_1, MR > MC (the MR curve lies above the MC curve) and the firm would be adding more to its revenues than to its costs. Because the firm is adding to its total profit at all output levels in which MR > MC then the firm should produce more. Likewise, at any output level above q_1, MR < MC and the firm would be adding more to its costs than to its revenues and should cut back on production.

   d) Because price exceeds average total costs this firm is earning an economic profit equal to area *bP1ce* in graph b). Recall that the profit per unit multiplied by the output level equals total profit. The profit per unit equals the price per unit (P_1) minus average total costs (point *b*). This is shown as line segment *bP1*. The output level is shown as line segment *0q1*, which is the same as line segment *be*. Hence, multiplying line segment *bP1* by line segment *be* (think of multiplying a width by a length) we get area *bP1ce*.

   e) I) Total revenue equals area *0P1cq1*. (TR = P × Q = *0P1* × *0q1* = *0P1cq1*).
      II) Total cost equals area *0beq1*. (TC = ATC × Q = *0b* × *0q1* = *0beq1*).
      III) Variable cost equals area *0afq1*. (VC = AVC × Q = *0a* × *0q1* = *0afq1*).
      IV) Fixed cost equals area *abef*. (FC = AFC × Q = *ab* × *af* = *abef*).

   Also note: Profit = TR − TC = *0P1cq1* − *0beq1* = *bP1ce*.

f) Because economic profits are being earned in this market, and given that there are no barriers to entry into a competitive market, we would expect to find additional entrepreneurs entering this market in an attempt to earn some economic profits for themselves. This larger number of sellers will increase market supply, decrease market price, and decrease the demand and marginal revenue curves facing firms until all economic profits are competed away. This is shown in the figure below. For convenience, only the relevant curves are shown. Notice that the market supply curve increases from S_0 to S_1, the market price falls from P_1 to P_2, and the demand and marginal revenue curves facing the representative firm decrease from d_1 to d_2. At price P_2, zero economic profits would be earned by firms because price equals average total cost—the profit per unit is zero. (Notice also that the demand curve facing the firm is just tangent to the low point on the ATC curve—this illustrates zero economic profits). Also note that the output level in the market will increase from Q_1 to Q_2, while the output level of individual firms will fall from q_1 to q_2 (because the profit-maximizing output level where MR = MC is now lower). How can there be a greater quantity supplied in the market when each individual firm is producing less? Because there are more firms. On balance, the firms collectively provide a greater quantity supplied in the market.

a)   b)

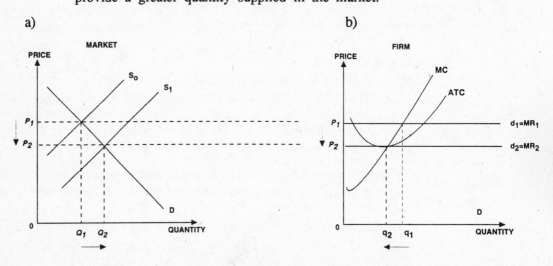

3. a) The normal profit is an amount of money the entrepreneur would have to make to just keep him or her in their current line of business. The normal profit equals the opportunity costs, or implicit costs of the entrepreneur. That is, the normal profit is a dollar figure which is equal to the greatest amount of money the person could have made in his or her highest alternative line of employment or business, plus the greatest amount of money the entrepreneur could have made with the funds invested in the firm if those funds were invested somewhere else. In sum, the normal profit equals the opportunity cost of both the entrepreneur's time and the financial capital (funds) invested in the firm.

    b) Accounting profit does not include the normal profit as a cost of production. Economic profit does. In other words, economic profit equals accounting profit minus the normal profit. (Notice that accounting profit will always be greater than economic profit). The economist treats the entrepreneur as another input into the production process. The cost to the firm for the entrepreneur is his or her normal profit. Moreover, this cost is a fixed cost—it will not vary with the amount of output produced.

c) Any dollar accounting profit is a relative number. What is considered a large accounting profit to one entrepreneur may be small to another. Accounting profits do not tell us whether entrepreneurs will likely enter or exit the market. On the other hand, an economic profit is an amount of money earned by the entrepreneur over and above what could have been earned anywhere else. That is a lot of money by any relative standard. Therefore, if economic profits are earned in a market, then you would expect more entrepreneurs to enter that market. Conversely, if economic losses are incurred (even if positive accounting profits are realized) then you would expect some of these entrepreneurs to exit the market. Information regarding whether economic profits, zero economic profits, or economic losses are being experienced by entrepreneurs indicates whether the market will be expanding, in equilibrium, or declining in the future.

4. An increase in fixed costs (FC) will increase average total cost (ATC). Average variable cost (AVC) and marginal cost (MC) will remain unchanged. The ATC curve will be the only curve that shifts up. Because MC has not changed (the MC curve has not shifted), and assuming the price in the competitive market (MR for the firm) has not changed, then the profit-maximizing output level will not change for the firm. However, its profits will decrease. If the firm was earning zero economic profits to begin with, then it will now lose money. If it was losing money before, then it will lose more now.

b. **Potential Essay Questions**

The following answers are annotated—they only indicate the general idea behind the answer.

1. If the price per unit (P) exceeds average total cost (ATC) then an economic profit is earned. (If P > ATC then an economic profit is earned.) If P = ATC then a zero economic profit (only a normal profit) is earned. If P < ATC then an economic loss is incurred (even though an accounting profit may be earned). If a loss is incurred then the firm should shut down if P < AVC.

2. If economic profits are currently being earned by firms operating within a competitive market then, over time, new entrants into the market will compete those profits away. This is because there are no barriers to entry to prevent the new entrepreneurs from entering the market. If zero economic profits (normal profits) are currently being earned then the market is in equilibrium. That is, there is neither an incentive for new entrepreneurs to enter the market, or for existing entrepreneurs to shut down their firms and exit the market (after all, the existing entrepreneurs are earning a normal profit—an amount of money just equal to what could be earned in their next-best alternative line of employment or business). If losses are incurred, some firms will shut down (the least efficient will shut down first). This causes a decrease in market supply and an increase in the market price. A higher market price will decrease the losses for the remaining firms. Over time the losses will disappear until a zero economic profit is earned for those firms which remain.

3. The profit-maximizing quantity to produce exists at that output level in which MR = MC. For the competitive firm P = MR. Therefore, in essence, at any price (P) above minimum average variable cost (AVC) all one has to do is to "bounce off" of the upward sloping marginal cost curve to determine the quantity supplied by the firm at that price. This is exactly what a supply curve does for us—it tells us what the quantity supplied will be at any price by "bouncing off" of the curve. (At any P < minimum AVC, the firm would shut down; there would be no quantity supplied.) Also note that as the price goes up, the quantity supplied goes up. Because the market supply curve is the

horizontal sum of all firms' upward sloping marginal cost curves above minimum AVC, then the market supply curve will also be upward sloping—also reflecting that as the price goes up the quantity supplied goes up; and vice versa (there is a direct relationship between the price and the quantity supplied).

4. The market supply curve is more elastic than the individual supply curves (which means there is a larger quantity supplied in response to an increase in price for the entire market) because as the price rises in the market, there is not only an increase in the output of existing firms, but there are also more firms whom have entered the industry that are producing output.

5. Economic profit includes the normal profit required by the entrepreneur as a cost of production. Accounting profit does not. The normal profit is the opportunity cost of both the time and the financial capital of the entrepreneur.

Chapter 10   Monopoly

I. CHAPTER AT A GLANCE

Rip this page out for quick and easy reference.

1. **For a competitive firm, marginal revenue equals price. For a monopolist, it does not. The monopolist takes into account the fact that its decision can affect price. (217)**

    The monopolist faces the market demand curve, it must reduce P to sell more.
    Hence, MR < P.

2. **If a monopolist deviates from the output level at marginal revenue, profits will decline. (219)**

    If MR > MC ⇒ ↑ Q (output level)
    If MR = MC ⇒ maximizing profit (minimizing losses)
    If MR < MC ⇒ ↓ Q

3. **a) The monopolist's price and output are determined as follows. (220)**

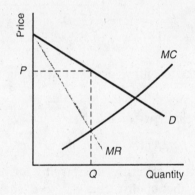

   b) A monopolist's profit is determined by the difference between ATC and price, as in the following diagram. (222)

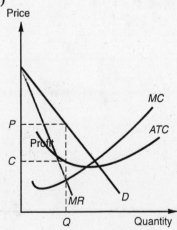

4. A price-discriminating monopolist does not lose revenue on previously-sold products, so its marginal revenue curve equals its demand curve. Thus, it will produce the same quantity as will a perfectly competitive firm. (225)

> *But, the <u>average</u> P it charges is greater than the competitive P.*

5. The welfare loss from monopoly is a triangle as in the graph below. It is not the loss that most people consider. They are often interested in normative losses that the graph does not capture. (226)

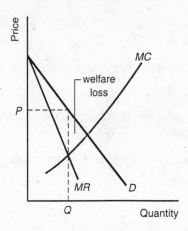

6. If there were no barriers to entry, profit-maximizing firms would always compete away monopoly profits. (229)

> **Know the different types of barriers to entry.*

> *The stronger the barriers to entry, the stronger the monopoly power.*

7. Economists generally favour government charging for monopolies because those charges do not raise the price the monopolist charges, and they tend to reduce the rent-seeking expenditures spent to get that monopoly. (231)

> *Government charging for a monopoly that it gives out would only increase the fixed costs to the monopolist. It would not change MC. Therefore, it would not change its output level or its P.*

II. MASTERY TEST

1. A monopolist has:

   a) no competitive producers of the same product.
   b) many competitors producing the same product.
   c) a few competitive producers of the same product.
   d) at least one competitive producer of the same product.

2. _____ make it possible for a monopoly to receive profits in the long run.

   a) mutual interdependence.
   b) free entry and exit.
   c) barriers to entry.
   d) homogenous products.

3. What is the result of government regulations increasing the cost of operating as a monopoly?

   a) New firms will be discouraged to enter the market.
   b) Minimum efficient scale of operations is increased.
   c) The firm's fixed costs are increased.
   d) All of the above.

4. A demand curve for the monopolist is:

   a) of unit elasticity throughout.
   b) the industry demand curve.
   c) perfectly inelastic.
   d) perfectly elastic.

5. The marginal revenue curve for the monopolist is:

   a) the market price.
   b) similar to the competitive firm's marginal revenue curve.
   c) below and to the left of the firm's demand curve.
   d) lower than the firm's demand curve and always higher than product price.

6. Bunny's Foods Co., a monopolist, sells 10 units at $100 per unit and 11 units when price is reduced to $99. Bunny's marginal revenue for the last unit sold is:

   a) $11.
   b) $99.
   c) $109.
   d) $89.

7. If Central Supply Co., a monopolist, has marginal revenue of $5, and marginal cost of $8, Central could increase profits by:

   a) lowering both price and output.
   b) increasing both price and output.
   c) increasing price and decreasing output.
   d) decreasing price and increasing output.

8. Which of the following statement(s) about price discriminating by Provincial Utilities, a monopolist, is true?

a) Provincial Utilities will charge higher prices to consumers who desire a product more than those who value it less.
b) Provincial Utilities will charge more to those consumers who have an inelastic demand.
c) Provincial Utilities will charge more to those consumers having few available substitutes.
d) All the above are true.

9. How is the perceived demand curve different for a monopolist from that of a competitive firm?

a) the marginal revenue curve is above the demand curve for a monopolist.
b) the market demand curve is the demand curve for a monopolist.
c) a competitive firm's demand curve is inelastic.
d) the marginal revenue curve for a competitive firm lies below the demand curve.

10. Under monopoly, resources are misallocated such that:

a) too few resources are used in other industries, too many are used by the monopoly.
b) too few resources are used by the monopoly, too many are used elsewhere.
c) resources are being used as efficiently as possible only by the monopoly.
d) consumers are being forced to pay a price below the MC of the monopolist.

11. What is meant by the term "deadweight loss"?

a) The difference between total revenue and accounting profit.
b) The difference between economic revenue and economic profit.
c) A lost opportunity to earn a greater pure economic profit by raising price above the level of marginal cost.
d) The welfare cost in terms of misallocated resources that are caused by monopoly.

12. A "natural monopoly" occurs when:

a) there are strong diseconomies of scale.
b) the ATC curve is always upward sloping.
c) the ATC curve is always downward sloping.
d) MC = ATC at its minimum point.

13. Price discrimination would probably offer the greatest opportunity in which of the following?

a) Wheat
b) Brain surgery
c) Oil
d) Groceries

14. Assume Big Oil Co. is a monopolist. At Big's output of 100 units MC = $33, MR = $33, AVC = $30, and ATC = $38. To maximize profit or minimize loss in the short run, Big should:

a) increase output.
b) continue producing 100 units.
c) shutdown.
d) not enough information given for an answer.

15. A price discriminating monopolist, other things being equal, would probably produce which of the following?

    a) More output than a nondiscriminating monopolist.
    b) Less output than a nondiscriminating monopolist.
    c) The same output as a nondiscriminating monopolist.
    d) Could be any of the above.

16. A community's only supplier of potable water (a pure monopolist) has a demand curve that is:

    a) downward sloping.
    b) perfectly inelastic.
    c) perfectly elastic.
    d) indeterminate.

17. If a monopolist lowers its price from $40 to $39 and increases output from 19 to 20, its marginal revenue would be:

    a) $760   b) $780
    c) $20   d) $1

18. Why is the monopolist's marginal revenue less than the selling price?

    a) Its marginal revenue curve is above its supply curve.
    b) the total revenue curve has a positive slope.
    c) in order to sell more, the price must be lowered on all units.
    d) the selling price is perfectly elastic.

19. When the marginal revenue is equal to marginal cost for a monopolist:

    a) marginal cost is equal to price.
    b) price equals marginal revenue.
    c) price is below marginal revenue.
    d) the monopolist is in equilibrium.

20. Profits are maximized for a monopolist when:

    a) price is maximized.
    b) production is at its most efficient level.
    c) costs are at their minimum.
    d) marginal revenue equals marginal costs.

21. If MC < MR, the monopolist should:

    a) increase production.
    b) maintain the same level of production.
    c) shut down.
    d) decrease the level of production.

22. How does a monopoly maximize profit or minimize losses?

    a) It adjusts output until price equals marginal cost.
    b) It adjusts output until marginal revenue equals marginal cost.
    c) By raising price.
    d) By lowering price.

23. If a monopolist is able to charge a different price for different customers, it is:

    a) price discriminating.
    b) maximizing profits.
    c) producing at the same output as a perfect competitor.
    d) All the above.

24. Your local public utility would charge a "socially optimum" price which is equal to its:

    a) average variable cost.
    b) average total cost.
    c) marginal cost.
    d) marginal revenue.

25. What does the welfare loss triangle show?
    a) Lost social fairness due to monopoly power.
    b) Unfair redistribution of income due to monopoly.
    c) Misallocated resources due to monopoly.
    d) Rent seeking expenditures by a monopoly.

When answering the following 5 questions (26-30), refer to the diagram below.

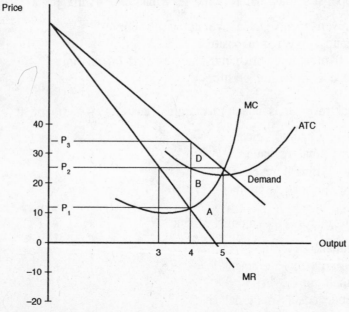

26. To maximize profit the monopolist will produce output _____ and charge a price
    _____

    a) 5; P_2.
    b) 4; P_2.
    c) 4; P_3.
    d) 3; P_2.

27. This monopolist is experiencing

    a) a profit equal to the $P_3 P_1 \times 5$.
    b) a loss equal to $P_2 P_1 \times 4$.
    c) a profit equal to area $P_2 P_1 \times 4$.
    d) a loss equal to area $P_2 P_3 \times 3$.

28. A perfect competitor in this situation would produce _____ quantity and charge _____ price.

    a) 5; P_2.
    b) 4; P_3.
    c) 4; P_1.
    d) a perfectly competitive firm would not produce at all faced with this cost and revenue information.

29. The welfare loss is represented by area(s)

    a) A.
    b) D.
    c) D, B and A.
    d) D and B.

30. If the monopolist were to expand production from 4 units to 5 units which of the following statements would be true?

    a) The additional benefit to society is the area from 4 to 5 under the ATC curve.
    b) The additional benefit to society is the area from 4 to 5 under the MC curve.
    c) The additional cost to society is the area from 4 to 5 under the MC curve.
    d) The additional cost to society is the area from 4 to 5 under the demand curve.

III. SHORT ANSWER EXERCISES AND PROBLEMS

a. Short Answer Exercises

1. Why can a monopolist charge a higher price than would exist in a competitive market?

2. Why does a monopolist face the market demand?

3. Is it possible for a monopolist to make an economic profit in the long-run? Why?

4. Why is marginal revenue less than the selling price for the monopolist?

5.   How does a monopolist determine its output?

6.   How are a monopolist's profits determined?

7.   How is the marginal revenue curve and the demand curve related for the perfectly price discriminating monopolist.

8.   What conditions must be present for a firm to be able to price discriminate?

9.   Which makes a potentially higher profit: the perfectly price-discriminating monopolist, or a ''normal'' monopolist?

10.   What is the estimated welfare loss to society from monopoly?

11.   What are some of the normative reasons which explain public opposition to monopoly?

12.   Name and describe three important barriers to entry.

13. What is the argument for the government charging for a monopoly?

b. **Problems**

1. Munchkin Products, a monopoly, faces the following price and quantity demanded market:

Price per unit	Quantity Demanded	Total Revenue	Marginal Revenue
$10	1	$	$
9	2		
8	3		
7	4		
6	5		
5	6		
4	7		

a) Complete the above table.
b) Graph Munchkin's total revenue curve in (1) below.
c) Graph Munchkin's demand and marginal revenue in (2) below.

   1. Total Revenue

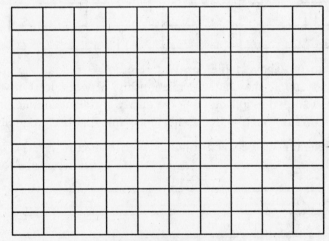

Quantity Demanded

2. Marginal Revenue

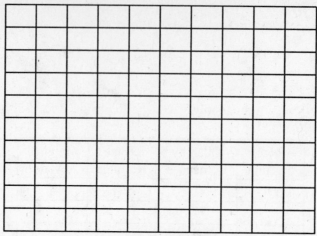

Quantity Demanded

2. Water Supply Inc., a monopoly, faces the following hypothetical demand schedule for its product.

Price	Quantity Demanded	Total Revenue	Marginal Revenue	Total Cost	Marginal Cost	Profit or Loss
$24	0			$13		
20	1			19		
16	2			22		
12	3			26		
8	4			34		
4	5			49		

a) Complete the above table for Water Supply Co.
b) Prepare a graph showing the relationship between total revenue and total cost.
c) Prepare a second graph showing the curves for demand, marginal revenue and marginal cost for Water Supply Co. Indicate the monopolist's output and price.

Graph showing relationship between total revenue and cost TR, TC, Profit, or Loss.

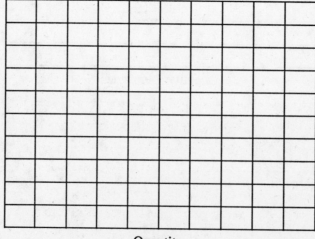

Quantity

Graph showing Demand, MC and MR, P, MC, MR

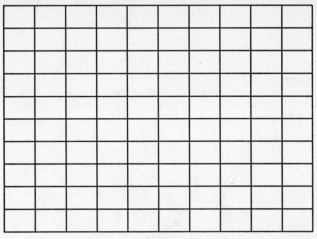

Quantity

3. Assume Company X's costs are as follows:

Output	Long-Run Total Cost	Long-Run Marginal Cost	Long-Run Average Cost
1	$ 50		
2	90		
3	120		
4	140		
5	150		

a) Complete the above table.
b) Show the company's Long-Run Marginal and Average costs on the graph below.
c) What reasons can you give for Company X's cost pattern?
d) How would you describe the market in which Company X operates?

Costs

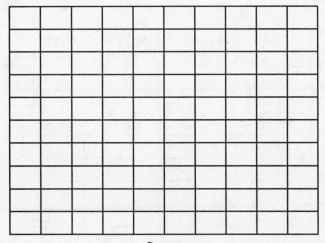

Output

IV. CHALLENGE PROBLEMS AND POTENTIAL ESSAY QUESTIONS

a. Challenge Problems

1. a) The figure below is a graph for a monopoly. Indicate the amount the monopolist will produce and the price it will charge in the figure. Shade the area representing any economic profit (or loss).

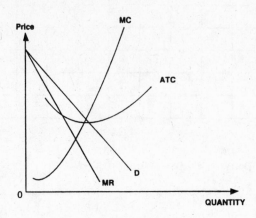

b) If economic profits are earned by a monopolist, then what is expected to happen over time? What if economic losses are incurred?

2. Assume your city government has been contracting with a single garbage collection firm whom has been granted an exclusive franchise, or sole right to pick up trash in the entire city. However, it has been proposed that the city be broken down into several, much smaller areas and then allow the numerous individuals and small companies whom would like to get into the business of collecting trash to competitively bid for garbage collection services in those areas. The government would then allow the lowest bidder to service the area for as long as service was acceptable to the residents in that area.

The city government has estimated the price residents are willing to pay for various number of garbage collections per month and the total costs per resident as shown in the following table.

Pickups (Q)	Price per Pickup (Demand)	Total Revenue (TR)	Marginal Revenue (MR)	Total Cost (TC)	Marginal Cost (MC)	Average Total Cost (ATC)
0	$4.20	0	—	$ 3.20	—	—
1	$3.80			$ 4.20		
2	$3.40			$ 5.60		
3	$3.00			$ 7.80		
4	$2.60			$10.40		
5	$2.20			$13.40		
6	$1.90			$16.80		

a) How much are the fixed costs per month of garbage collection per resident in any given area?

b) Fill in the table above. Given that the current garbage collection firm that the city has contracted with has a monopoly in garbage collection services, what is the current number of collections residents receive per month and the price charged residents for each collection? What is the economic profit received from each resident by the monopoly firm?

c) If competitive bidding were allowed and a competitive market for garbage collection services developed, what would be the number of collections per month and the price charged residents per collection? What is the economic profit received from each resident by the competitive firms?

d) Based on the above analysis should the city government allow competitive bidding? Why? Would you expect there to be any quality differences between the monopolistic versus the competitive trash collection firms?

e) Draw an appropriate graph of your solutions to (b) and (c) above and insert your numbers onto the graph.

3. Illustrate the output level and the price charged by the monopoly in the figure below. What would the price and output level be if this was a competitive market? Explain what is meant by "welfare loss" associated with a monopoly. Illustrate the area representing welfare loss in the figure below.

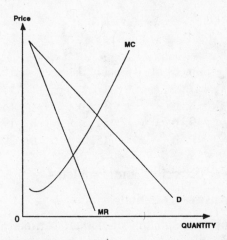

4. Suppose you are in the business of staging concerts. You have just contracted to stage a concert in a local theater next year. Your featured band will be "Beevus and the Boneheads," a red-hot rock group. The total cost of staging the concert is $10,000. This cost includes all band fees, the rental of the theater, security, insurance, etc., and it is independent of how many people attend the concert. Your market research indicates that attendance at the concert will vary as shown below depending on the price of an admission ticket. What ticket price should you charge to maximize profit? Briefly explain.

Ticket Price	Attendance
$20	771
$18	979
$16	1,133
$14	1,327
$12	1,559
$10	1,625
$ 8	1,803

b. **Potential Essay Questions**

1. Will the elasticity at the price that the non-price-discriminating monopolist charges be elastic or inelastic? Why?

2. What are the conditions which could cause any firm, including a monopolist, to incur economic losses?

3. Explain why, without barriers to entry, there would be no monopoly?

4. Show graphically the welfare loss from monopoly, and explain why it may understimate the general public's view of the social loss from the presence of monopoly.

V. ANSWERS

II. **Mastery Test**

1. a	6. d	11. d	16. a	21. a	26. c
2. c	7. c	12. c	17. c	22. b	27. c
3. d	8. d	13. b	18. c	23. a	28. a
4. b	9. b	14. b	19. d	24. d	29. d
5. c	10. b	15. a	20. d	25. c	30. c

III. **Short Answer Exercises and Problems**

a) **Short Answer Questions**

1. Due to restriction of output, barriers to entry and zero competition.

2. Because it is the only seller in the market.

3. A monopolist can make a profit in the long run.
    Competitors are prevented from entering the market due to barriers to entry. Long-run profits are protected.

4. The monopolist faces a downward sloping demand curve. To sell more, the monopolist lowers the price on *all* units sold. Its marginal revenue will equal P minus the revenue it loses from selling previous units at a lower price. The monopolist's MR will be less than the price for which it can sell the next unit.

5. Output is determined at MC = MR. At that point, profits are maximized.

6. First determine its output (from (5) above. Then determine its price and average total cost at that point. The difference between ATC and price is profit per unit. To find total profit, multiply this difference by output.

7. The marginal revenue and demand areas for a perfectly price-discriminating monopolist will be one and the same.

8. In order to price discriminate, a firm must be able to segment its markets or customers. That is, it must be able to determine which markets or customers have the more inelastic demand for the good or service, and then charge those people the higher price. (Recall that an increase in price when demand is inelastic will increase total revenue. Because price discrimination is charging people different prices for the same good or service where those price differences *are not a reflection of cost differences,* then a higher price charged translates into higher profits.) The firm must also be able to prevent resale.

9. The perfectly price-discriminating monopolist. It is able to maximize profit on **each** customer, and therefore will produce more output and make a higher profit than the normal monopolist.

10. As measured by Harberger and others, relatively small. About .5% of GDP. Normative measures of the welfare cost can increase that loss significantly.

11. 1. Barriers to entry. Some feel that monopolies are unfair and inconsistent with freedom. Monopolies prevent people from being free to enter whatever business they want and are undesirable on normative grounds.

    2. The income distributional effects of monopoly. Some believe that monopoly profits transfer income from ''deserving'' consumers to ''undeserving'' monopolists.

    3. The possibility that government-created monopoly encourages management to spend a lot of resources in rent seeking. Depending on the amount of competition for monopolies, management will spend up to the total expected amount of profit from their monopoly position.

12. 1. Natural ability. Possessing abilities not available to other firms.

    2. Increasing returns to scale. When sufficiently great, it is not efficient for two or more firms to be in the same market.

    3. Government granted monopolies. Government granted exclusive franchises for operating in a given area.

13. The government tax becomes a fixed cost to the monopoly. This additional FC increases ATC and reduces profit. The government tax transfers some of the monopoly profits back to society, and reduces the incentive for monopoly rent seeking. In addition, the tax should have no effect on output, because it does not become a part of the monopolist's MC.

b. Problems

1. (Note: Calculating Marginal Revenue (MR) from discrete numbers leaves a slight ambiguity in the answer. The marginal concepts could be associated with either the "above" or the "below" number.)

Price	Quantity Demanded	Total Revenue	Marginal Revenue
$10	1	$10	$10
9	2	18	8
8	3	24	6
7	4	28	4
6	5	30	2
5	6	30	0
4	7	28	−2

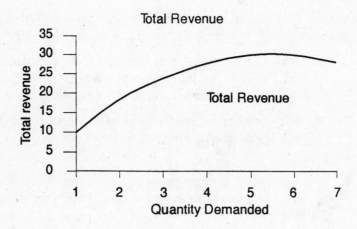

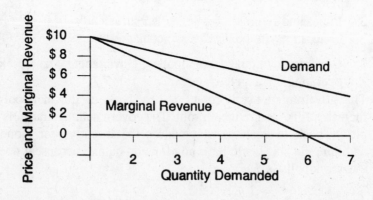

2. a) (Note: Calculating Marginal Revenue (MR) from discrete numbers leaves a slight ambiguity in the answer. The marginal concepts could be associated with either the "above" or the "below" number.)

PRICE	QUANTITY DEMANDED	TOTAL REVENUE	MARGINAL REVENUE	TOTAL COST	MARGINAL COST	PROFIT OR LOSS
$24	0	$	$	$13	$	−$13
20	1	20	20	19	6	−1
16	2	32	12	22	3	10
12	3	36	4	26	4	10
8	4	32	−4	34	8	−2
4	5	20	−12	49	15	−29

b)

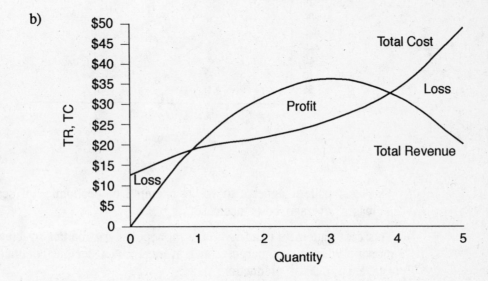

c)

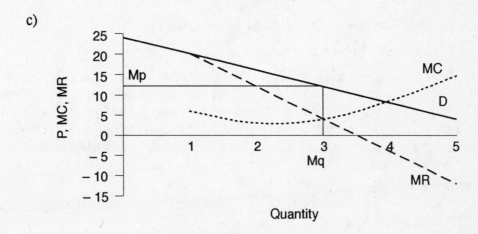

3. a)

Output	Long-Run Total Cost	Long-Run Marginal Cost	Long-Run Average Cost
1	$50	$50	$50
2	90	40	45
3	120	30	40
4	140	20	35
5	150	10	30

b)

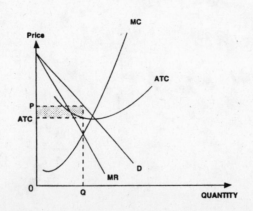

c) This cost pattern appears to be an example of economies of scale. As output increases, average costs decrease.

d) This cost pattern is indicative of a monopoly type market structure. In a natural monopoly, long-run marginal and average costs decline continuously over the relevant range of production.

IV. **Challenge Problems and Potential Essay Questions**

a) **Challenge Problems**

1. a) See the figure below. The monopolist will produce Q because that is the output level in which MR = MC for the last unit produced. The monopolist will charge price P. This is determined by bouncing off of the demand after you have determined the profit-maximizing quantity to produce. Because P > ATC the firm is earning an economic profit equal to the shaded area.

b) Whenever economic profits are earned in any market then there is always a tendency for new entrepreneurs to want to enter the market to soak up some profits for themselves. However, that is usually very difficult in a monopolized market because it is usually characterized by very strong barriers to entry. Therefore, economic profits are likely to persist for quite some time—at least for as long as the barriers to entry are successful in preventing potential competitors from entering the market. If losses are incurred, then like any other firm, the monopolist will shut down if P < AVC in the short run. No firm can sustain losses in the long run.

2. a) $3.20. Recall that fixed costs equal total costs when output is zero (because variable costs are zero when output is zero).

   b) See the table below. The profit maximizing monopoly will produce where MR = MC. This occurs at 3 trash collections per month. The price charged will equal $3.00 per collection. The economic profit for the monopoly will equal $1.20 per resident.

Pickups (Q)	Price per Pickup (Demand)	Total Revenue (TR)	Marginal Revenue (MR)	Total Cost (TC)	Marginal Cost (MC)	Average Total Cost (ATC)
0	$4.20	0	—	$ 3.20	—	—
1	$3.80	$ 3.80	$3.80	$ 4.20	$1.00	$4.20
2	$3.40	$ 6.80	$3.00	$ 5.60	$1.40	$2.80
3	$3.00	$ 9.00	$2.20	$ 7.80	$2.20	$2.60
4	$2.60	$10.40	$1.40	$10.40	$2.60	$2.60
5	$2.20	$11.00	$0.60	$13.40	$3.00	$2.68
6	$1.90	$11.40	$0.40	$16.80	$3.40	$2.80

   c) For a competitive firm price equals marginal revenue (P = MR). Therefore, a competitive trash collection market would give rise to 4 collections per month at a price of $2.60 per collection. The competitive firms would earn a zero economic profit (a normal profit would still be earned—a profit just sufficient to cover the opportunity costs of the entrepreneurs' time and financial capital invested in the businesses).

   d) Yes, because the price would be lower and the quantity of trash service would be greater. One might also expect the competition for garbage collection to result in better service.

   e) See the figure below. Note that the monopolist will produce where the MR and MC curves intersect, and then charge that price determined by "bouncing off" of the demand curve. The monopolist's economic profit is equal to the shaded area. The competitive outcome is determined graphically by the point of intersection between the MC and D curves; note P = ATC and there are no economic profits.

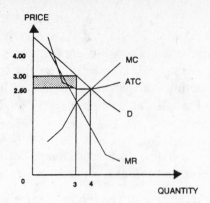

3. See the figure below. The monopoly would produce Qm and charge price Pm. The competitive outcome would be Qc and Pc. (As you would expect, the monopolist charges a higher price and produces less than a competitive market.) Welfare loss is the amount by which the marginal benefits to society (measured by the price people are willing to pay on the demand curve) exceed the marginal costs to society (measured by the marginal cost curve) for those units which would be produced in a competitive market but are not produced in a non-competitive market. This is shown as the shaded area in the figure below. Note that whenever production occurs at P = MC then social marginal benefits (P) equal social marginal costs (MC)—we have an efficient output level; the competitive outcome. However, if P > MC then output is too low from society's perspective; the non-competitive outcome.

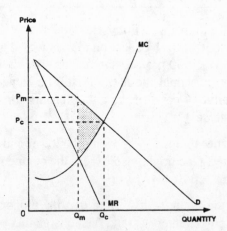

4. The profit-maximizing price is $12. It generates maximum revenues of $18,708. Since all costs of staging the concert are fixed costs, a price which maximizes revenues also maximizes profit. Profit will equal $8,708 (TR − TC = $18,708 − $10,000).

b) Potential Essay Questions

The following answers are annotated—they only indicate the general idea behind the answer.

1. It will be elastic. Because MC cannot be negative (except when a subsidy is received), and because the profit-maximizing quantity to produce exists at an output level in which MR = MC, then the firm will produce an output level in which MR is positive. MR is positive only in the elastic price range along a straight line demand curve. (Recall that as the price falls in the elastic portion of a demand curve then total revenue will rise. This means that marginal revenue must be positive.)

2. Any firm can suffer economic losses if: 1) demand is relatively weak, and/or 2) costs are relatively high.

3. If there were no barriers to entry, then potential competitors would be able to enter the market and compete these profits away.

4. Empirical studies suggest the loss from monopoly is not a big problem. However, the general public usually also adds some normative arguments against the presence of monopolies. Some members of the general public add the reduction of individual liberty if government action created the monopoly. There are also the redistributional effects, issues of fairness, and the ''wasted'' resources devoted to firms trying to secure monopoly power from government.

Chapter 11   MONOPOLISTIC COMPETITION, OLIGOPOLY, AND STRATEGIC PRICING

I. CHAPTER AT A GLANCE

Rip this page out for quick and easy reference.

1. A concentration ratio is the percentage of industry output that a specific number of the largest firms have. (237)

    A four-firm ratio of 60% means the four largest firms account for 60% of industry sales.

2. Four distinguishing characteristics of monopolistic competition are: (240)

    1. *Many sellers in a highly competitive market;*
    2. *Differential products, but firms still act independently;*
    3. *Multiple dimensions of competition; and*
    4. *Easy entry of new firms in the long run so there are no long-run profits.*

    Know these as well as the distinguishing characteristics of all 4 market structures.

3. The equilibrium of a monopolistic competitor is: (241)

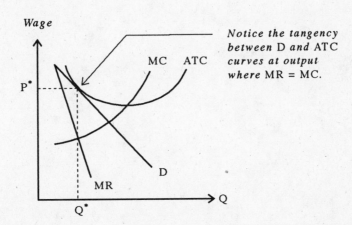

Notice the tangency between D and ATC curves at output where MR = MC.

Also Note: Only a zero economic profit in the long run where P = ATC. But, P > MC which implies underproduction from society's perspective.

4. Advertising allows a firm to differentiate its products from those of its competitors. (243)

    The primary goal of advertising is to shift the firm's demand curve to the right.

    Sometimes advertising results in a firm being able to enjoy economies of scale and therefore lower ATC.

    Usually ATC is higher because of advertising—is it worth it?

5. If oligopolies can limit the entry of other firms and form a cartel, they increase the profits going to the combination of firms in the cartel. (246)

> *There is an inherent tendency for collusion (getting together to avoid competing). However, holding firms together is difficult because of a tendency to cheat.*

6. In the contestable market model of oligopoly, pricing and entry decisions are based only on barriers to entry and exit not on market structure. Thus, even if the industry contains only one firm, it could still be a competitive market if entry is open. (248)

> *So: 2 extreme models of oligopoly behavior:*
>
> *(1) Cartel model: Firms set a monopoly price*
>
> *(2) Contestable market model: An oligopoly with no barriers to entry sets a competitive price*
>
> *Most real world oligopolies are in between.*

7. Exhibit 10 on page 255 of the textbook gives a summary of the central differences among the four various market structures. (254)

> **Study this exhibit! (Makes for "nice" exam questions!)*

II. MASTERY TEST

1. Which of the following is a characteristic of monopolistic competition?

   a) Homogeneous product
   b) Interdependence of producers
   c) No advertising
   d) A significant number of producers

2. Monopolistic competitors:

   a) earn economic profits in the long run.
   b) face downward sloping demand curves.
   c) face perfectly elastic demand curves.
   d) face perfectly inelastic demand curves.

3. Monopolistically competitive firms advertising expenditures may:

   a) lower the consumer's purchase price.
   b) help differentiate a firm's product.
   c) shift the demand curve to the right.
   d) All of the above.

4. As more firms enter a monopolistically competitive industry:

   a) ATC falls.
   b) economic profits increase.
   c) each firm's demand curve shifts to the left.
   d) advertising expenditures decrease.

Answer the following question (5) by referring to the diagram below.

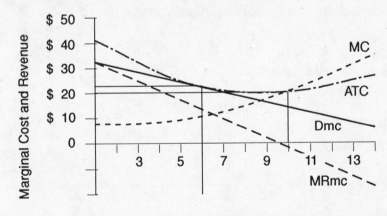

5. In the long run, this firm will produce _____ units of output and charge a price $ _____ (approximately).

   a) 7; $22.
   b) 9; $18.
   c) 7; $10.
   d) 6; $24.

Answer the next 2 questions (6 and 7) by referring to the diagram below.

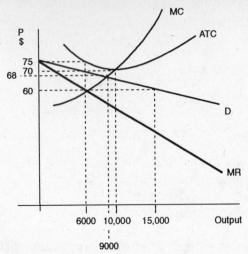

6. This firm in the short run will produce

   a) 6,000 units of output and earn an economic profit of $60,000.
   b) 9,000 units of output and earn an economic profit of $18,000.
   c) 10,000 units and earn zero profit.
   d) 6,000 units and earn economic losses of $30,000.

7. In the long run

   a) new firms will enter.
   b) price will be $70.
   c) this firm will go out of business.
   d) the demand curve will shift to the right.

8. Mutual interdependence in an oligopolistic industry results from:

   a) a large number of firms in the industry.
   b) large industry size.
   c) a few firms produce the largest share of total output.
   d) no competition among the firms.

Four Firm Concentration Ratio

Industry	Ratio (%)
A	75
B	25
C	89
D	51

9. In the table above, which industry is most competitive?

   a) A   b) B
   c) C   d) D

10. In the table on page 194, which industry is most oligopolistic?

    a) A   b) B
    c) C   d) D

11. An oligopolist facing a kinked demand curve will:

    a) match price cuts, but not increases.
    b) match price increases.
    c) not match price decreases.
    d) act independently of other producers.

12. A kinked demand curve helps explain:

    a) different kinds of advertising.
    b) homogeneous products.
    c) sticky prices in oligopolies.
    d) why oligopolies form cartels.

13. Which of the following are necessary conditions for oligopolistic industries?

    a) barriers to entry
    b) interdependence of firms
    c) small number of firms, or industry dominance by a small number of firms
    d) All of the above.

14. Oligopolistic and monopolistic competitors are similar in that:

    a) they produce differentiated products.
    b) they are both interdependent.
    c) long-run economic profits are zero.
    d) producers face perfectly elastic demand curves.

15. Long-run equilibrium price and output for monopolistic competitors will be at a point where:

    a) $MC > MR$.
    b) $MC < MR$.
    c) economic profits will be positive.
    d) the firm does not produce its output at the minimum point on the ATC curve.

16. The concentration ratio does not give a complete picture of the structure of the economy because:

    a) the data is out of date.
    b) the indexes measure sales instead of profits.
    c) many firms are conglomerates, and often span a variety of different industries.
    d) market share measurements do not take into consideration the mergers of many corporations with each other.

17. Strategic decision making means:
    a) considering a rival's expected response to a decision you are making.
    b) economic decision making.
    c) competitive decision making.
    d) monopolistic decision making.

In answering the following 2 questions (18 and 19), refer to the payoff matrix below.

Firm A's Strategies

		does not cheat	cheats
Firm B's Strategies	**does not cheat**	① A $ 15,000 profit / B $ 15,000 profit	② A $ 100,000 profit / B $ 20,000 loss
	cheats	③ A $ 20,000 loss / B $ 100,000 profit	④ A $ 0 profit / B $ 0 profit

18. This payoff matrix represents the strategic dilemma facing a duopoly. The best thing for both firms would be to

a) cooperate and achieve the result in box 1.
b) coopeate and achieve the result in box 4.
c) cheat and achieve the result in box 2.
d) cheat and achieve the result in box 3.

19. The competitive solution reached when both firms cheat is represented by

a) box 1.
b) box 2.
c) box 3.
d) box 4.

20. If various sellers can influence the market price of a product:

a) no firm has any monopoly power.
b) demand is elastic.
c) the market is monopolistically competitive.
d) demand is inelastic.

21. Marginal cost for a monopolistically competitive firm is less than price in long-run equilibrium because:

a) demand is downward sloping.
b) demand is perfectly elastic.
c) accounting profits are positive.
d) economic profits are positive.

22. Lower average costs of production can be the result of advertising when there are:

a) movie stars involved.
b) well known brand names.
c) diseconomies of scale in production.
d) economies of scale in production.

23. Members of a cartel can be successful in increasing prices when they:

   a) plan output to where MC = cartel price.
   b) produce no more than their assigned quota.
   c) invite new firms to enter the market.
   d) are producing at their lowest ATC.

24. Collusion is most likely to occur in which market structure?

   a) monopolistic competition.
   b) oligopoly
   c) perfect competition.
   d) monopoly.

25. Pricing and output decisions in the contestable market model are based on:

   a) ease of entry and exit.
   b) market structure.
   c) the degree of product differentiation.
   d) the four firm concentration ratio.

26. Attempts to establish a "brand name" would

   a) lower ATC.
   b) not affect demand for the product.
   c) increase ATC.
   d) attract other firms into the industry.

27. A situation in which the dominant firm in an industry sets a price which the other firms then adopt is called

   a) kinked demand.
   b) price-leadership.
   c) limit pricing.
   d) strategic pricing.

28. The market structure that produces where average costs are minimized in the long run is

   a) perfect competition.
   b) monopoly.
   c) oligopoly
   d) monopolistic competition.

29. Experimental economists have found

   a) game structure is irrelevant to the outcome.
   b) game structure is an important variable in deciding the solution.
   c) if the payoff to cheating is small, people tend to cheat more.
   d) competitive solutions are more likely with a small number of competitors.

30. Under oligopolistic competition, in the long run the price of the product

   a) always equals MC.
   b) is greater than ATC.
   c) equals ATC.
   d) may be anywhere between the perfectly competitive price and the monopoly price.

III. SHORT ANSWER EXERCISES AND PROBLEMS

a. Short Answer Exercises

1. List the problems encountered in determining market structure.

2. What is a concentration ratio?

3. The four firm cancentration ratios for the tobacco and clothing industries are respectively 98.9 and 6.6. What can you conclude about the structure of these industries?

4. What is a strategic decision? Why is it important for economic modelling?

5. Compare the relative state of independence between monopolistic competitors and oligopolists.

6. How do monopolistic competitors and perfect competitors differ?

7. Describe the long-run opportunities of the monopolistic competitor versus the monopolist.

8. Describe the role of advertising in monopolistic competition.

9. What are the advantages of advertising for the consumer?

10. What are the characteristics of a cartel model of oligopoly?

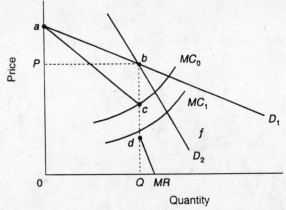

11. The diagram above represents the kinked demand curve which some oligopolists perceive that they face. Currently the price is P and output is Q. Refer to this diagram to explain why prices are sticky.

12. How and where is an oligopolist's price usually set?

13. How does the contestable market theory of oligopoly judge an industry's competitiveness?

14. Explain why a cartel with no barriers to entry might achieve a competitive solution.

15. a) In a prisoner's dilemma type of situation, what would be the best strategy for each prisoner to follow?
    b) What strategy does each prisoner actually follow?

---

16. Cooperative solutions sometimes occur when the benefits from cheating aren't too great, but eventually these solutions will tend to break down. Why?

b. **Problems**

1. Assume the below graph is for a monopolistic competitor.

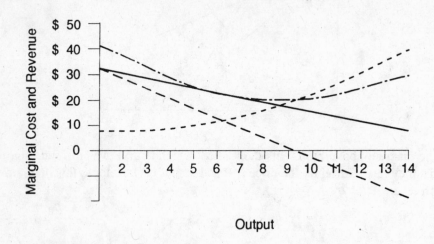

a) Identify the following curves:

   1. demand
   2. marginal revenue
   3. marginal cost
   4. average total cost.

b) At what level will the monopolistic competitor set output and price in the long run?
c) At what level of output and price would economic profits be zero?
d) At what price and output is ATC at its lowest?

2. Moline Barge Co., an oligopolist, believes that its competitors will not match a price increase it is considering, but will match any price cuts Moline made. This suggests its demand curve would be highly elastic if it raised prices, but would become relatively inelastic if it cut prices.

Illustrate below in graph form, the following:

i) Moline's hypothetical initial demand, and the "kink" in the curve at the point of a price cut. (Assume that demand becomes less elastic at the point of the price cut.)

ii) Illustrate Moline's initial marginal revenue and the shift in marginal revenue below the kink.

iii) Sketch in Moline's marginal cost curve at a location between the original marginal revenue curve and the shifted marginal revenue curve.

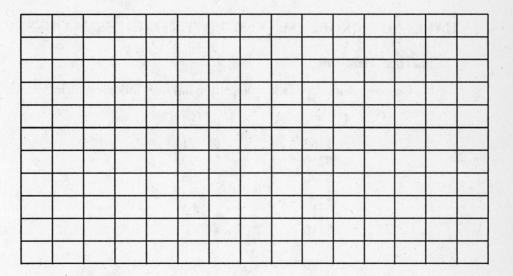

a) What relationships on your graph determine Moline's optimal level of output and price to maximize profits?

b) Would there be any advantage for Moline to cut prices to gain market share based on your graph?

c) Based on your analysis, what would be your prediction about the stability of prices in an oligopoly?

d) If oligopolists formed formal or informal cartels, would your answer to (c) above be any different?

3. The below table indicates some information for the "Zippy" industry.

Annual Sales
($ in millions)

Firm A $300
Firm B 200
Firm C 150
Firm D 100
All other firms 500

a) What is the 4 firm concentration ratio for this industry?

b) Assume that Zippy is the railroad industry. What would happen to the concentration index if we redefined Zippy as the railroad car industry? As the transportation industry?

IV. CHALLENGE PROBLEMS AND POTENTIAL ESSAY QUESTIONS

a. Challenge Problems

1. Suppose a monopolistic competitor has the following demand and cost schedules:

Q	P	TC
0	$260	$ 471
1	$250	$ 593
2	$240	$ 656
3	$230	$ 693
4	$220	$ 709
5	$210	$ 760
6	$200	$ 840
7	$190	$ 960
8	$180	$1,112

a) Compute the profit-maximizing price, output, and amount of economic profit.

b) Now suppose new competitors enter the market and take away some of the monopolistically competitive firm's customers, leaving it with the new demand schedule shown below. What is the new profit-maximizing price, output, and amount of economic profit?

Q	P	TC
0	$200	$ 471
1	$190	$ 593
2	$180	$ 656
3	$170	$ 693
4	$160	$ 709
5	$150	$ 760
6	$140	$ 840
7	$130	$ 960
8	$120	$1,112

c) Draw a graph comparing your solutions for this monopolistically competitive firm for (a) and (b) above. Insert your numbers into the graph.

2. It is often said: "Advertising doesn't cost, it pays!" Assume a firm undertakes a successful advertising campaign to better differentiate its good or service from its competitors. Also assume some economies of scale can be experienced if this firm expands its scale of operation.

a) If the advertising campaign is indeed successful in distiguishing the firm's product from its competitors product in either real or imaginary terms, what is expected to happen to the firm's demand? Will the demand for the firm's output likely become more elastic or more inelastic? Why?

b) What is likely to happen to the firm's costs of production over time? Why?

c) What will likely happen to the firm's economic profit over time? Why? Is it true that advertising sometimes "doesn't cost, it pays!"?

3. In a recent consent decree, airlines agreed to stop a practice in which they had signaled planned fare increases in the computer reservation system and then waited to see if other airlines would follow suit. After this consent decree, travel agents have noticed that airlines often raise their prices on Friday nights and often, but not always, lower those prices on Monday morning. Can you give a likely explanation for this airline action?

4. Al's and Bob's are two garages operating in a small prairie town. They each do spring tune-ups and are both wondering about a spring advertising campaign. If Al's advertises in the local newspaper, the profits for the 3 spring months will be $3,000 for him. Bob's will lose $1,000 in extra profits and vice versa. If both Al's and Bob's advertise then neither one will end up with any extra profits for those three months. If neither advertise they will both make their usual extra $1,000 profit for these three months.

a) Construct a payoff matrix for this duopoly. Be sure to include the players, the possible strategies, and the potential outcomes.

b) What will Al's and Bob's do if they don't trust each other?

c) What would they be better off to do?

5. a) Suppose two other garages in a small town in the Maritimes agree to collude and charge the monopoly price for tune-ups. They agree to divide the monopoly output equally between them. Use the diagram below to determine the collusive price and the amount each firm will produce. What is the profit of each firm?

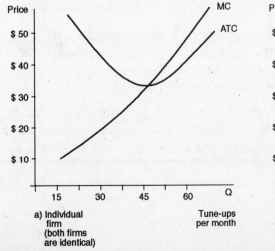

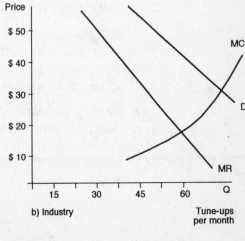

b) Suppose one garage decides to cheat and increase its output of tune-ups to the firm's maximizing output at a price of $50. What is this output, and what would be the short run profit for this firm? What will happen in the long run?

b. **Potential Essay Questions**

1. Compare and contrast the four market structures. What are some difficulties one may encounter in determining the market structure of a particular real-world market?

2. What are the ways in which a firm can differentiate its product from its competitors? What is the over-riding objective of product differentiation?

3. Why is there a tendency for an oligopoly to form a cartel? Is collusive activity more or less likely given a smaller number of firms in the market?

4. What is the difference between the contestable market model and the cartel model of oligopoly? How are they related?

V. ANSWERS

II. **Mastery Test**

1. d	6. d	11. a	16. c	21. a	26. c
2. b	7. c	12. c	17. a	22. d	27. b
3. d	8. c	13. d	18. a	23. b	28. a
4. c	9. b	14. a	19. d	24. b	29. b
5. a	10. c	15. d	20. c	25. a	30. d

III. **Short Answer Exercises and Problems**

a. Short Answer Exercises

1. a) Defining the industry; b) defining the relevant market of a given industry; c) deciding what is to be included in an industry.

2. A concentration ratio is the percentage of the total industry output the top firms of the industry have. The four-firm concentration rate is the percentage the top four firms in the industry have. The presumption is that a ratio over 60 percent is monopolistic, 40 to 60 is oligopolistic, and under 40 is monopolistically competitive.

3. The tobacco products industry is monopolistic and the clothing industry is monopolistically competitive.

4. A strategic decision means taking into explicit account a rivals expected response to a decision you are making. The economist's model of a market where there is strategic decision making will not have a definite prediction of price and output. In oligopoly therefore, there are a variety of rational decisions.

5. A monopolistic competition market has many firms each producing a differentiated product. The firms are independent of each other and will earn no long-run economic profits. An oligopolistic market has a few firms, each producing a differentiated (but similar) product. The firms are interdependent and engage in strategic pricing. They are constantly aware of how competitors will react to output and pricing decisions.

6. Monopolistic competitors produce a differentiated output. They face a downward sloping demand curve, and restrict output at the intersection of MR = MC. Perfect competitors produce an undifferentiated output. They face a horizontal demand curve and restrict output at the intersection of MR = MC = P.

7. The monopolistic competitor makes zero economic profits in the long run. The monopolist has the possibility of making economic profits in the long run.

8. Advertising plays an important role in differentiating products; shifts the demand curve for the product to the right; increases price (and costs); allows the firm to enjoy economies of scale.

9. Differentiated products bring satisfaction to some consumers. Consumers gain a sense of trust from ''knowing'' the products.

10. A cartel is a combination of firms that act as if it were a single firm or monopoly. Each firm has a quota so that total output is consistent with joint profit maximization. There is a uniform price.

11. If the firm raises its price above P, the demand is perceived to be elastic (ab). Other firms will tend not to follow suit so this firm will lose a lot of business and TR ↓. A decrease in price brings similar action from other firms—inelastic demand. Decreasing price will not increase the firm's market share by much, so TR ↓ (bf). Since MR is discontinuous, MC can change without bringing a corresponding price and quantity change.

12. Somewhere between the competitive price and the monopolistic price, determined by the structure of the industry and the level of barriers to entry.

13. It judges more by performance and barriers to entry than by structure of the industry.

14. ''Outside competition'' can break down cartels with no barriers to entry. Demand in the long run for these firms would be very elastic, so P = MC = ATC or close to it.

15. a) Each player would be best off if both deny.
    b) The actual best strategy will be that each will confess because it is the best choice regardless of what the other does.

16. Cooperative solutions tend to break down as the benefits of cheating become larger. Also, as the number of competitors increases, cooperation will tend to break down.

b. Problems

1. a)

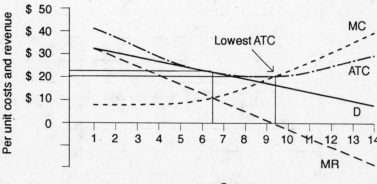

b) At MC = MR. Price is about $22. Output is between 6 and 7 units.
c) The same as b) above. ATC = D. Price about $22. Output between 6 and 7 units.
d) At MC = ATC. Price and ATC are about $19, and quantity is between 9 and 10 units.

2. a) MR = MC. Produce quantity q and price at p.

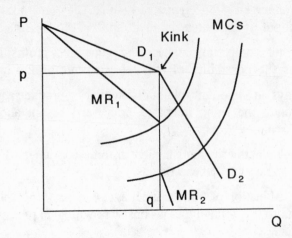

   b) The kinked demand curve illustrates that profits would be maximized at the point of the kink. There would be no advantage in cutting price.
   c) If there is no profit advantage to raise or lower prices due to competitive factors, prices would tend to be stable.
   d) If all the producers in an oligopoly cartel acted together to raise prices, there would be a greater opportunity for long-run economic profits.

3. a) 60 percent. (750/1,250)
   b) The ratio will rise as the industry is more narrowly defined, and fall as the industry is more broadly defined.

V. Challenge Problems and Potential Essay Questions

a. Challenge Problems

1. a) Price = $190, output = 7, and economic profit = $370. See the table below.

Quantity	Demand (Price)	Total Revenue	Marginal Revenue	Total Cost	Marginal Cost
0	$260	$0	—	$ 471	—
1	$250	$ 250	$250	$ 593	$122
2	$240	$ 480	$230	$ 656	$ 63
3	$230	$ 690	$210	$ 693	$ 37
4	$220	$ 880	$190	$ 709	$ 16
5	$210	$1,050	$170	$ 760	$ 51
6	$200	$1,200	$150	$ 840	$ 80
7	$190	$1,330	**$130**	$ 960	**$120**
8	$180	$1,440	$110	$1,112	$152

b) Price = $140, output = 6, and economic profit = $0. See the table below.

Quantity	Demand (Price)	Total Revenue	Marginal Revenue	Total Cost	Marginal Cost
0	$200	$0	—	$ 471	—
1	$190	$190	$190	$ 593	$122
2	$180	$360	$170	$ 656	$ 63
3	$170	$510	$150	693	$ 37
4	$160	$640	$130	$ 709	$ 16
5	$150	$750	$110	$ 760	$ 51
6	$140	$840	**$ 90**	$ 840	**$ 80**
7	$130	$910	$ 70	$ 960	$120
8	$120	$960	$ 50	$1,112	$152

c) See the figure below.

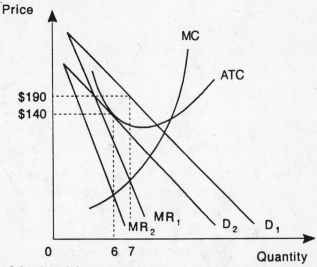

2. a) A successful advertising campaign, or anything else which is successful in positively differentiating a firm's good or service from its competitors, will increase the demand for the firm's output *and* increase the inelasticity of demand for the firm's good or service. The demand curve will become more inelastic (steeper) because there are now fewer suitable substitutes for the product, or it is now considered to be a "necessity."

b) Although advertising will shift up a firm's short-run ATC curve, the firm's costs of production are likely to fall over time as the firm expands its scale of operation (to satisfy the increased demand for its output) and economies of scale are experienced.

c) The firm's economic profit will likely rise as its revenues rise (due to the increased demand, and inelasticity of demand, for its product) and its costs fall (if economies of scale are experienced). Even if costs rise, revenues may rise more than costs increasing profit. Advertising can pay off.

3. The airline industry is an oligopoly. The demand curve for airline services appears from this action to be kinked around the "going-market price." Before the consent decree, many airlines which had signaled a price increase may have often found that the other airlines did not follow suit. Consequently, an airline's signaled price increase could cause a significant reduction in its ticket sales and its revenues. After the consent decree, an airline which increases its prices Friday night can reduce its air fares back to where they were on Monday morning before too many ticket sales and revenues are lost if the other airlines do not follow with their own price increases.

4. a)

		Al's	
		Advertise	Not Advertise
Bob's	Advertise	Profit for Al's $0 / Profit for Bob's $0	Profit for Al's −$1,000 / Profit for Bob's $2,000
	Not Advertise	Profit for Al's $3,000 / Profit for Bob's −$1,000	Profit for Al's $1,000 / Profit for Bob's $1,000

b) Since they can't trust each other, they will both advertise.

c) They would be better off to neither one advertise.

5. a) They will each produce 30. The profit maximizing output for the industry is 60. The profit maximizing price is $50 and ATC is $40 at output of 30 for each firm, so profit's are $10 × 30 = $300 for each firm.

b) The cheater will produce where MC = MR at an output of 55. See the figure above. This firm will now make a profit of $550. The non-cheater will only be able to sell 5 tune ups now instead of 30. His profits will decline.

As time goes on, the other firm (the non-cheater) will start to produce more as well and eventually price to both firms will fall. The potential is for a competitive situation to be reached with zero economic profit.

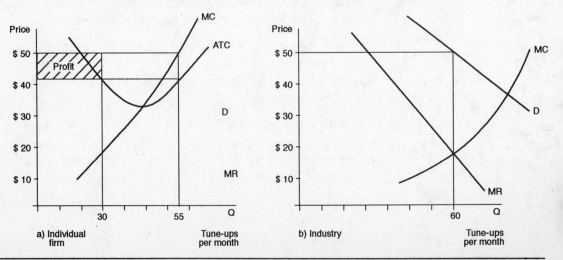

a) Individual firm   Tune-ups per month

b) Industry   Tune-ups per month

b. Potential Essay Questions

The following answers are annotated—they only indicate the general idea behind the answer.

1. Each profit-maximizing firm, regardless of the market it is operating within, will produce where MR = MC. Moveover, in all market structures there is always a tendency for new firms to enter the market when economic profits are being earned. However, the market structures differ in the ease with which new firms can move into the market. Indeed, the stronger the barriers to entry, generally the less competitive the market, and the greater the probability that the existing firms can earn economic profits in the long run. See Exhibit 10, page 255 of the textbook, for additional differences between the market structures. The difficulties one may encounter in applying a market structure classification in the real world is determining what is the relevant market (the whole world, or a town within a nation?), and what is to be included in the industry (do you use a two-digit or four-digit classification?).

2. Firms can differentiate their good or service in either real or imaginary terms. The objective of differentiation is to increase the demand for the product and to increase the inelasticity of demand.

3. Forming a cartel enables the firms to avoid competing, thereby increasing their profits individually and collectively. A cartel is, in essence, a monopoly. Cartels are designed to (1) set prices; (2) carve out markets—to agree not to compete on each other's turf; or (3) to set production quotas (which limits market supply and then, indirectly, determines market price). Although cartels are illegal in Canada there is still a tendency for firms to want to get-together informally—to undertake informal, or implicit collusion. The smaller the number of firms, the more likely collusion will be undertaken, and the more likely any collusive activity will be continued over time.

4. The cartel model argues that oligopolistic firms will come together to behave as a monopoly in terms of their pricing and output decisions because it is in their self-interest to do so—they'll make more money. (However, there is always a tendency for a firm to want to "cheat" and the mere rumor of cheating can cause a break-down of the collusion.) The contestable market model argues that an industry that looks like an oligopoly (because there are a few dominant firms in the industry) could set highly competitive prices and produce a competitive output level. What is important in pricing and output decisions, according to the contestable market model, is not the number of firms in the industry, but the strength of the barriers to entry that exist in the market. If there are few, if any barriers to entry, then a competitive price and output level will be observed. These two models are related in that the stronger the barriers to entry usually the fewer the number of firms and the greater the probability for collusion.

Chapter 12　COMPETITION IN THE REAL WORLD

I.　CHAPTER AT A GLANCE

Rip this page out for quick and easy reference.

1. **The monitoring problem is that employees' incentives differ from the owner's incentives. Because monitoring these employees is expensive, some economists are studying ways to change the situation. (259)**

    An incentive-compatible contract is needed to match the goals of both parties.

2. **Corporate takeovers, or simply the threat of a takeover, can improve firms' efficiency. (251)**

    The competitive pressures a firm faces limit its laziness and x-inefficiency.

3. **When competitive pressures get strong, individuals often fight back through social and political pressures. Competition is a process—a fight between the forces of monopolization and the forces of competition. (262)**

    —Everyone applauds competition—except for themselves.

    —Competitive markets will exist only if suppliers or demanders don't collude.

4. **A natural monopoly is an industry with strong economies of scale so the average cost is continually falling. It can be demonstrated graphically that as a number of firms in a natural monopoly increases, the average cost of producing a fixed number of units also increases. (264)**

    Examples of natural monopoly include local telephone service, cable TV and electric utilities. Gov't regulatory boards often regulate the prices charged.

5. **Firms protect their monopolies by (1) advertising and lobbying, (2) producing products as nearly unique as possible, and (3) charging low prices. (266)**

    Firms will spend money and time to obtain monopoly power until the marginal cost equals the marginal benefit.

II. MASTERY TEST

1. Economic models generally assume that firms attempt to maximize

   a) sales.
   b) revenues.
   c) profits.
   d) market share.

2. The monitoring problem is that

   a) short-run and long-run goals for the firm are often inconsistent.
   b) managers and shareholders always share the same objectives for the firm.
   c) employees' incentives differ from the owners' incentives.
   d) most real-world production takes place in owner-operated businesses.

3. Incentive-compatible contracts

   a) ensure that the firm's goals and the manager's goals match.
   b) ensure that manager's have the right to maximize their own incomes.
   c) are designed to protect employees from shareholders.
   d) reduce the power of managers and put decision making into the hands of owners.

4. The structure of corporations in Canada is such that

   a) there is no monitoring problem.
   b) there is a monitoring problem as evidenced by the high managerial salaries.
   c) managers receive relatively low pay compared to those in other countries.
   d) managers are paid in exact accordance with their marginal productivity.

5. X-inefficiency

   a) occurs when monopolists are "lazy" and don't push to keep costs down.
   b) means firms operate more efficiently than they technically could.
   c) means monopolists are maximizing short-run and long-run profits.
   d) occurs when monopolists keep costs low by refusing to adopt new technology.

6. A lazy monopolist

   a) would never survive in today's world.
   b) is limited by the degree of competitiveness faced by the firm.
   c) tries to eliminate X-inefficiency.
   d) All of the above.

7. A corporate takeover

   a) is welcomed by the lazy monopolist as it reduces the competitive pressure.
   b) benefits managers by creating more management positions.
   c) puts competitive pressure on a lazy monopolist.
   d) increases the advertising expenditures and therefore the costs of doing business.

8. Economists believe that

   a) some highly motivated individuals will seek efficiency for its own sake and for these managers the profit motive is unnecessary.
   b) employee pride is all that is needed for profit maximization to occur.
   c) well intentioned individuals do not need to be motivated.
   d) holding down costs without the profit motive takes stronger will power than most people have.

9. Monopoly triumphs over perfect competition because

   a) monopoly is in the long run more efficient.
   b) competition keeps wages and prices too high.
   c) government emphasizes other social goals besides efficiency
   d) they are beneficial for consumer's who ultimately have the power of the consumer $.

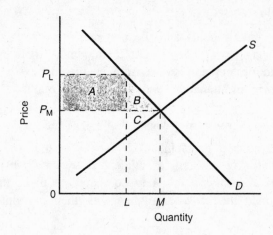

10. In the diagram above, shaded area A represents

    a) additional income to suppliers producing OL if they prevent new suppliers from entering and producing LM.
    b) the loss to suppliers kept out of the market so they don't have much incentive to fight entry restrictions.
    c) the total loss to demanders from restricted entry.
    d) the cost to demanders of organizing.

11. In the diagram above, shaded area C represnts

    a) additional income to suppliers producing OL if they prevent new suppliers from entering and producing LM.
    b) the loss to suppliers kept out of the market so they don't have much incentive to fight entry restrictions.
    c) the total loss to demanders from restricted entry.
    d) the cost to demanders of organizing.

12. A patent

    a) guarantees that a monopolist will enjoy monopoly profits for the life of the patent.
    b) gives information to potential competitors that can erode the monopoly position provided by the patent.
    c) is designed to encourage additional producers to copy the patented article and thereby to ensure competition in the market place.
    d) makes it legal for firms to practice reverse engineering.

13. Regulatory boards

    a) control the price of natural monopolies to ensure monopoly profits.
    b) have the job of encouraging new entrants into decreasing cost industries.
    c) create X-inefficiency.
    d) must screen every cost so as to ensure that the regulated price is "fair."

14. Which of the following would *not* be a method of protecting monopoly?

    a) Advertise
    b) Maximize profit
    c) Produce hard to copy outputs
    d) Establish a trademark

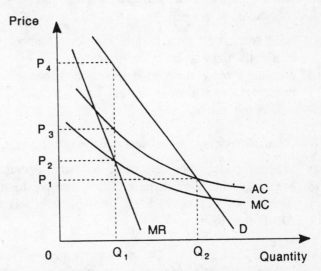

15. Refer to the above figure which represents a natural monopoly. Which of the following statements is true?

    a) An unregulated monopoly would produce Q1 and charge price P4.
    b) If the government regulatory board set the selling price equal to the marginal cost, the firm would be sustaining losses.
    c) If the government regulatory board set the selling price so that only a zero economic profit, or "fair" rate of return were earned, it would set the price at P1.
    d) The effect of X-inefficiency for this firm would be to shift its average cost curve up.
    e) All of the above.

16. If long-run losses are expected of firms in a decreasing cost industry, we can expect that:

    a) the product price will rise as firms leave the industry.
    b) new firms will enter the industry.
    c) the product price will fall.
    d) the product will be produced by perfectly competitive firms.

17. A monopolist earning economic profits will:

    a) spend money on advertising for greater market penetration.
    b) hire a lobbyist to help defeat unfriendly legislation.
    c) use competitive pricing to discourage competition.
    d) All of the above.

18. Perfect monopoly producers:

    a) have many competitors producing the same product.
    b) have a few competitors producing the same product.
    c) have no competitors.
    d) have at least one competitor.

19. Which of the following statements are incorrect?

    a) The monopolist always charges a higher price for its product than does an oligopolist.
    b) The monopolist will always charge the highest price possible for its product.
    c) Society's overall well-being is always reduced under a monopoly.
    d) All of the above are incorrect.

20. If a public utility faces a decreasing average total cost throughout its range of output, then the utility should:

    a) be characterized as a natural monopoly, since it can produce the market output more efficiently than several firms.
    b) encourage more firms to enter since market efficiency is increased with several firms.
    c) be able to earn only a normal profit.
    d) All of the above.

21. What conditions may prevail when real-world firms differ from the profit-maximizing model?

    a) Production does not take place in owner-operated businesses.
    b) Many decision makers have little incentive to hold down their pay and other costs.
    c) Employee's incentives differ from owner's incentives.
    d) All of the above.

22. Assume the Central Power Co. is a natural monopoly. Also assume it is forced by regulators to establish a maximum price equal to long-run marginal cost. This will result in:

    a) either profits or losses depending on the efficiency of the monopoly.
    b) losses to the monopoly.
    c) normal profits to the monopoly.
    d) excessive profits to the monopoly.

23. Why would a monopolist engage in competitive pricing?

    a) To discourage new entrants to the market
    b) To maximize profits
    c) Both a. and b.
    d) Neither a. nor b.

24. Why do most consumers tend to accept supplier imposed restrictions?

   a) There is little incentive to fight collusion.
   b) Costs of organizing are higher than those of the suppliers.
   c) Little political power.
   d) Government restrictions on consumers.

25. What conditions generally lead to competitive markets:

   a) demand is limited.
   b) supply is limited.
   c) collusion between suppliers and demanders.
   d) no collusion between suppliers and demanders.

26. What rights do patents grant?

   a) legal right to produce a good.
   b) reverse engineering.
   c) financial controller.
   d) proxy.

27. What conditions lead to natural monopoly?

   a) The LRATC curve shows constant returns to scale.
   b) LRATC is the same regardless of the number of firms producing the good.
   c) one firm can produce the entire output at a lower ATC than two or more firms.
   d) one firm can produce the entire output at a higher ATC than two or more firms.

28. If demand is relatively inelastic over the range of production for a natural monopoly, the monopolist will:

   a) advertise more.
   b) sell more.
   c) charge a higher price.
   d) charge a lower price.

29. What criteria do regulatory boards try to use when setting the price of a natural monopoly?

   a) The price includes all costs plus a normal return on investment.
   b) The price remains stable over the long-run.
   c) The price covers all the accounting costs.
   d) $P = MC$

30. As the number of firms increase in a natural monopoly, the average cost of producing a:

   a) variable number of units is indeterminate.
   b) constant number of units remains the same.
   c) constant number of units decreases.
   d) constant number of units increases.

III. SHORT ANSWER EXERCISES AND PROBLEMS

a. Short Answer Exercises

1. How are the goals of real-world firms determined?

2. Explain what is meant by the monitoring problem?

3. Why are managers sometimes given incentive compatible contracts?

4. What are some of the intermediate goals that sometimes become the focus of firms?

5. What is the nature of X-inefficiency in a monopoly?

6. How can potential corporate takeovers improve the efficiency of a firm?

7. Why should competition be seen as a dynamic process and not as a static situation?

8. When will suppliers find it in their interest to restrict entry?

9. What cost structure is characteristic of natural monopolies?

10. Name several ways firms protect their monopoly.

11. How do firms determine how much monopoly to buy?

12. Why are perfect monopolies rare?

13. An argument has been made that utilities, as natural monopolies, should set rates at their marginal costs. Discuss.

14. Agriculture has many of the conditions for almost perfect competition. Does the real-world reflect this market structure in agriculture? Why or why not?

b. Problems

1. The curves on the below graph represent the following:

ATC1 = Average total cost for efficient monopolist.
ATC2 = Average total cost for lazy monopolist.
MR = Marginal Revenue
D = Demand

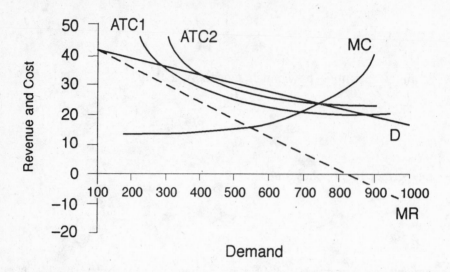

Required:

a) Show the Price (Pm) and Quantity (Qm) amounts for a profit maximizing monopolist.
b) Show the ATC (Clm) for the lazy monopolist at the profit maximizing equilibrium.
c) Show the ATC (Cm) for the efficient monopolist at the profit maximizing equilibrium.
d) Mark with an X the area of the profits that characterize X-inefficiency management.

2. Public utilities, characterized as natural monopolies are usually subject to local regulations in regard to pricing. Some regulators suggest pricing at MC = D. Theoretically, this would produce maximum efficiency for the public.

On the graph below are hypothetical Average Total Cost, Marginal Cost and Demand curves for a natural monopoly. (Assume economies of scale.)

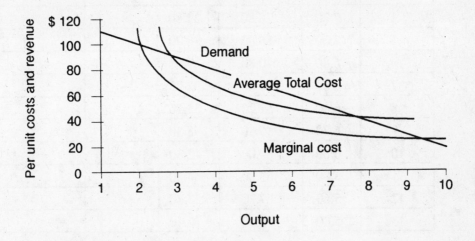

a) Describe the relationship between Average Total Cost and Marginal Cost at the point where Marginal Cost = Demand? What is the long-term viability of this monopoly if price is set at Marginal Cost = Demand?

b) If price is set at Marginal Cost = Demand, what are the alternatives available to the regulator to ensure continuing supply of the utility service?

3. Complete the revenue, cost, profit, etc. table for Monopgen Company shown below and graph the following data:

    Total Revenue
    Total Cost
    Total Profit

A. Indicate on your graph Monopgen's output if management is attempting to maximize profits. Label it "A".
B. Indicate on your graph Monopgen's output if management is attempting to maximize revenues without incurring operating losses. Label it "B".
C. Indicate on your graph Monopgen's output if management is attempting to earn $10 as a "satisfactory level" of profits. Label it "C".

RATE OF OUTPUT	PRICE	TOTAL REVENUES	TOTAL COST	TOTAL PROFIT	MARGINAL COST	MARGINAL REVENUE
1	$7.80	$ 7.80	$14.00	−6.20	$3.50	$7.40
2	7.60	15.20	17.50			
3	7.40	22.20	20.75			
4	7.20	28.80	23.80			
5	7.00	35.00	26.70			
6	6.80	40.80	29.50			
7	6.60	46.00	32.25			
8	6.40	51.20	35.10			
9	6.20	55.80	38.30			
10	6.00	60.00	42.30			
11	5.80	63.80	48.30			
12	5.60	67.20	57.30			
13	5.40	70.20	70.40			

Total Costs and Revenues

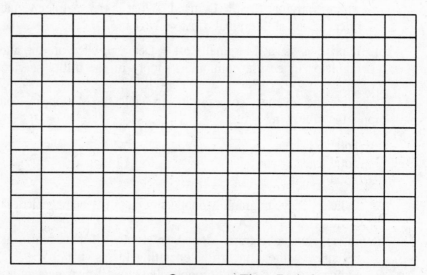

Output per Time Period

IV. CHALLENGE PROBLEMS AND POTENTIAL ESSAY QUESTIONS

a. Challenge Problems

1. Why might a government granting a monopoly to a firm in an industry which experiences economies of scale over the range of output desired by consumers, and then regulating the prices charged by the monopoly be justified? What are some examples of this?

2. As computer technology has developed, pricing has become far more complex, with prices varying more for different buyers and discount plans becoming more prevalent. One company, Canadian Lock and Supply, has been quoted as saying it spends 50 percent of its corporate strategy sessions in setting prices.

   a) Why has this change occurred? Is multiple pricing consistent with economic theory?

   b) All the firms who follow a multiple-price strategy would consider their industries to be very competitive. The multiple prices, however, tell us that the firms are not perfectly competitive. Which of the assumptions of perfect competition is not present here which can help account for the multiple-price strategy? Can a market be very competitive and have a multiple-price strategy?

3. Professional sports is big business. Have you noticed that the sports pages of your local newspaper often devote as much space to the "business" of sports as to the competition on the field, court or ice? The professional leagues of baseball (American and National Leagues), basketball (National Basketball Association), football (National and Canadian Football Leagues), and hockey (National Hockey League) are unique to the North American business landscape in that government has granted them legal cartel status. Why has government done this?

4. The high cost of medical care can be illustrated using demand and supply analysis. Both demand and supply are highly inelastic. Over time, demand has been increasing faster than supply, resulting in higher prices, as well as greater revenues to the various entities involved in supplying health care services. Let's focus on the role of physicians alone when it comes to the supply of health care. What role has the CMA (Canadian Medical Association) played in creating entry barriers into the health care profession which have restricted the supply of health care? How does this illustrate the influence of the invisible handshake (social forces) and the invisible foot (political forces) in real-world markets?

b. Potential Essay Questions

1. What role do profits play in ensuring competition?

2. Define the monitoring problem and state its implications for economics. What helps place a limit on firm's laziness, or X-inefficiency?

3. What is a natural monopoly? What are some examples? What role does government often play in natural monopolies?

4. How can the standard models of monopoly and perfect competition still be useful when applied to real-world industries which are neither monopolistic nor perfectly competitive?

V. ANSWERS

II. Mastery Test

1. c	6. b	11 c	16. a	21. d	26. a
2. c	7. c	12. b	17. d	22. b	27. c
3. a	8. d	13. d	18. c	23. a	28. c
4. b	9. c	14. b	19. d	24. b	29. a
5. a	10. a	15. e	20. a	25. d	30. d

III. Short Answer Exercises and Problems

a. Short Answer Exercises

1. Profit plays a role, but actual goals depend upon the incentive structure embodied in the firm's organizational structure.

2. The monitoring problem occurs because real-world production doesn't take place in owner-operated businesses. Managers may seek to maximize their own incomes at the expense of profits for the firm and its owners. When the incentives of owners and employees differ like this, it is called the monitoring problem.

3. These contracts are designed to ensure that the goals of managers and owners are the same or compatible. A self-interested manager will maximize the firm's profit if her contract requries her to do so.

4. Intermediate goals: growth in sales, cost reduction for long-term profit improvement, status quo.

5. X-inefficiency describes the level of laziness managers allow themselves. Rather than attempting to maximize profits for the firm, they set a goal to earn enough profits to keep the absentee stockholders satisfied.

6. Managers fear corporate takeovers because they might lose their jobs. They then take steps to prevent the takeovers and in the process are forced to improve overall efficiency.

7. The competitive process involves a continual fight between monopolization and competition. Decision makers hate competition for themselves, but not for others. When pushed, they tend to push back. The invisible forces of the hand, foot and handshake are pushing against each other.

8. Entry restrictions will be undertaken by suppliers if it increases their income by more than it costs to restrict entry.

9. In a natural monopoly, because of economies of scale it is cheaper for one firm to produce a good than for two or more firms to produce it.

10. Advertising, lobbying, new improved products, competitive pricing, predatory business practices.

11. By the relationship of marginal cost to marginal benefit. For example, the expected marginal cost of a lobbying effort for a particular piece of legislation, is measured against the expected marginal benefit gained from it.

12. Monopoly profits send out signals to other firms. Those signals cause competition from other firms who want to get some of that profit for themselves. They attack the monopoly through political or economic means.

13. If the utility is in an economies of scale cost pattern, its MC < AC. This means the utility would have to price its output at less than AC. The utility would be operating at a loss, and would have to be subsidized to stay in operation.

14. Canada along with most other producing nations has a myriad of laws, regulations, and programs that prevent agricultural markets from working competitively. Canada markets are characterized by price supports, acreage limitations, and quota systems. The government emphasizes other social goals besides efficiency.

b. **Problems**

1.

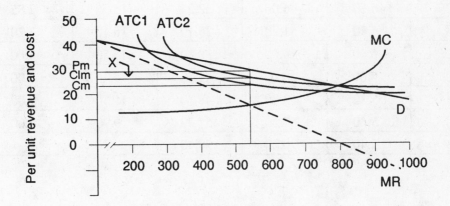

a) For the profit maximizing monopolist, price and quantity are determined by the relationship between MC and MR. Quantity would be set at between 500 and 600 units, priced at about $30.

b) ATC for the lazy monopolist (Clm) is about $25 at the profit maximizing equilibrium.

c) ATC for the profit maximizing monopolist is about $23.

d) X on the graph indicates the area of profits lost to the X-inefficiency management.

2. a) In this situation, ATC > MC at MC = D ATC is greater than demand, which means that this natural monopoly would operate at a long term loss if price is set at D = MC.

b) Alternatives available to the regulator to assure continuing service include:

1. Subsidizing the utility to provide a fair return on their investment.
2. Government operation of utility, and absorbing any losses as a public service.
3. Changing the pricing structure to allow the utility to earn a "normal" profit.

3.

RATE OF OUTPUT	PRICE	TOTAL REVENUES	TOTAL COST	TOTAL PROFIT	MARGINAL COST	MARGINAL REVENUE
1	$7.80	$ 7.80	$14.00	−$6.20	$ 3.50	$7.40
2	7.60	15.20	17.50	−2.30	3.25	7.00
3	7.40	22.20	20.75	1.45	3.05	6.60
4	7.20	28.80	23.80	5.00	2.90	6.20
5	7.00	35.00	26.70	8.30	2.80	5.80
6	6.80	40.80	29.50	13.75	2.75	5.20
7	6.60	46.00	32.25	13.95	2.85	5.20
8	6.40	51.20	35.10	16.10	3.20	4.60
9	6.20	55.80	38.30	17.50	4.00	4.20
10	6.00	60.00	42.30	17.70	6.00	3.80
11	5.80	63.80	48.30	15.50	9.00	3.40
12	5.60	67.20	57.30	9.90	13.00	3.00
13	5.40	70.20	70.40	−.20		

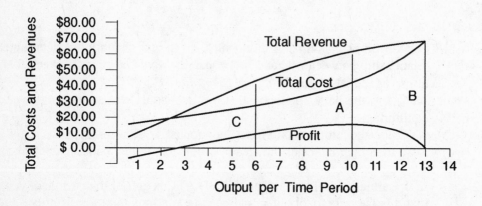

IV. Challenge Problems and Potential Essay Questions

a. Challenge Problems

1. Economies of scale result in lower average (per unit) costs. If economies of scale are extensive then the firm which expands first will end up as the sole survivor over time—the largest firm with the lowest average cost. As a monopoly it may then "gouge" consumers with very high prices. Government realizes this and grants a monopoly to a firm under the condition that its price will be regulated to prevent any "price-gouging." Some examples include public utilities and the cable T.V. companies.

2. a) The computer industry has become much more competitive. New technologies have enabled many new firms to enter the industry which used to be dominated by IBM. There are not only a growing number of firms offering computer technologies, but the products being offered are becoming increasingly more differentiated (because of the growth in technology)—responding to the specific, varying, and growing needs of consumers. These firms are scurrying for the profits to be had. The greater number of firms has reduced the probability for collusion. The competition has resulted in paying close attention to price—strategic pricing. But, wherever possible, if the consumer's elasticity of demand can be determined, these firms will charge a higher price to the consumer with the more inelastic demand (the consumer whom is less price conscious but maybe more service conscious—"service after the sale" is a form of product differentiation). Indeed, these firms try to create a more inelastic demand for their product as they try to increase the demand for their product. This can be accomplished by more successfully differentiating their product from competitors in either real (technology) or imaginary terms. Moreover, the degree to which a higher price can be charged is limited to how effectively the firm is in differentiating its good. Multiple-pricing is entirely consistent with economic theory.

   b) The assumption of perfect competition that is not present here is "firms sell a homogeneous (identical) good." Differentiation allows for multiple-pricing and still constitutes an extremely strong form of competition.

3. Government recognizes that to preserve the competitive spirit of the game on the field or the court requires a lack of competition in the front offices. Imagine teams competing for fans in perfectly competitive markets. The better teams would be more profitable and would be able to attract the better players coming out of school. Over time, only a few teams would dominate the sport—boring! In order to preserve spectator support for the game the leagues (which are effectively cartels) have established rules to govern the practices of the varous clubs (franchises). These rules and procedures limit "business" competition in order to preserve athletic competition.

4. The CMA virtually controls, and limits, the supply of physicians. It accredits medical schools and restricts admission practices of these schools in the name of "quality." Numerous qualified applicants to medical schools are turned away every year. It also controls internships and residency training programs by approving or disapproving hospitals that administer these programs. Hospitals need cheap interns and therefore succumb to CMA pressure. Provincial governments, with the support of the CMA, also require physicians to pass a provincial licensing exam before practicing medicine. This can be an effective way of controlling the supply of physicians from abroad by changing the difficulty of the exam or other costs of getting a license. There are many other social and political (invisible handshake and foot) forces at play in the nursing, health insurance, and drug business as well. In all cases, barriers to entry limit supply and drive prices up.

b. Potential Essay Questions

The following answers are annotated—they only indicate the general idea behind the answer.

1. Whenever profits are large then firms will be attracted to the industry. As firms enter the industry competition pushes prices down, increases output, and reduces profits. Although barriers to entry may be encountered, they are rarely insurmountable over time. However, any policy which reduces the strength of those barriers to entry is recommended—with the exception of some government created barriers to entry in the case of a natural monopoly, and patents which reward innovations over time.

2. The monitoring problem is that employee's incentives differ from the owner's incentives. It is a problem especially considering that most business activity is undertaken by corporations where there is a separation of ownership and control. The implication is that many real-world firms may not have profit-maximization, and an efficient use of resources which it requires, as a primary goal. But, the laziness or X-inefficiency of firms is still limited by international competition and the threat of a takeover.

3. A natural monopoly exists when economies of scale are extensive (the long-run average cost curve is downward sloping). Over time the one firm which expands and realizes lower average costs of production and charges a lower price will be the sole survivor. Given their eventual monopoly status then they are free to charge a monopoly price. Some examples include local utilities, the phone company and cable T.V. companies. Often, natural monopolies have their prices regulated by government.

4. They illustrate the reasoning process behind all real-world business decisions—the application of marginal benefits and marginal costs to business decisions. Marginal analysis is a useful way to look at many real-world problems. It provides insights and often clarifies events which would otherwise be unintelligible.

Chapter 13   COMPETITION AND
INDUSTRIAL POLICY

I. CHAPTER AT A GLANCE

Rip this page out for quick and easy reference.

1. **Canadian anti-combines legislation has evolved since the late 1800s. (270)**

    Competition policy is carried out through anti-combines legislation.

    A combine is a combination of firms that act like a single firm.

2. **Three areas of anti-competitive behaviour addressed in the Competition Act of 1986 include: price-fixing, merger, and the "abuse of a dominant position." (272)**

    Price-fixing: Combining together with other firms and setting a uniform price.

    Merger: Combination of firms; e.g., acquisition, takeover.

    Abuse of dominant position: Defines a number of specific anti-competitive acts, (listed in #3 below).

3. **There are four ways of abusing a dominant position. (272)**

    1) fighting brands
    2) withholding of resources required by competitors
    3) adoption of product specifications that would prevent competitors from entering the market or that would be incompatible with those of competitors
    4) pricing below cost

4. **Mergers can be horizontal, vertical, or conglomerate, and there are many reasons why firms might want to merge. (274)**

    Horizontal merger: two companies in the same industry merge
    Vertical merger: a firm merges with its supplier
    Conglomerate merger: two firms in unrelated industries merge: reasons—1) to achieve economies of scale; 2) to get a good buy; 3) to diversify; 4) to ward off a takeover bid; 5) to strengthen their political-economic influence.

5. **There are at least seven reasons to object to a merger proposal. (274)**

    The reasons are:

    1) The extent of foreign competition
    2) Whether one of the parties to the merger is "failing."
    3) The availability of close substitutes
    4) The existence of barriers to entry
    5) How competitive the industry will be after the merger
    6) The likelihood that the merger would remove an effective competitor
    7) The nature and extent of innovation in the relevant market

6. **A number of restrictive practices are prohibited under the Competition Act. (275)**

   They are:

   1) *Price discrimination*
   2) *Predatory pricing*
   3) *Resale price maintenance*
   4) *Bid-rigging*
   5) *Misleading advertising*
   6) *Deceptive marketing*
   7) *Exclusive dealing*
   8) *Tried selling*

7. **Nationalization and Privatization might lead to greater economic efficiency. (277)**

   Nationalization refers to the case of federally or provincially owned firms; e.g., crown corporations. The government can then influence pricing decisions so that more is supplied to consumers at a lower price. Privatization refers to the case where government attempts to find private buyers for publicly owned government businesses. The purpose is to reduce the rising costs of maintaining crown corporations.

8. **Industrial policy refers to the government's role in actively determining the structure of industry in Canada. (279)**

   The idea is to have government pick "winners" and channel funds to these high-growth industries—but can government do this?

9. **Economists can find reasons for and against an activist industrial policy. Most would probably come out against an activist role for government, given the invisible feet of politics and law. (279)**

   Economic decisions made for political reasons inevitably involve waste—cost of an activist industrial policy.

   Cooperation by firms with government and universities can result in more productive research—benefit of an activist industrial policy.

   *What do you think—does the cost outweigh the benefit?

II. MASTERY TEST

1. The competitiveness of markets should be judged by

    a) the structure of the market.
    b) the number of firms in the market.
    c) the performance of the firms in the market.
    d) the type of product being produced.

2. Deciding what constitutes a market is particularly difficult in Canada because

    a) many firms produce the same products.
    b) international trade affects Canadian markets to a large degree.
    c) so many firms collude to set prices.
    d) companies are always merging.

3. A combine is

    a) a combination of firms that act like a single firm.
    b) a shared monopoly.
    c) to restrict output to the monopoly level.
    d) All of the above.

4. The most important element of the 1879 National policy was

    a) the reduction of import taxes.
    b) the decision to reduce all barriers to trade.
    c) the introduction of protective tariffs.
    d) the decision to import cheaper products from abroad.

5. In 1889, a new government act

    a) made it a criminal offence to "unduly" limit competition or "unreasonably" enhance price.
    b) made it a criminal offence to "encourage" unnecessary and undue competition.
    c) increased protective tariffs for large Canadian producers.
    d) created monopoly as the market of performance.

6. In 1910, the Anti-combines Act

    a) gave the government complete power in court to convict anyone found to be following monopolistic practices.
    b) resulted in the disappearance of competition.
    c) gave legal status to price fixing.
    d) established procedures for investigating "restrictive business practices."

7. In 1986 the Competition Act

    a) created the Competition Tribunal.
    b) reversed all other anti-competitive policies in favour of monopoly.
    c) made everything a criminal offence.
    d) focused on market structure.

8. Abuse of dominant position includes all but which of the following:

   a) Pricing below cost to drive out competition
   b) Withhold resources required for competitors to produce
   c) Fighting brands
   d) Pricing above cost in order to maximize monopoly profits

9. A takeover occurs when

   a) two firms combine into one.
   b) a shell corporation buys an existing firm and market concentration doesn't change.
   c) three or more firms combine to alter the market concentration.
   d) a large firm buys a small firm.

10. The buyout of one firm by another is called

    a) a takeover.
    b) a predatory arrangement.
    c) an acquisition.
    d) never occurs.

11. Double Pac Man is a

    a) form of green mail.
    b) friendly takeover.
    c) golden parachute.
    d) form of hostile takeover.

12. Poison Pill strategy:

    a) the target of a hostile takeover makes itself unpalatable by doing something "stupid."
    b) the target of the takeover "pays off" the company trying to take-over.
    c) the target of the hostile takeover looks for a "white knight" firm.
    d) management resigns in protest of a hostile takeover.

13. To ensure that managers act in the shareholders interest in the case of a takeover bid, managers are sometimes offered a

    a) green mail.
    b) golden parachute.
    c) poison pill.
    d) government job as a backup.

14. The term given to the merging of two companies in the same industry is

    a) vertical merger.
    b) hostile takeover.
    c) horizontal merger.
    d) conglomerate merger.

15. The term given to the combination of two firms engaged in unrelated business activity is

    a) horizontal merger.
    b) conglomerate merger.
    c) vertical merger.
    d) friendly acquisition.

16. Why would two unrelated firms want to merge? Choose which of the following is <u>incorrect</u>.

   a) to achieve economies of scope.
   b) to diversify.
   c) to strengthen their political economic influence.
   d) to become more attractive for a takeover bid.

17. How do mergers reduce competition? Choose which of the following is <u>incorrect</u>.

   a) They could remove an effective competitor.
   b) They lower barriers to entry.
   c) They could eliminate the availability of close substitutes.
   d) They could reduce foreign competition.

18. Loss leading is an exception to the illegal practice of

   a) resale price maintenance.
   b) predatory pricing.
   c) price discrimination.
   d) bid rigging

19. If three potential bidders for the contract to supply janitorial services to federal government buildings in Ottawa meet to coordinate their bidding, so they all get a share of the work, this is called

   a) deceptive marketing.
   b) bid rigging.
   c) predatory pricing.
   d) price discrimination.

20. Copying machines that require owners to buy paper from the same copy company is an example of

   a) exclusive dealing.
   b) misleading advertising.
   c) bid-rigging.
   d) tied selling.

21. A difficulty with crown corporations is that

   a) the government can exercise control over pricing.
   b) the government can ensure more output is supplied to consumers.
   c) bureaucrats charged with running the firm may decide to inflate costs in their own interests.
   d) they are more efficient than monopolies.

22. Information that is skewed to deliver only the impact that the informer wants to convey is called

   a) informer information.
   b) impacted information.
   c) competitive information.
   d) regulated information.

23. The benefits from deregulation are all but which of the following?

   a) More competition
   b) Reduced price
   c) Reduced service
   d) Competition with foreign firms on a level playing field.

24. Japan's Ministry of International Trade and Industry (MITI) is an example of:

   a) a passive industrial policy.
   b) an activist industrial policy.
   c) a restrictive bureaucracy.
   d) a military-industrial complex.

25. In Canada, economists oppose an activist industrial policy for all but one of the following reasons.

   a) Creation of more inefficiency and waste
   b) Impacted information
   c) Possibility for graft
   d) The encouragement of research cooperation between government and the private sector.

26. A criticism of the structural criterion for competition is that

   a) structure is a good indicator of future performance.
   b) relevant market and industry are hard to determine.
   c) it leaves the court too much contextual judgment.
   d) it is against the populist values of society.

27. The Bagel Chip Company is concerned about an unfriendly takeover by Mom's White Bread Company. Bagel Chip buys the Rye Company for twice its market value as a defense. This strategy is known as:

   a) double whammy.
   b) greenmail.
   c) poison pill.
   d) golden parachute.

28. Computers-R-Us merges with Computers Sales Company. This is an example of:

   a) crossover merger.
   b) vertical merger.
   c) conglomerate merger.
   d) horizontal merger.

29. An example of a vertical merger would be:

   a) A computer manufacturing company merging with a micro-chip producing company.
   b) A computer manufacturing company merging with a department store company.
   c) A computer manufacturing company merging with another computer manufacturer.
   d) A computer manufacturing company merging with a construction company.

III. SHORT ANSWER EXERCISES AND PROBLEMS

a. Short Answer Exercises

1. What was the main impact of the National Policy in 1879?

2. What was the main problem with the Anti-Combines legislation of 1889?

3. What was it about the Anti-Combines Act of 1910 that made it so difficult to enforce?

4. List two of the major changes introduced by the Anti-Combines Act of 1986.

5. How might a firm be seen as a predator by some and an aggressive competitor by others?

6. List the anti-competitive acts referred to as abuse of dominant position.

7. Davetec, a shell corporation, is planning to "merge" with Petec, a small clerical manufacturer in Peteborough. How would this merger be described in more technical language?

8. Describe what is meant by a hostile takeover.

9. a) Sutec, a small producer of natural vitamin supplements found itself the target of a hostile takeover by the large Sun Vitamin Co. Describe a "poison pill" strategy that Sutec might employ to prevent the takeover.

   b) Describe "greenmail" as it applies to the Sun takeover bid for Sutec.

10. What do firms sometimes do to protect shareholders from management's interest overriding shareholders' interest?

11. Identify each of the following as a vertical, horizontal, or conglomerate merger.
    a) One shoe factory buys another shoe factory _____
    b) An apple orchard owner buys an apple juice company _____
    c) A telephone company buys a pop company _____

12. Why might two unreleated firms want to merge?

13. Identify each of the following as price discrimination, predatory pricing, resale price maintenance, bid-rigging, misleading advertising, or deceptive marketing.
    a) Children pay a lower price for movies _____
    b) The customer believes that when they purchase a lawn mower that servicing will be free when in fact it is not _____
    c) The customer believes that the blade on the new lawn mower is unique in that it will never need sharpening (in fact, this is not true) _____
    d) Concrete manufacturers agree to cooperate and bid together on a project so that they can each share equally in the job _____

e) A producer of flannel shirts won't allow the shirts to be sold by retailers at less than the suggested price _____

f) A tire producer gives the fourth tire free _____

14. Describe the problems associated with trying to regulate the price of a natural monopoly.

15. What is the purpose of deregulation?

16. What are the costs and benefits of an activist industrial policy?

b. **Problems**

1. Answer the following questions based on the Figure shown below representing a monopoly.

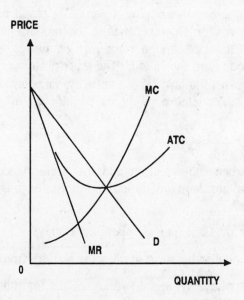

a) Illustrate the monopoly price and quantity outcome on the graph.

b) Assume this monopoly was regulated to achieve a competitive price and quantity. Illustrate this outcome on the graph.

c) Assume a monopolist is regulated so that its price will always just be able to cover all of its average total cost so that the monopolist will be able to earn a "fair" rate of return. What is a potential problem with this?

IV. CHALLENGE PROBLEMS AND POTENTIAL ESSAY QUESTIONS

a. Challenge Problems

1. What general criteria should be used to determine when it is rational for government to regulate business?

2. For each of the following situations determine what type of business practice is being undertaken.

   a) Pepsi-Cola Corporation buys Pizza Hut and Kentucky Fried Chicken.

   b) A bakery corporation buying up a grocery store chain.

   c) Company X and Company Y are each trying to buy each other.

   d) Company X is threatening to buy out Company Y but really doesn't want to acquire Company Y. Instead, it wants payment from Company Y to halt the takeover bid.

   e) Company X is trying to buy out Company Y but Company Y doesn't want to be taken over.

   f) A steel manufacturer buys up all other steel manufacturers.

3. Canadian auto manufacturers sell their models at a lower price on the west coast in an effort to remain competitive with Japanese imports. This has upset many car dealers on the east coast who view this as price discrimination and therefore a violation of anti combines legislation. Which anti combines law are these dealers referring to? What possible defense might the auto manufacturers claim?

4. Suppose a grocery store is interested in buying a particular brand name of canned tomato soup from a food processing vendor. However, before the vendor agrees to deliver any cans of tomato soup the grocer is required to sign a contract guaranteeing that the grocery store will buy all of its canned goods from the vendor. The grocery store objects because it argues that such a requirement is against the law. Which anti-combines law would the grocer argue is being broken? What possible defense might the vendor claim?

b. Potential Essay Questions

1. Explain the difference between the structure and the performance methods of judging competition. In the real world are there any definitive criteria for judging whether a firm has violated anti-combines laws?

2. Briefly describe the history of Canadian Competition Policy.

3. What is one advantage and one disadvantage of takeover activity from society's perspective?

4. What is meant by industrial policy? What are two arguments for and two arguments against having an activist industrial policy? Why has there been more serious consideration of an activist industrial policy for Canada in recent years?

V. ANSWERS

II. Mastery Test

1. c	6. d	11. d	16. d	21. c	26. b
2. b	7. a	12. a	17. b	22. b	27. c
3. d	8. d	13. b	18. a	23. c	28. d
4. c	9. b	14. c	19. b	24. b	29. a
5. a	10. c	15. b	20. d	25. d	

III. Short Answer Exercises and Problems

a. Short Answer Exercises

1. Protective tariffs: taxes on imports were introduced in the National Policy of 1879. These taxes sheltered Canadian producers from cheap imports. During 1870's and 1880's these firms did not adopt cost decreasing technology because protective tariffs excluded foreign imports.

2. The law made it a criminal offence to stifle competition by "unduly" limiting competition or "unreasonably" enhancing price. The wording of the act was so ambiguous that it had little effect on the way business operated.

3. Merger and monopoly were criminal offences and they were hard to prove "beyond a reasonable doubt."

4. This act placed merger and monopoly under civil law where the standards of proof were easier. The other major change was a shift to performance rather than structure as the basis for judgement of anti-competitive behaviour.

5. A firm that lowers price could be a predator trying to drive competitors out of business by pricing below cost. A firm that lowers price could be doing so as the result of efficient organization and the adoption of new technologies.

6.
   - Fighting brands (a firm producing two similar products provides a discount on one of its products to capture the market)
   - Withholding resources (a firm acquires a vital resource and refuses to supply it to competitors)
   - Product specifications incompatible with competition
   - Pricing below cost

7. Davetec exists primarily to buy up the other company. This is a takeover. Little real "merging" is taking place.

8. A hostile takeover occurs when one firm doesn't want to be taken over, that is, the managers don't want it taken over. In a hostile takeover the management of each corporation presents its side to the shareholders of both corporations and the shareholders of the corporation that is the takeover target, decide.

9. a) Sutec could buy the small producer of fruit leather located in the same town. The fruit leather company has run up a large debt from poor business practices so once Sutec acquires this debt ridden company, Sutec is no longer desirable.

   b) In the case of a greenmail, Sun Co. would be hoping for a payment from Sutec to "persuade" Sun Co. to drop its takeover bid.

10. Golden Parachute. This is a strategy whereby top managers are promised large payouts should a takeover occur. Presumably they would then make decisions regarding takeovers in the best interests of the shareholders.

11. a) horizontal merger
    b) vertical merger
    c) conglomerate merger

12. a) to achieve economies of scope
    b) to get a good buy
    c) to diversify
    d) to ward off a takeover bid
    e) to strengthen their political-economic influence

13. a) price discrimination
    b) deceptive marketing
    c) misleading advertising
    d) bid-rigging
    e) resale price maintenance
    f) predatory pricing

14. It is hard to get an honest figure for costs. Impacted information benefits managers at the expense of consumers and prevents regulatory agencies from getting the correct information.

15. To allow competition to replace regulation as an effective way of keeping prices down.

16. Costs: Possible graft and waste associated with political rather than economic decisions.
    Benefits: If the government successfully chooses, winners, gains will come from increased cooperation and international competitiveness.

b. Problems

1. a) See Figure below. The monopoly price and quantity would be P_m and Q_m (any profit-maximizing firm will produce where MR = MC and then charge the highest price market demand will bear at that output level).

   b) See Figure below. The competitive price and quantity are P_c and Q_c. The competitive outcome exists where P = MC = minimum ATC.

   c) If the monopolist is regulated whereby the price it is able to charge will always be sufficient to cover all of its average total cost of production then there is little incentive for the monopolist to keep its costs down.

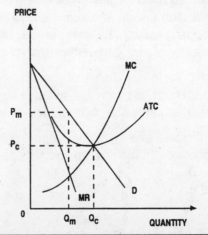

IV. Challenge Problems and Potential Essay Questions

a. Challenge Problems

1. Government should regulate business only when the benefits outweigh the costs.

2. a) Conglomerate merger (designed to achieve economies of scope).
   b) Vertical merger
   c) Double Pac Man
   d) Greenmail
   e) Hostile takeover
   f) Horizontal merger

3. The Competition Act prohibits price discrimination if it has the effect of lessening competition. The auto manufacturers could claim that the lower prices on the west coast do not result in less competition but are instead a consequence of the intense competition that exists on the west coast.

4. The Competition Act prohibits tied selling in which the buyer must agree to deal exclusively with one seller and not to purchase goods from competing sellers. The vendor may claim that this is not reducing competition.

b. Potential Essay Questions

The following answers are annotated—they only indicate the general idea behind the answer.

1. The judgement by structure method argues we should judge competitiveness of markets by the structure of the industry. For example, by using the concentration ratios. The judgement by performance approach argues we should judge the competitiveness of markets by the performance (behaviour) of firms in that market. That is, by comparing the price and output level to that expected under competitive market conditions and by looking at the strength of the barriers to entry which exist in the market. In the real world there are no definitive criteria for judging whether a firm has violated the antitrust statutes because both the structure and performance criteria have ambiguities. History has shown that a firm is not at fault or in the clear until the courts make the call.

2. One of the major problems associated with the judgement-by-structure criterion is that if a firm has driven its competition out of the market because it produced the best product at the cheapest possible price—because it is the most efficient—it may be found guilty of breaking the law (monopolizing) for doing what it's supposed to do—produce the best product at the lowest possible cost. Another problem is the difficulty of defining what the relevant market is. Is it the local, national or international level which is most relevant for determining the degree of competition? A benefit of this approach is its practicality. It limits the issues the courts look at. Another advantage is that this approach can be a predictor of future performance. Although a firm may be charging a low price now, when the competition is gone, it will not be able to resist exercising its monopoly power.

   One of the problems with judging the degree of competition on the basis of performance is that it requires a case-by-case analysis by the courts. This could be quite cumbersome. One of the advantages is that a few, or even one firm may be providing a high quality product at the lowest possible cost and should not have to be found guilty of anti-combines for this reason. That is, bigness of business is not necessarily bad for society.

3. One advantage is that the threat of a takeover will keep managers on their toes—adding competitive pressure to the economy. To avoid being a takeover target, managers will be more apt to minimize costs. A disadvantage is that managers spend too much time playing the takeover game and too little tilme overseeing the truly productive activities of the firm—like "real" investment that creates jobs and future economic growth over time.

See pp. 270–271 for a brief history until 1986 with the passage of the Competition Act. Highlights of the Competition Act should include the Competition Tribunal, the switch to judgement by performance, mergers, and restrictive practices.

4. An industrial policy is a government's formal policy toward business. Two arguments for an industrial policy are (1) that it will create gains from cooperation among firms, and (2) that it will channel funds to high growth industries. Two arguments against having an activist industrial policy are (1) graft and (2) the inevitable waste inherent in bureaucracy. The recent increased interest in whether the Canadian government ought to adopt a more activist industrial policy stems from the concern with Canadian industry's ability to effectively compete in the global economy—especially considering the relatively more stringent Competition Law that Canadian firms must contend with compared to those found in other countries.

Chapter 14   WORK AND THE LABOUR MARKET

I. CHAPTER AT A GLANCE

Rip this page out for quick and easy reference.

1. **Applying rational choice theory to the supply of labour tells us that the higher the wage, the higher the quantity of labour supplied. (283)**

    > *The higher the wage, the more "expensive" it is to "goof-off." So, we work more; or at least more people decide to work. As wages increase the quantity supplied of labour also increases $\Rightarrow$ upward sloping S curve for labour.*

    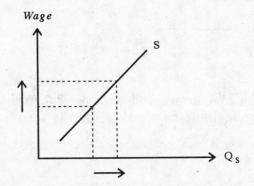

2. **An increase in the marginal tax rate is likely to reduce the quantity of labour supplied because it reduces the net wage of individuals and hence, via individuals' incentive effect, causes them to work less. (286)**

    > *Higher marginal tax rates reduce the incentive to work.*

3. **To determine a firm's derived demand curve for labour, you look at the marginal revenue product, because that tells you how much additional money the firm will make from hiring an additional worker. (290)**

    > **A firms D for labour curve is its MRP curve!*
    >
    > *For competitive firm; if*
    >
    > *MRP > wage $\Rightarrow$ hire more workers*
    >
    > *MRP = Wage $\Rightarrow$ Employing* profit-maximizing quantity of workers
    >
    > *MRP < Wage $\Rightarrow$ hire fewer workers*

4. **Because a monopolist's marginal revenue is below a competitive firm's price, its demand for labour will be lower, assuming all else equal. (292)**

    > *Competitive firm: MRP = MPP $\times$ P*
    > *Monopoly firm: MRP = MPP $\times$ MR*

---

5. **A monopsony is a market in which only a single firm hires labour. A bilateral monopoly is a market in which a single seller faces a single buyer. (297)**

Monopsony will hire fewer workers and pay a lower wage compared to the competitive outcome.

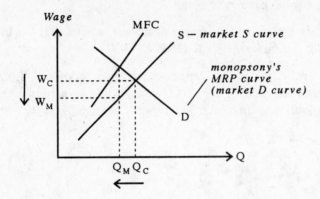

6. **Real world labour markets are complicated and must be explained by all three invisible forces; the invisible hand, the invisible handshake, and the invisible foot. (299)**

What we see in the real world is a consequence of the interaction of these 3 forces.

7. **Three types of discrimination are: (300)**

   (1) discrimination based on individual characteristics that will affect job performance;

   (2) discrimination based on correctly perceived statistical characteristics of the group; and

   (3) discrimination based on individual characteristics that don't affect job performance or are incorrectly perceived.

   You can think of discrimination as treating equals unequally, or treating unequals equally.

II. MASTERY TEST

1. Which of the following would <u>not</u> be categorized as a nonmarket activity?

    a) Illegal or black market selling
    b) Weeding your neighbours garden for $8/hour pay
    c) Tuning up your own car
    d) weeding your own garden

2. How much a person will change his or her hours of work in response to a change in the wage rate is called

    a) the black market effect.
    b) the opportunity cost effect.
    c) the incentive effect.
    d) All of the above.

3. When wages rise

    a) the opportunity cost of leisure increases.
    b) the opportunity cost of leisure decreases.
    c) you will buy more leisure.
    d) the participation rate declines.

4. All but which of the following influence the market supply of labour?

    a) Individuals either/or decision to enter or leave the labour market
    b) Individuals decision to work more or less hours
    c) The cost of leisure
    d) The marginal product of labour

5. High marginal tax rates

    a) increase people's incentive to work.
    b) increases the relative price of non-market activities.
    c) create a negative incentive effect on people's incentive to work.
    d) have been on the decline for some time in Canada.

6. The elasticity of the supply of labour is affected by all but which of the following?

    a) The elasticity of individual supply curves
    b) Individuals entering and leaving the labour force
    c) The type of market being discussed
    d) The extent to which the labour supply is backward bending.

7. If very few workers enter or exit a labour market as the wage rate changes, the labour supply is:

    a) perfectly elastic.
    b) perfectly inelastic.
    c) elastic.
    d) inelastic.

8. Employed workers prefer _____ labour supplies, while employers prefer _____ labour supplies.

   a) elastic, inelastic
   b) inelastic, elastic
   c) elastic, elastic
   d) inelastic, inelastic

9. Which of the following tends to increase the elasticity of demand for labour?

   a) inelastic demand for the good that workers make
   b) quickly falling marginal productivity of factor inputs
   c) many substitutes for labour in production
   d) labour makes up a small portion of production costs

10. Entrepreneurship

    a) is a type of specialized piece of capital equipment.
    b) is a type of creative labour.
    c) ensures that all labour receives equal wages.
    d) refers to the fact that many labourers have virtually no skills at all.

11. Labour productivity is determined by the:

    a) average output per worker.
    b) MPP of labour.
    c) total output of all workers.
    d) MRP of labour.

12. If a firm hires additional workers without employing any additional factors for labour to work with, ultimately labour's:

    a) MPP declines.
    b) average product declines.
    c) total product declines.
    d) a and b
    e) All of the above

13. The MRP curve for a monopolist is equal to:

    a) marginal factor cost times MPP.
    b) MPP times MR of output.
    c) marginal factor cost times MR.
    d) MPP times price of output.

14. An increase in the demand for labour could be caused by

    a) a decrease in the productivity of workers.
    b) a decrease in the price of the product.
    c) a decrease in the demand for the product produced by workers.
    d) an increase in the price of a substitute input like capital (machines).
    e) All of the above.

15. If the ratio of the marginal product to the price of an input is equal for all inputs employed, then a firm realizes:

a) production maximization.
b) cost minimization.
c) revenue maximization.
d) b and c

16. If the firm's "MP_{labour}/wage rate" is greater than "$MP_{nonlabour\ inputs}$/nonlabour costs", then the cost-minimizing firm will:

a) hire additional workers.
b) lay off workers.
c) hire additional nonlabour inputs.
d) b and c

17. Both unions and monopsonists tend to:

a) increase wages above competitive labour market level.
b) decrease wages below competitive labour market level.
c) decrease hiring below competitive labour market level.
d) increase hiring above competitive labour market level.

18. Which of the following statements is *not* a reason why firms often make an effort to treat their workers fairly?

a) Unions are a dominant force in most labour markets.
b) Government rules mandate that firms treat labour fairly.
c) Fairness improves long-term profitability of a firm.
d) It is in firms' self-interest to be fair to workers.

19. If market supply of an input decreases, market input price _____ and employment of the input _____.

a) decreases, increases.
b) increases, increases.
c) increases, decreases.
d) decreases, decreases.

20. The derived demand by firms for labour input arises from:

a) government regulations.
b) consumers demand for the firm's output.
c) management's personal needs.
d) marginal costs and marginal benefits.

21. Why will a monopolist hire fewer workers than a competitive firm?

a) The monopolist's MR < P.
b) The monopolist's MR > P.
c) The monopolist is more interested in maintaining the lowest possible total cost.
d) A monopolist's sales are less than a competitive firm's sales.

22. Big Microchip Company in a major corporate takeover, monopolizes the supply of microchips in Canada. As a result of the monopolization of the market:

a) The profit maximizing level of workers in the industry will remain the same.
b) The profit-maximizing level of workers in the industry will increase.
c) The MRP of labour will shift out.
d) The MRP of labour will shift down.

23. A monopsonist hires the 5th worker for a wage of $15, and this worker has a MRP of $15. What is the economic result?

a) The monopsonist has a loss.
b) There is no change in the monopsonist's profits.
c) The monopsonist's profit falls.
d) The monopsonist's profit rises.

Use the following information for items 24, 25, and 26.
Amalgamated Manufacturing is hiring capital and labour. The price of labour is $5 and the price of capital is $10.

---

24. If MP of labour is 15, and the MP of capital is 40:

a) the firm is paying too much for capital.
b) the firm is cost-minimizing the combination of capital and labour.
c) the firm should purchase more capital and less labour to minimize costs.
d) the firm should purchase more labour and less capital to minimize costs.

25. If the MP of labour is 10 and the MP of capital is 20, and the price of its product is $1, if the firm produces one more unit of output, total cost will rise by:

a) $.50   b) $1
c) $2   d) $10

26. The MP of labour is 10 and the MP of capital is 20, and the price of its product is $1. This firm should maximize profit by:

a) producing more output.
b) producing less output.
c) producing the same output.
d) none of the above.

27. The change in total revenue a firm receives from hiring an additional unit of an input is:

a) MP of an input.   b) MRP of an input.
c) total revenue.   d) MFC of an input.

28. Assume textbooks are sold in a competitive market at $30 and that the price of textbooks doubles to $60. The MRP of labour used to produce textbooks would:

a) be cut in half.
b) double.
c) remain the same.
d) could not be determined without more data.

29. If a firm plans to maximize profits, it should hire labour up to the point where:

   a) MRP > wage.
   b) MRP is maximized.
   c) MRP of labour is zero.
   d) MRP of labour = wage paid to labour.

30. If a monopoly firm takes over a competitive industry:

   a) there would be no change in quantity of labour hired.
   b) there would be an increase in the quantity of labour hired.
   c) MRP of labour would decline more rapidly if labour inputs increase.
   d) MRP of labour would increase.

III. SHORT ANSWER EXERCISES AND PROBLEMS

a) **Short Answer Exercises**

1. Provide the correct term for the following definitions.

   a) factor market in which individuals supply labour services for wages to firms that demand labour services

   b) higher wages result in labour choosing to sacrifice leisure in order to increase work activity

   c) higher income results in a reduction of work activity in order to increase nonmarket pursuits

   d) labour services that involve high degrees of organizational skills, concern, and creativity

   e) average output per worker

   f) technology results in a reduction of labour demand as machines replace labour

   g) the pay for different types of jobs remains a fixed percentage despite changes in demand and supply conditions in labour markets

   h) a firm in which the union controls hiring

   i) a firm in which all workers must join the union

   j) laws that prevent union membership from being a requirement of continuing employment

2. List three negative incentives that affect productivity.

   a)

   b)

   c)

3. List three forces that influence the elasticity of labour supply.

   a)

   b)

   c)

4. List four forces that influence the elasticity of labour demand.

   a)

   b)

   c)

   d)

5. State four factors that determine a firm's demand for labour.

   a)

   b)

   c)

   d)

6. What is the cost minimization condition?

7. What is the profit-maximizing quantity of labour for any firm to employ? Why?

8. Refer to the figure below for a perfectly competitive labour market to answer the following questions.

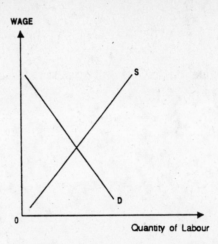

a) Who are the suppliers and who are the demanders of labour? Why does the labour supply curve slope upward? Why does the demand curve for labour slope downward?

b) Indicate the equilibrium wage and equilibrium quantity of labour seeking and finding a job in the figure above. Why is this an equilibrium?

c) Suppose this is an unskilled labour market. What impact would a minimum wage have on this market?

9. Explain how the three invisible forces interact in determining the equilibrium wage and quantity of workers employed in any real-world labour market?

10. List three sources of labour market imperfections.

a)

b)

c)

11. What are three categories of discrimination in labour that affect hiring?

a)

b)

c)

12. List eight types of regulations on the workplace mandated by government as a result of social views of fairness.

a)

b)

c)

d)

e)

f)

g)

h)

13. What are two reasons for the decline in union membership in Canada?

a)

b)

14. What is an efficiency wage?

15. What is institutional discrimination?

16. Give a brief history of unions in Canada?

b. Problems

1. The table below shows hypothetical individual labour supply schedules for two people. Respond to the questions that follow.

Wage	Mrs. A Hours/Day	E_s	Wage	Mrs. B Hours/Day	E_s
$7	7		$5	8	
8	8		6	9.5	
9	8.5		7	12	

a) Determine the respective supply elasticities of Ms. A and Ms. B as their wage rates increase and place them on the table.

b) Assess the relative importance of the income effect and substitution effect to Ms. A and Ms. B.

2. The table below shows the relationship between additional labour units employed and production holding all other factor inputs constant for a hypothetical firm. Assuming that the firm can sell as much of its output as it desires at $10 per unit, determine labour productivity, marginal physical product, and marginal revenue product as additional labour units are employed.

Depict the firm's demand curve for labour in the graph below the table.

Numbers of Workers	Total Product	Labour Productivity	MPP	MRP
3	100			
4	150			
5	185			
6	200			
7	210			

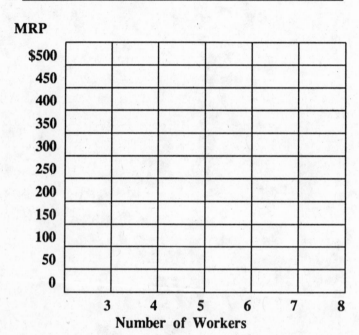

MRP

$500
450
400
350
300
250
200
150
100
50
0

3   4   5   6   7   8
Number of Workers

3. The table below shows the labour supply schedule that a hypothetical monopsony firm faces. Determine the total cost and marginal cost of employing labour at the given quantities in the schedule (columns 3 and 4).

(1) Q_{labour}	(2) Wage	(3) Total cost of labour	(4) Marginal Factor Cost	(5) MRP	(6) $MFC_{minwage}$
1	$20			$80	
2	25			70	
3	30			60	
4	35			50	
5	40			40	
6	45			30	

a) Using the information in the first five columns above, construct curves reflecting supply, marginal factor cost, and marginal revenue product.

Wages, MFC, MRP

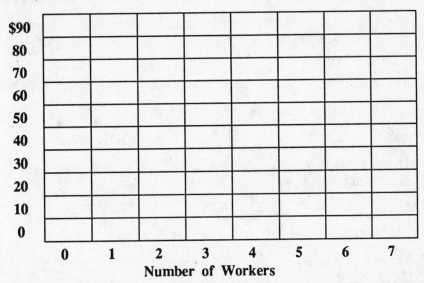

Number of Workers

b) If you are the monopsony employer seeking to maximize profits, how many workers would you hire and what wage would you pay?

c) Assume a minimum wage of $40 per day is established. Fill in column 6 in the table and sketch in the new marginal factor cost curve on the model.

d) As a profit-seeking monopsonist, how many workers will you hire with the minimum wage in effect?

IV. CHALLENGE PROBLEMS AND POTENTIAL ESSAY QUESTIONS

a. Challenge Problems

1. Consider demand and supply in a labour market. For each of the following situations determine whether there would be an increase or a decrease in demand, or supply of labour. Furthermore, indicate the impact on the equilibrium wage rate (W) and the equilibrium quantity (Q) of labour. (You may want to use a graph of demand and supply curves for labour to help you correctly predict the impact on the wage and quantity of labour employed given a shift in the demand or the supply curve.)

a) The demand for the product workers are producing increases.

b) It is Christmas Day, and workers value their leisure time more highly.

c) The other factory in town is now offering a higher wage rate.

d) The fringe (non-monetary) benefits of this job have increased substantially. Now more lucrative health and dental coverage is provided, as well as a retirement program, paid vacation, etc.

e) The price of a machine, which is a substitute for this labour, is now less expensive and its productivity has increased substantially due to an increase in technology.

f) The firms in this industry have successfully convinced government to impose stricter tariffs and import quotas on a foreign good which is a substitute for the good produced by these workers.

g) The government has just adopted an "open-door" immigration policy.

h) Workers are now more productive.

2. Complete the table below for a perfectly competitive employer.

a) Is this firm selling its output in a competitive or non-competitive (e.g., monopolistic) product market? How do you know?

Number of Workers	Total Product Per Hour	Marginal Physical Product Per Hour (MPP)	Price of Product (P)	Marginal Revenue Product (MRP)
18	13	—	$2	—
19	22		$2	
20	29		$2	
21	34		$2	
22	37		$2	

b) Interpret what is meant by the term "marginal revenue product" (MRP)?

c) Why does the MRP decline as additional workers are employed?

d) Assume the wage rate in the labour market is $12 per hour. How many workers should this competitive employer hire? Generally speaking what is the profit-maximizing quantity of labour to employ for the perfectly competitive employer?

e) How many workers should this competitive employer hire if the wage rate is $9 per hour?

f) Graph this firm's MRP of labour curve. What is this competitive firm's demand curve for labour?

g) What would change if this firm was selling its output as a monopolist (or any other non-competitive firm in the product market)?

3. Refer to the figure below for a monopsony labour market to answer the following questions.

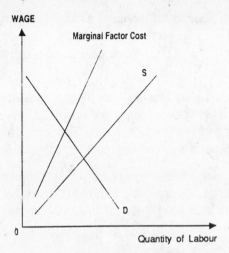

a) Indicate in the figure above the quantity of workers a monopsony employer would employ and the wage rate that would be paid. Why does the monopsonist employ this quantity of workers and pay this wage?

b) Indicate in the figure above the quantity of workers employed and the wage rate if this were a perfectly competitive labour market.

c) Suppose the workers in this monopsony market unionize. Indicate in the figure above the highest wage the union could receive without causing any reduction in the amount of workers the monopsonist would otherwise employ—i.e., without causing any unemployment among these workers?

d) What is a bilateral monopoly? Is it possible that a bilateral monopoly could give rise to a wage and quantity of workers employed that would occur under competitive market conditions? Why?

4. Most Canadian companies are increasingly having to compete in a global economy. Moreover, many of the larger firms have production facilities in other countries. The increased competition in the global economy has required many firms to more aggressively use the least-cost combination of inputs in their production processes in order to survive. However, many Canadians are concerned about the apparent loss of jobs to low-wage countries like Mexico. Let's suppose that for a particular industry the marginal physical product of Canadian workers is 21 units per hour, while the wage rate is $7 per hour. In Mexico, suppose the marginal physical product of workers in the industry is 6 units per hour, while the wage rate is $1.50 per hour. Assume all other costs of production are the same in both countries. If you were a firm in this industry where would you locate? If Canada is to maintain jobs at home, or better yet, if Canada is to provide for not only more jobs for Canadians but higher-paying jobs as well, then what must occur for this to be achieved? Can you think of any national policies which you think might be effective?

b. Potential Essay Questions

The following answers are annotated—they only indicate the general idea behind the answer.

1. What is the shape of the labour supply curve? Why does it take on this shape? What could cause the labour supply curve to become more elastic? What is meant by an increase in the supply of labour? What could cause an increase in the supply of labour?

2. What does it mean to say the demand for labour is a "derived demand"? What could cause the market demand for labour to be relatively inelastic? What does it mean if there is an increase in the market demand for labour? What could cause an increase in the demand for labour?

3. What is any firm's demand curve for labour? How does a firm derive its demand curve for labour? What is the difference between an employer's demand curve for labour that is selling its output in a perfectly competitive product market and an employer's demand curve for labour that is selling its output in a non-competitive (e.g., monopoly) product market?

4. What is a monopsony? How does a monopsonist determine the quantity of workers employed and the wage it pays? How does this compare with the competitive labour market outcome? What is a bilateral monopoly? Could a bilateral monopoly result in a competitive labour market outcome?

V. ANSWERS

II. Mastery Test

1. b	6. d	11. a	16. a	21. a	26. a
2. c	7. d	12. d	17. c	22. d	27. b
3. a	8. b	13. b	18. a	23. b	28. b
4. d	9. c	14. a	19. c	24. c	29. d
5. c	10. b	15. b	20. b	25. a	30. c

III. Short Answer Exercises and Problems

a. Short Answer Exercises

1.
   a) labour market
   b) substitution effect
   c) income effect
   d) entrepreneurship
   e) labour productivity
   f) Luddite reasoning
   g) wage contour
   h) closed shop
   i) union shop
   j) right to work laws

2.
   a) high marginal income tax rates
   b) off-the-books work effort to avoid recognition and taxation
   c) means-based assistance, which penalizes those who work and generate income

3.
   a) elasticity of individual labour supply curves
   b) willingness and ability of individuals to enter and leave labour markets in response to changes in wage
   c) type of market under considerations

4.
   a) elasticity of demand for the firm's product
   b) relative importance of the factor in the production process
   c) availability of factor substitutes
   d) degree to which marginal productivity falls with an increase in labour employment

5.
   a) changes in demand for a firm's product
   b) the firm's structure (mpp)
   c) changes in the other factors of production that a firm employs
   d) a change in technology

6. The ratio of marginal product to the price of an input is equal for all inputs: $MP_l/w = MP_c/P_c = MP_x/P_x$, where w = wage rate, l = labour, c = capital, and x = any other input

7. *The profit-maximizing quantity of labour for any firm to employ exists at that quantity of labour in which the MRP = MFC for the last worker employed.* MRP is the extra revenue generated to the firm from the employment of the last worker. The MFC is the extra cost of employing the last worker. MFC = Wage, if the firm is a competitive employer. Note that if MRP > MFC then that last worker employed is adding more to the firm's revenues than to its costs. Keep hiring workers until MRP = MFC because it's profitable. If MRP < MFC then lay off workers until MRP = MFC. (The output level associated with the quantity of labour in which MRP = MFC will be the output level in which marginal revenue from production just equals marginal cost of production—the profit-maximizing quantity to produce. So there's two ways to look at how to maximize profits!)

8. a) Workers do the supplying and employers (businesses) do the demanding of labour in a labour market. The supply curve slopes upward. More people will look for a job as the wage rises because the opportunity cost of leisure increases as the wage increases. The demand for labour slopes downward because businesses are interested in minimizing their costs. If labour is relatively more expensive they will use more machines or another substitute for labour.

   b) The equilibrium wage is W1 and the equilibrium quantity of labour employed in this market is Q1 as shown in the figure below. This is an equilibrium because the quantity demanded of labour (Q1) equals the quantity supplied of labour (Q1)—there is neither a shortage nor a surplus of labour at this wage rate.

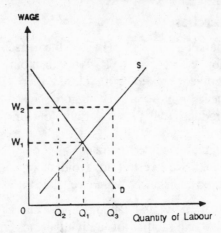

   c) A minimum wage is a wage set by government above equilibrium such as W_2. It would create a surplus of labour supplies Q_3 and firms demand which is Q_3—unemployment.

9. The three invisible forces are the invisible hand (economic forces of demand and supply), invisible handshake (social forces), and invisible foot (legal or government forces).

   Social forces of "fairness," seniority, and discrimination as well as the legal forces of child labour laws, comparable worth laws, equal opportunity laws, and laws governing unions etc., all effect the labour market along with the economic forces of supply and demand.

10. a) monopsony
    b) bilateral monopoly
    c) union

11. a) discrimination based on individual characteristics that affect job performance
    b) discrimination based on individual characteristics that do not affect job performance
    c) correctly or incorrectly perceived statistical characteristics of groups

12. a) minimum wage laws
    b) comparable worth laws (pay equity)
    c) anti-discrimination laws
    d) work day and compensation regulations
    e) child labour laws
    f) safety and health regulations
    g) sexual harassment restrictions
    h) collective bargaining laws

13. a) Laws that unions have encouraged government to establish on work conditions have reduced the need for union protection in the workplace.

b) The relative reduction of manufacturing as a source of employment has undermined the base of union activity.

14. Wages paid above marginal revenue in order to keep workers happy and productive.

15. This is demand side discrimination in which the structure of the job makes it difficult or impossible for certain groups to succeed.

16. Unions began in Canada in Toronto and Hamilton in the late 1800's. The Dominion Trades and Labour Congress began to organize studies to achieve higher wages. Businesses opposed unions' right to strike and in the early years the law was on the side of business. Unions were seen under the law as monopolistic restraints on trade and an intrusion into management rights.

In the 1920's and 30's opinion began to shift and unions were given more recognition by management. In 1936 the Canadian Congress of Labour was formed. In 1939, it became a criminal offence to fire a worker for belonging to a union. The Rand formula of 1945 forced all employees to pay union dues whether they were members or not. Measures such as a government supervised strike vote and penalties for illegal strikes strengthened the union movement. In 1950, the Canadian Labour Congress was formed.

b. **Problems**

1. a)

Wage	Mrs. A Hours/Day	E_s	Wage	Mrs. B Hours/Day	E_s
$7	7		$5	8	
8	8	1.0	6	9.5	.94
9	8.5	0.5	7	12	1.58

b) Both workers are willing to put in more hours at work in response to higher wages, which indicates the substitution effect is a more powerful influence than the income effect for both of them.
The substitution effect has a more powerful influence on Ms. B's willingness to sacrifice leisure for work at higher wages than on Ms. A's.

2.

Number of Workers	Total Product	Labour Productivity	MPP	MRP
3	100	33.3		
4	150	37.5	50	$500
5	185	37	35	350
6	200	33.3	15	150
7	210	30	10	100

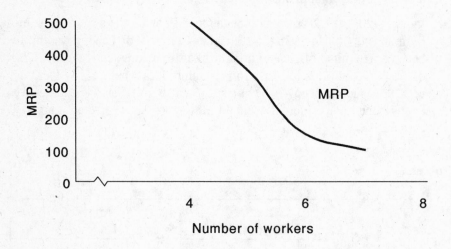

3. a), c)

(1) Q_{labour}	(2) Wage	(3) Total Cost of Labour	(4) Marginal Factor Cost	(5) MRP	(6) $MFC_{minwage}$
1	$20	$20	$20	$80	$40
2	25	50	30	70	40
3	30	90	40	60	40
4	35	140	50	50	40
5	40	200	60	40	40
6	45	270	70	30	40

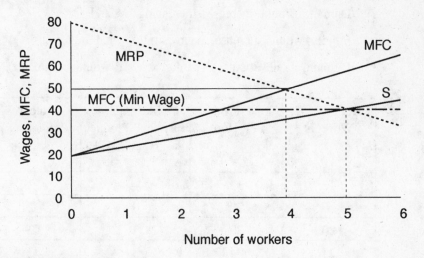

b) 4 workers, $35 a day
d) 4 workers

IV. Challenge Problems and Potential Essay Questions

a. Challenge Problems

1. a) The demand for labour would increase, increasing W and Q. (The increase in the demand for the product increases the price of the product. The higher price for the product increases workers' marginal revenue product—MRP = MPP × P—which is the competitive firms' demand for labour.)

   b) The supply of labour would decrease on Christmas Day, which would increase W and decrease Q on Christmas Day.

   c) Supply would decrease, increasing W and decreasing Q.

   d) Supply would increase, decreasing W and increasing Q.

   e) Demand would decrease, decreasing W and Q.

   f) Demand would increase, increasing W and Q.

   g) Supply would increase, decreasing W and increasing Q.

   h) Demand would increase (workers' MRP would be greater), increasing W and Q.

2.

Number of Workers	Total Product Per Hour	Marginal Physical Product Per Hour (MPP)	Price of Product (P)	Marginal Revenue Product (MRP)
18	13	—	$2	—
19	22	9	2	$18
20	29	7	2	14
21	34	5	2	10
22	37	3	2	6

   a) The firm is selling its output in a competitive product market because the selling price of the product ($2) remains the same as the firm's output expands—the firm can sell as much as it wants at $2. Because the firm does not have to reduce the price of its output in order to sell more, then it is a price-taking competitive firm.

   b) The marginal revenue product tells us the amount of revenue generated to the firm from the employment of the last worker hired.

   c) The MRP declines as additional workers are employed because the marginal physical product (MPP) declines as additional workers are employed. (The MPP declines because of diminishing returns.)

   d) The firm should employ 20 workers (and maybe another part-time worker). Any profit-maximizing firm should continue to employ workers up to the point where the MRP = MFC ("marginal factor cost"—the extra cost of employing an additional unit of a factor of production such as labour; the MFC is equal to the wage rate for the perfectly competitive employer). Note that the optimal number of workers (or any other factor) to employ is simply an application of benefit-cost analysis. The extra benefit to the employer of hiring an additional worker is the MRP. The extra cost of an additional worker is the MFC (marginal factor cost).

The 19th and the 20th workers' MRP > MFC (note again that MFC is equal to the wage rate for the competitive employer) so they should be hired. These workers will be adding more to the firm's revenues than to the firm's costs. So, hire them. The 21st and 22nd workers are not paying for themselves (their MRP < wage). So, don't hire them.

e) The firm should now employ 21 workers.

f) Any firm's demand curve for labour is its MRP curve for labour. At any given wage rate, just read off of the MRP curve to determine the quantity demanded of labour by the firm. This is exactly what any demand curve does for us—it tells us what the quantity demanded will be at any given price (in this case the price is the wage). See the figure below.

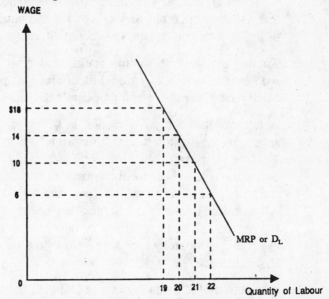

g) If this firm was selling its output as a monopolist then it would have to reduce its price in order to sell additional units of output. Before, for the firm selling its output in a competitive product market, MRP = MPP × P. But, now, for the monopolist, MRP = MPP × MR. (MR is ''marginal revenue''). Note that for the monopolist, MR < P. Therefore, the MRP of additional workers employed would be lower. Hence, the monopolist's demand for labour curve (its MRP curve) would be more inelastic (steeper) and the monopolist will therefore employ fewer workers at any wage rate. *(Hopefully, this outcome intuitively make sense. Think of it this way: the monopoly produces less and therefore hires fewer workers.)*

3.

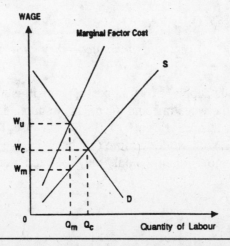

a) The monopsony would hire Q_m workers and pay the wage of W_m. This is because, like any firm, the profit-maximizing quantity of workers to employ exists at that quantity of workers where the MRP = MFC of the last worker employed (if the MRP > MFC then hire more workers; if MRP < MFC then hire fewer workers.) MRP = MFC at Q_m workers—where the two curves intersect. (Recall that a firm's MRP curve is its demand curve for labour. The monopsonist's demand for labour curve is the market demand for labour curve because the monopsonist, by definition, is the only demander in the market.) The monopsonist only has to pay W_m to entice Q_m workers into the market (this is determined by reading off of the labour supply curve).

b) If this were a perfectly competitive market the equilibrium quantity and wage would be Q_c and W_c (where the market demand and supply curves intersect). Note that a monopsonist hires fewer workers and pays a lower wage than if the firm was hiring workers in a perfectly competitive labour market.

c) The highest wage this union could receive which would not alter the amount of workers the monopsony would otherwise employ would be W_u. It is still true that MRP = MFC for the last worker employed, but now workers are getting paid more.

d) A bilateral monopoly is a market in which there is only one buyer and only one seller. In the labour market this would be a monopsony employing unionized workers. It is possible a bilateral monopoly could give rise to a competitive outcome. This is because the two sides will negotiate a wage between W_m, what the monopsonist would want to pay, and W_u (or some other wage above W_m), the wage desired by the union. Somewhere between these two wage rates will likely lie the outcome. The negotiations could result in a perfectly competitive outcome— W_c and Q_c—whereby each side's monopoly power will have been cancelled out by the other side.

4. The productivity for the money spent (MPP/P) may be greater in Mexico (6/1.50 = 4) than in Canada (MPP/P 21/7 = 3) for some firms in this industry as these numbers imply. Assuming all other costs are the same, then firms will find it cheaper to produce their products in a low-wage country, like Mexico. If so, some Canadian jobs will be lost. In order to preserve Canadian jobs, then one of two things, or some combination of the two, must occur. Either wages must fall and/or productivity must rise in Canada. This will bring about a more favourable MPP/P ratio and make Canadian workers look more attractive to businesses. Because lower wages are not a desirable option, then it is imperative to increase Canadian workers' productivity. Any policy designed to do so is worthy of consideration.

b. Potential Essay Questions

The following answers are annotated—they only indicate the general idea behind the answer.

1. The labour supply curve slopes upward illustrating the direct (positive) relationship between the wage rate and the quantity supplied of labour. It slopes upward because of the work-leisure tradeoff. That is, because there is increasing opportunity costs associated with working more (we have to give up ever more valuable leisure time as we work more), then the only way we can be enticed into working more is to be paid more.

The labour supply curve could become more elastic (which means a greater percentage increase in the number of labour hours made available in the market given any percentage increase in the wage) if there is a greater incentive to work (e.g., lower marginal tax rates, not taking a legal job looks bleak), or if there is a greater number of people who are willilng to enter the labour force if wage rates rise (e.g., an open-door immigration policy).

The scope of the market also effects the elasticity of supply. The elasticity of supply of labour facing one firm in a small town will likely be far greater than that for all firms in that town considered as a whole. If one firm increases its wage then many workers will respond to that higher wage. On the other hand, if all firms increase their wages then new entrants into the market will be required to increase the quantity supplied.

An increase in the supply of labour means a greater quantity of labour will be supplied at any particular wage (more people are willing and able to work at the current wage). This could be caused by a reduced opportunity cost of working (less has to be given up in order to work a legal job, or, the standard of living associated with not working a legal job looks less appealing).

2. The demand for labour is derived from the demand for the product the labour is employed to produce. The greater the demand for the product, the greater the amount of the product produced, and the greater the demand for the labour used in its production. It takes more workers to produce more output. (Alternatively viewed, the greater the demand for the product, the higher its price. The greater the price, the greater the MRP of labour and therefore the greater the demand for labour.)

The demand for labour (or any other input) will be relatively inelastic (which means there will be a relatively small decrease in the quantity demanded given any percentage increase in the wage) if: (1) the demand for the good is inelastic; (2) labour is a relatively very important input into the production process; (3) this type of labour is difficult to find or it is expensive to employ a suitable substitute; and (4) the marginal productivity falls quite rapidly as more workers are employed.

An increase in the market demand for labour means more workers will be employed at any wage rate. This could be caused by anything which increases workers' MRP (because the MRP curves are the firms demand curves for labour). This could be accomplished by: (1) an increase in the demand for the product produced (as explained above), (2) the greater the number of firms employing the labour which sells its output in competitive product markets (competitive firms' MRP for workers is greater); (3) anything which increases the productivity of the workers (an increase in MPP will increase MRP); and an increase in technology (if that increases worker's MRP).

3. A firm's demand for labour curve is its MRP for labour curve. It slopes downward indicating that each additional worker's MRP decreases as more workers are employed. This occurs because of declining MPP (due to diminishing marginal returns). For a competitive firm: MRP = MPP × P. For a non-competitive firm (monopoly): MRP = MPP × MR (marginal revenue). In both cases the MRP will decline because MPP declines as additional workers are employed. However, because MR < P for a monopolist then the monopoly's MRP curve decreases more rapidly as additional workers are employed. Therefore, the monopoly's demand for labour curve is more inelastic—steeper. Hence, the monopoly will hire fewer workers (as well as any other input) than if it was selling its output in a competitive market.

4. The term "monopsony" means "one buyer." In the labour market that means there is only one employer. The monopsonist's MRP curve is the market demand curve because the monopsony is the only demander (employer) in the market. The monopsony also faces the market supply curve. The market supply curve tells the monopsony the wage rate which will have to be offered in the market to get any given number of workers to look for a job. Because the market supply curve is upward sloping then the monopsony will have to increase the wage rate to entice more workers to enter the market. Moreover, because the monopsony will have to pay not only the last worker hired the higher wage, but all previously employed workers the higher wage as well, then the MFC (marginal factor cost) of each additional worker employed will exceed the wage rate paid that last worker. This translates into a MFC curve which lies above the market supply of labour curve.

Like any other firm, the monopsony will hire workers up to the point where the MRP equals the MFC of the last worker employed. This exists at the point of intersection between the two curves. The monopsony will then pay the wage rate determined by reading off the market labour supply curve. The result is a lower wage and fewer workers employed than would occur if this labour market was competitive.

A bilateral monopoly is a monopsony employing unionized workers. So, it's a bilateral monopoly because there is monopoly power on both sides. It's possible that the monopoly power of the two sides will be cancelled out giving rise to a competitive wage and quantity of labour employed.

Chapter 15   NONWAGE AND ASSET INCOME: RENTS, PROFITS, AND INTEREST

I.   CHAPTER AT A GLANCE

Rip this page out for quick and easy reference.

1. a)   **Rent is the income from a factor of production that is in fixed supply. (310)**

    A fixed supply means the supply curve is perfectly inelastic (vertical).

    b)   **As long as land is perfectly inelastic in supply, landowners will pay the entire burden of a tax on land, as in the graph below. (310)**

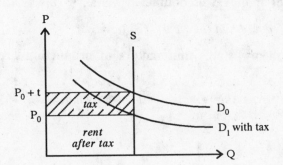

2.   **Rent seeking is the restricting of supply in order to increase its price. It is an attempt to change the institutional structure and hence the underlying property rights. (311)**

    Rent seeking is an attempt to make more money by trying to create ownership rights or institutional structures that favour you.

3.   **Normal profits are the amount that an entrepreneur can get by supplying entrepreneurship to the market. Economic profits are the entrepreneur's return above and beyond normal profits. (312)**

    Normal profits equal the opportunity cost of the entrepreneur (an amount of profits just sufficient to keep the entrepreneur in that line of business).

4.   **An entrepreneur seeks market niches because within those niches lie economic profits. (313)**

    To make economic profits may also require rent seeking behaviour.

5. a)   **Interest is the income paid to savers—individuals who produce now but do not consume now. (313)**

    The "i" is the reward for foregone current consumption to savers but is the cost of borrowing to businesses (and other borrowers).

    b)   **The loanable funds theory of interest says the interest rate is determined by the forces of demand and supply.**

    Demand comes from firms wanting funds for capital expansion. Supply is from household saving.

6. **Interest plays an essential role in the present value formula. (316)**

   Present Value (PV) is determining the <u>current worth</u> of money received in the future. The greater the interest rate or time frame, the smaller the PV.

7. a) **PV = X/i states the annuity rule: Present value of any annuity is the annual income it yields divided by the interest rate. (318)**

   For example:

   $40 received annually for 30 years when i = 8% = .08 ⇒

   $$\frac{\$40}{.04} = \$500 \ value \ today.$$

   b) **The rule of 72 states that 72 divided by the interest rate is the number of years in which a certain amount of money will double in value. (318)**

   $100 at 6% will double in 12 years (72/6 = 12)

8. **Marginal productivity theory states that factors of production are paid their marginal revenue product. (319)**

   Also depends on ownership rights—who owns what.

II. MASTERY TEST

1. What institutional structure needs to be in place in order for markets to function in an orderly way?

   a) property rights
   b) well-developed infrastructure
   c) democratic government
   d) All of the above

2. A tax placed on a good or service will fall entirely on the seller when

   a) supply is more inelastic than demand.
   b) supply is less elastic than demand.
   c) supply is perfectly inelastic.
   d) supply is perfectly elastic.

3. When a supply curve is fixed at a specific amount, the return to the seller is called

   a) pure rent.
   b) quasi-rent.
   c) economic profit.
   d) opportunity cost.

4. Any payment to a factor above its opportunity cost of employment is referred to as

   a) seller surplus.
   b) quasi-rent.
   c) rent.
   d) All of the above

5. The return to an entrepreneur on risk-taking activity is termed

   a) human capital.
   b) economic profit.
   c) quasi-rent.
   d) profit.
   e) b and c

6. A return to an entrepreneur above and beyond his or her opportunity cost of risk taking is

   a) normal profit.
   b) economic profit.
   c) quasi-rent.
   d) profit.
   e) b and c

7. Given competitive conditions, the typical firm will in the long run earn

   a) quasi-rent.
   b) pure rent.
   c) normal profit.
   d) economic profit.
   e) a and c

8. Exploiting a market niche results in an entrepreneur

   a) earning an economic profit
   b) becoming a rent seeker.
   c) driving down the market price.
   d) reducing competition.
   e) b and d

9. At an interest rate of 7 percent, the present value of an income flow of $10,000 expected five years from now will be _____ its present value at an interest rate of 6 percent.

   a) greater than
   b) equal to
   c) less than

10. How is the present value of a given income flow at a specified rate of interest influenced by the time period in which it will be received?

    a) The longer the time period before it is received, the more its present value will decrease.
    b) The longer the time period before it is received, the more its present value will increase.
    c) Its present value is not influenced by when it will be received.
    d) Its present value will increase over the first five years, then decrease.

11. The annuity rule approximates the present value of an annuity more closely

    a) the higher the rate of interest.
    b) the lower the rate of interest.
    c) the longer the time period of the annuity.
    d) the shorter the time period of the annuity.

12. Interest payments are received by

    a) individuals who supply resources to the economy.
    b) entrepreneurs when they borrow from savers.
    c) businesses who borrow to invest.
    d) individuals who produce now but don't consume now.

13. All economists agree that

    a) the demand for money affects the short term interest rate.
    b) short-term interest rates determine long-term interest rates that reflect short-term trends.
    c) short-term and long-term rates move in opposite directions.
    d) only real changes matter.

14. At a 12% interest rate, $1 fifty years from now has a P.V. equal to

    a) $.05.
    b) 0.
    c) $.50.
    d) $5.00.

15. According to the rule of 72, the sum of $5,000 invested today at 8 percent interest will be worth approximately $10,000 in

   a) 10 years.
   b) [72/(5,000 × 8%)] years.
   c) (72/8%) years.
   d) (72/8) years.

16. Modern economic analysis suggests that the payment made to a factor is influenced by

   a) the supply of that factor.
   b) its derived demand.
   c) its marginal productivity.
   d) all of the above

17. Traditional marginal productivity theory attempts to explain

   a) the distribution of income.
   b) the source of property rights.
   c) the returns to unspecified factors of production.
   d) all of the above

18. If the county places a new real estate tax on downtown property, which is in fixed supply:

   a) the quantity of downtown property will decline, and the land owners will bear the burden of the tax.
   b) the quantity of downtown property will remain the same and the land owners will pass the burden of the tax on to the users.
   c) the quantity of downtown property will remain the same and the land owners will bear the burden of the tax.
   d) the quantity of downtown property will decline and the users will bear the burden of the tax.

19. Refer to Exhibit 1 in the textbook.

   a) The curve labeled (S) is the owner's opportunity cost.
   b) The curve labeled (S) is relatively elastic.
   c) The curve labeled (S) is relatively inelastic.
   d) The curve labeled (S) is perfectly inelastic.

20. Refer to the textbook chapter Exhibit 1.

   a) The burden of a tax (t) is shared equally by the owner and the user.
   b) The burden of a tax (t) falls totally on the user.
   c) The burden of a tax (t) falls totally on the owner.
   d) The burden of a tax (t) would have to be indeterminate.

21. Refer to the textbook Exhibit 1.
   Given the tax (t), the after-tax price received by the owner:

   a) is the same as the before-tax price, P_O
   b) is the same as the before-tax price, P_1
   c) lies in between P_O and P_1 as a result of the tax.
   d) rises from P_1 to P_O as a result of the tax.

22. Refer to the textbook Exhibit 2.
The supply curve on this graph is:

a) perfectly elastic.
b) perfectly inelastic.
c) relatively elastic.
d) illustrates a resource that is in fixed supply.

23. Refer to the textbook Exhibit 2.
If the price is set at S_O, the supplier will:

a) not recoup her opportunity cost.
b) withdraw the resource from the marketplace.
c) will be operating at a loss.
d) not earn a quasi-rent.

24. Refer to the textbook Exhibit 2.
The owner of this resource represented by point A on the supply curve:

a) would be willing to supply the resource at a price of S_O.
b) would be willing to supply the resource at a price less than S_O.
c) will not supply the resource at any price below P_O.
d) will not supply the resource at any price above P_O.

25. A quasi-rent is clearly a component of the individual's new salary when:

a) a department store clerk is given the opportunity to become the department manager.
b) a college professor gives up a promising academic career to work in the inner city.
c) a professional football player retires and becomes a volunteer at a local youth center.
d) a successful attorney leaves her profitable law practice and accepts a position as a public defender.

26. The least likely example of rent-seeking behaviour would be:

a) the American Bar Association attempting to restrict law school enrollments.
b) going on to graduate school to qualify for a better position.
c) lobbying efforts by a trade association for a higher import tariff on a competitive product.
d) A manufacturer making a large campaign contribution to a politician in hopes of getting a government contract.

27. A business owner-manager is seeking to receive _____ for her entrepreneurial activity and risk taking.

a) profit
b) interest
c) wages
d) rent

28. Payments necessary to business owners to keep the resources in the market are:

a) rents.
b) economic profits.
c) normal profits.
d) wages.

III. SHORT ANSWER EXERCISES AND PROBLEMS

a. Short Answer Exercises

1. Provide the appropriate terms for the following definitions.

   a) the rights to use specified property as one sees fit

   b) the set of laws that govern economic behaviour

   c) laws that set limits on the use of one's property

   d) the theory that factors of production are paid their marginal revenue product

2. Which body of economic thought holds that the interest rate is determined by the demand for and supply of savings?

3. Which body of economic thought holds that the interest rate is determined by the demand for and supply of money?

4. Express the present value formula and explain the variables.

5. Express the annuity rule and explain the variables.

6. Provide the term for the income return generated by each economic resource from the traditional perspective.

   a) capital

   b) entrepreneurship

   c) land

   d) labour

b. Problems

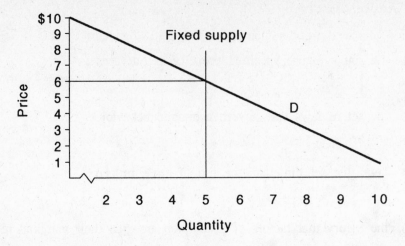

1. Work with the fixed supply model provided to respond to the questions that follow.

   a) What is the value of the rent generated in this market?

   b) Sketch in a tax of $1 per unit (paid by buyers) on the model.

   c) As a result of the tax, what is the new market price?

   d) What is the value of the rent generated after the tax?

2. Complete the table below. Given an annual payment of $1,500, determine the present value using the annuity rule and the annuity table for each of the time periods and interest rates provided.

Annual Cash Flow	Interest Rate	PV Annuity Rule	PV Annuity Table (10 years)	PV Annuity Table (50 years)
$1500	3%			
$1500	9%			
$1500	15%			

3. Complete the table below, given an income flow of $1,000 at alternative specified future periods at alternative rates of interest. Discount the future return using your textbook present value table to determine the present value for each case.

Income Flow	Interest Rate	Time Period Received	Present Value
$1,000	6%	10 years hence	
$1,000	6%	20 years hence	
$1,000	12%	10 years hence	
$1,000	12%	20 years hence	

a) With a given rate of interest, how does the time period affect the present value of a given expected income flow?

b) For a given flow of income expected at a specific future time, how does the rate of interest affect the present value?

IV. CHALLENGE PROBLEMS AND POTENTIAL ESSAY QUESTIONS

a. Challenge Problems

1. a) What happens to the demand curve when buyers have to pay a tax on an item?

   b) What happens to the supply curve when sellers have to pay a tax on an item?

   c) Suppose the supply of land is perfectly inelastic (vertical) and a tax is imposed on renters of the land. Who bears the burden of the tax?

   d) Suppose the demand for an item is perfectly inelastic (.e.g., some form of medicine like insulin). If sellers have to pay a tax then who bears the burden of the tax?

2. a) Your very rich Uncle has just passed away and left you a large sum of money. You have determined that you will need $100,000 in 15 years to fund your child's college education (it's a great school!). How much should you set aside today in an interest-bearing account which guarantees a 6% annual interest rate for the next 15 years?

   b) You have just retired. Your pension (retirement) plan presents you with two options. You can receive a lump sum payment of $200,000, or a guaranteed annual payment of $20,000 for the next 15 years (if you predecease the flow of payments then the money will be paid to your designed beneficiary). The expected interest rate over the next 15 years is 9%. Which option should you select? Why?

   c) Congratulations! You've just bought your first home. You now have 30 years of fixed monthly house payments to go. Is the first or the last house payment the most difficult to make financially? Why?

   d) Because there's nothing like being prepared you visit your local mortician to buy a plot. You are offered a "wonderful" deal. The graveyard you have chosen has an established reputation of keeping the grounds in beautiful condition. The mortician has informed you that it is expected to cost $40 a year to properly care for your gravesite. Therefore, he has asked you to pay him $1,000 now for the meticulous care of your grave for eternity. Is this part of the deal making the mortician money or not? (Assume an interest rate of 5%).

3. If entrepreneurs are successful in establishing barriers to entry to prevent potential competitors from entering their markets then they can increase the likelihood of economic profits for themselves—at least for as long as those barriers to entry are effective in keeping potential competitors out of their markets.

   a) How can the attempt to create barriers to entry be considered rent seeking behaviour on the part of firms?

   b) What are some examples of barriers to entry which firms may try to establish?

   c) One barrier to entry for entrepreneurs is to create a niche in the market for themselves. This can be accomplished by differentiating (distinguishing) their good or service from all other competitors—in either real or imaginary terms. How can product differentiation motivated by rent seeking behaviour on the part of firms be beneficial to society?

b. **Potential Essay Questions**

   1. What determines the distribution of income in a market-oriented economy?

   2. Explain rent seeking and its relationship to property rights.

   3. Why do entrepreneurs search out market niches?

   4. What role do entrepreneurs play in a market-oriented or capitalist economy?

V. ANSWERS

Mastery Test

1. a	6. e	11. c	16. d	21. a	26. b
2. c	7. c	12. d	17. a	22. c	27. a
3. a	8. a	13. a	18. c	23. d	28. c
4. d	9. c	14. b	19. d	24. a	
5. d	10. a	15. d	20. c	25. a	

Short Answer Exercises and Problems

a. **Short Answer Exercises**

   1. a) property rights
      b) contractual legal system
      c) zoning laws
      d) marginal productivity theory

   2. classical economics

   3. Keynesian economics

   4. $PV = A_1/(1+i) + A_2/(1+i)^2 + A_3/(1+i)^3 + ... + A_n/(1+i)^n$, where A_n = the amount of money received in periods in the future and i = the interest rate in the economy

   5. $PV = X, i$, where X = an infinite income flow and
      i = the rate of interest

   6. a) interest
      b) profit
      c) rent
      d) wages

b. Problems

1. a) $30

   b)

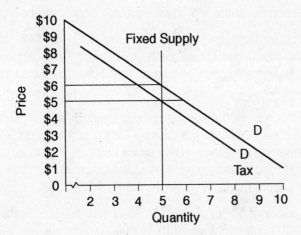

   c) $5

   d) $25

2.

Annual Cash Flow	Interest Rate	PV Annuity Rule	PV Annuity Table (10 years)	PV Annuity Table (50 years)
$1500	3%	$50,000	$12,795	$38,595
$1500	9%	$16,667	$ 9,630	$16,440
$1500	15%	$10,000	$ 7,530	$ 9,990

3.

Income Flow	Interest Rate	Time Period Received	Present Value
$1,000	6%	10 years hence	$560
$1,000	6%	20 years hence	$310
$1,000	12%	10 years hence	$320
$1,000	12%	20 years hence	$100

a) The longer the time period the income flow will be received, the lower its present value.

b) The higher the interest rate, the lower the present value.

Challenge Problems and Potential Essay Questions

a. Challenge Problems

1. a) The demand curve decreases (shifts down equal to the amount of the tax).

    b) The supply curve decreases (shifts up equal to the amount of the tax).

    c) The suppliers (owners; landlords). (See Exhibit 1 on p. 310). This tells us that the suppliers of any factor which has an inelastic supply (and not necessarily a perfectly inelastic supply) will bear the biggest burden of any tax imposed on the user of that factor.

    d) Buyers. The supply curve will shift up equal to the tax and the equilibrium price will rise equal to the amount of the tax because the demand for the item is perfectly inelastic. The tax will be entirely borne by the buyer. (Only when demand is perfectly inelastic can a tax imposed on a supplier be entirely passed on to the consumer in the form of a higher price—otherwise the supplier will have to bear part of the tax.)

2. a) $42,000. The present value of $1 in 15 years is $0.42 (see Exhibit 5a on page 317). So the present value of $100,000 in 15 years in $42,000. Using reverse logic: if you put $42,000 into an interest-bearing account at 6% then it would accrue $100,000 (approximately) in 15 years.

    b) You should select the lump-sum payment of $200,000 because that present value is greater than the present value of $20,000 for the next 15 years which is $161,200. (In Exhibit 5b on p. 317, the value of $1 received for 15 years has a present value of $8.06 when the interest rate is 9%. Therefore, the present value of $20,000 for 15 years has a present value of $161,200—equal to $20,000 times 8.06.)

    c) The first house payment is the most difficult to pay financially because the present value of future fixed dollar payments will be lower. (The discount factor is the rate of inflation—inflation, expressed as a percent, erodes the value of a dollar over time.)

    d) This part of the deal is making the mortician money. The present value of $40 for eternity is only $800 ($40/.05—see p. 317.)

3. a) If barriers to entry are successful they will enable the entrepreneur running the firm to earn an economic profit. An economic profit is a profit above the entrepreneur's opportunity cost (above the normal profit). Therefore, the entrepreneur is able to earn quasi rent. Also note that the attempt to restrict supply (through the establishment of barriers to entry) in order to increase the price suppliers receive (profit entrepreneurs receive) is rent seeking behaviour by definition.

    b) There are many potential barriers to entry. Some examples include: government laws, regulations, patents and copyrights (as well as other legal barriers), technological, financial, social factors (the most extreme could be the threat of violence), sole ownership over a strategic input, and the firm's ability to differentiate its product from competitors in either real or imaginary terms. The list could go on. But, anything which can keep potential competitors from successfully entering the market is a barrier to entry.

    c) Successful product differentiation by a firm will likely be rewarded with quasi rent (economic profit) going to the entrepreneur who has found or created a niche in the market. Society can benefit due to the wider variety of products and higher quality products from which consumers can choose. Many consumers are willing to pay a little more for variety, quality and the opportunity to have their individual tastes satisfied.

b. Potential Essay Questions

The following answers are annotated—they only indicate the general idea behind the answer.

1. Although the forces of demand and supply determine the relative prices (payments) of inputs, it's really the ownership control over inputs which primarily determines the distribution of income in a market-oriented economy. Those who control more (posses ownership rights over) inputs, or control more scarce, more expensive inputs make more money.

2. Rent seeking is the restricting of supply in order to increase price. It is an attempt to change the institutional structure and hence the underlying property rights. Many people try to achieve property rights over loss of things so they can restrict its supply to increase the price they receive—to increase their income.

3. To make an economic profit. Entrepreneurs not only try to search out market niches but they may very well practice rent seeking by trying to establish barriers to entry to preserve any economic profits for themselves.

4. They help achieve an efficient allocation of a nation's scarce resources into the production of those goods and services most desired by society. The profit motive ensures this.

Chapter 16   WHO GETS WHAT? THE DISTRIBUTION OF INCOME

I. CHAPTER AT A GLANCE

Rip this page out for quick and easy reference.

1. **A Lorenz curve is a geometric representation of the size distribution of income among families in a given country at a given time. (324)**

    Shows the relative equality of the distribution of income. The farther below the diagonal line the more <u>unequal</u> the distribution of income.

2. **From 1965 to 1980, income equality in Canada decreased. From 1980 to 1992, it increased at higher levels of income and it fell at lower levels of income. (325)**

    When income distribution becomes "more equal," the Lorenz curve is closer to the diagonal.

    Factors contributing to equality of distribution are:

    1) Welfare programs
    2) Unemployment insurance
    3) Social security
    4) Progressive taxation
    5) Growth

3. **The low income cut-off is defined by Statistics Canada as the level at which 56.2 percent of income is spent on food, clothing and shelter given 1986 family expenditure and income data. (326)**

    Canada doesn't have an official definition of poverty because poverty is relative. Consider some of the types of statistical and data problems that economists face when trying to define poverty.

4. **Canada's income distribution is similar to that of other industrialized nations. (328)**

    Much income inequality in Canada is caused by discrimination and other socioeconomic factors. Know what these are.

5. **Three problems in determining whether an equal income distribution is fair are: (335)**

    (1) people don't start from equivalent positions;
    (2) people's needs are different; and
    (3) people's efforts differ.

    When most people talk about believing in equality of income, they usually mean an equality in opportunity to earn income.

6. **Three side effects of redistribution of income include the labour/leisure incentive effect, the avoidance and evasion incentive effects, and the incentive effect to look more needy than you are. (335)**

    *Know these as well as the different kinds of taxes.

---

7. **Expenditure programs used to redistribute income include the Canada Pension Plan, Old Age Security, the Guaranteed Income Supplement and public assistance (welfare) programs. (337)**

> *Know these as well as the other specific types of government programs.*

> *The overall effect has been to create a more equal distribution of income. But, not without its costs.*

II. MASTERY TEST

1. The Canadian size distribution of income

   a) ranks families by their income and tells how much the richest 20% and the poorest 20% receive.
   b) ranks families by their salaries and tells how much the poorest 30% and the richest 30% receive.
   c) says that in 1993 the top 20% of Canadian families received 1/2 the income.
   d) is such that the ratio of the income of the top 20% compared to the bottom 20% is 20:1.

2. A perfectly equal distribution of income would be represented by a Lorenz curve that is

   a) above the diagonal.
   b) diagonal.
   c) vertical.
   d) below the diagonal.

3. In 1993, the lowest 20% of families received _____ of the income and the top 20% received _____ of the income.

   a) 100%; 4.7%
   b) 4.7%; 100%
   c) 4.7%; 43.9%
   d) 20%; 20%

4. All but which of the following contribute to equality in the distribution of income?

   a) Welfare programs
   b) Unemployment insurance
   c) Progressive taxation
   d) Recession

5. The official poverty line in Canada is

   a) an income of $36,000.
   b) 50% of the average income.
   c) there is no official definition of poverty.
   d) is calculated before transfers are made.

6. The low income cut-off is based on

   a) the percent of family income spent on luxuries.
   b) the percent of family income spent on food, shelter, and clothing.
   c) the number of transfer programs a family qualifies for.
   d) the number of school age children in the family.

7. All but which of the following complicate the poverty issue?

   a) Cost of living in urban areas is higher than rural areas
   b) Unreported income
   c) Transfers of goods
   d) Updating figures

8. The LIM

    a) adjusts median family income for the differential effects of adult and children on family expenditures.

    b) adjusts median family income for the differential effects of rural and urban living on family expenditures.

    c) is 1/4 of adjusted median family income.

    d) gives the same estimates of poverty as does the low income cut-off.

9. Costs of poverty to society include all but which of the following?

    a) Increased levels of crime

    b) Society as a whole suffers when some of its members are hungry

    c) Discontent amongst the have nots

    d) Demographic changes

10. Progressive tax systems result in

    a) a less equal distribution of income.

    b) a more equal distribution of income.

    c) no change in the distribution of income.

    d) affects only the absolute level of income in the economy.

11. Which of the following is not a socioeconomic characteristic contributing to income inequality?

    a) Gender

    b) Profits

    c) Type of job

    d) Race

12. Women receive about _____ of the pay that men do for the same job. About _____ of this difference is explained by discrimination.

    a) 60%; 1/4

    b) 70%; 1/4

    c) 70%; 1/2

    d) 50%; 1/2

13. Jane and Jim are equally qualified as a cook. Jim is hired simply because he is male. This is

    a) supply-side discrimination.

    b) demand-side discrimination.

    c) supply-side sociological discrimination.

    d) demand-side institutional discrimination.

14. Pay equity laws

    a) help to close wage gaps based solely on gender.

    b) close wage gaps based on race.

    c) close wage gaps based on age.

    d) close wage gaps based on geographic location.

15. Class structure in Canada today compared to earlier periods is different due to

    a) the shrinking size of the middle class.
    b) the reversal of the pyramid.
    c) the tremendous growth in the relative size of the middle class.
    d) the relative growth of the lower class.

16. All but which of the following government policies contribute to a "fair" income distribution?

    a) Affirmative action laws
    b) Minimum wage laws
    c) Social welfare programs
    d) Sales tax

17. The "fairness" of the distribution of income is generally interpreted as a concern for

    a) normative economics.
    b) positive economics.
    c) equality of income.
    d) equality of opportunity.
    e) a and d

18. Canadians tend to think that "fairness" suggests

    a) equality.
    b) inequality.
    c) diversity.
    d) an equal distribution of income.

19. All but which of the following constitute negative effects of redistribution programs?

    a) Incentive effects from taxes may cause a switch from labour to leisure
    b) Equality of opportunity
    c) Tax avoidance leading to decreased reporting of income
    d) Incentive effects may cause people to try to look needy

20. Some economists don't believe that taxation for redistribution should take place because

    a) when the rich do well, the benefits spill over to the poor.
    b) entrepreneurs pay taxes.
    c) growth will fail to occur.
    d) all of the above.
    e) a and c only.

21. Which of the following is not a reason why the poor do not vote themselves an improved distribution of income?

    a) The poor face legal obstacles to voting.
    b) The poor are not organized to vote as a block.
    c) Individuals vote with other issues as a priority.
    d) Higher-income people are better able to influence political outcomes because of their financial position.

22. The overall structure of taxes in Canada can be described as

    a) highly progressive.
    b) moderately regressive.
    c) roughly proportional.
    d) highly regressive.

23. A tax system where the average tax rate decreases as income increases is

    a) proportional.
    b) regressive.
    c) progressive.
    d) neutral.

24. In 1994, the Unemployment Insurance Act was changed so as to

    a) give benefits to the disabled.
    b) provide more long term benefits to the unemployed.
    c) encourage job sharing in families.
    d) remove the disincentive to work.

25. The negative income tax is in essence a(n)

    a) break even income tax.
    b) work experience programme.
    c) guaranteed annual income.
    d) unemployment insurance scheme.

III. SHORT ANSWER EXERCISES AND PROBLEMS

a. Short Answer Exercises

1. Name and describe the two distributional issues of concern to economists today.

2. Exhibit 1 in your text shows a Lorenz curve of the 1993 Canadian income distribution. Describe that distribution in words and numbers.

3. Between 1965 and 1980, did the size distribution of income become more or less equal? Why?

4. How do demographic factors affect the size distribution of income?

5. Why doesn't Canada have an official definition of poverty?

6. What is the low income cut-off?

7. How is poverty connected to crime?

8. Give an example of a) demand-side workplace discrimination; b) supply-side sociological discrimination; c) demand-side institutional discrimination.

   a)

   b)

   c)

9. What is different about today's class structure in comparison to earlier periods?

10. How have tensions caused by unfair distribution of income have been dealt with in Canada?

11. What is "equality of income" short for in discussions of "fairness" of income distribution?

12. Name <u>3</u> important side effects that economists have found in programs to redistribute income.

a)

b)

c)

13. Why don't the poor use their votes to make sure income is redistributed to them from the rich?

14. Identify the following tax systems.

a) income redistributed from the rich to the poor

b) income redistributed from the poor to the rich

c) the average tax rate decreases as income increases

15. Given the following descriptions, name each program to redistribute income.

a) Provides monthly benefits to retired contributors _____

b) Provides insurance for workers who are temporarily unemployed

_____

c) Provides federal assistance to provinces for welfare progams

_____

16. What is a negative income tax?

b. Problems

1. Using information provided in Exhibit 1a in the text, determine the quintile income shares of families and complete the table below.

	Percentage of Families	Income Share
Highest Income	20%	
Next	20%	
Next	20%	
Next	20%	
Lowest Income	20%	

2. Given the two tax schedules below, determine the tax burden, marginal tax rate, and average tax rate for the incomes given in the table.

Schedule A Income	Tax Rate	Schedule B Income	Tax Rate
$0 to $10,000	0%	$0 to $20,000	10%
$10,001 to $50,000	10%	$20,001 to $50,000	12%
$50,001 to $100,000	15%	$50,001 to $80,000	14%
$100,001 to $900,000	20%	$80,001 to $100,000	16%
over $900,000	40%	$100,000 to $500,000	18%
		Over $500,000	20%

Family Income	Schedule A			Schedule B		
	Tax Burden	Marginal Rate	Average Rate	Tax Burden	Marginal Rate	Average Rate
$ 30,000						
$ 75,000						
$150,000						

3. Given the information in the table below, fill in column 3 and sketch a Lorenz curve in the income distribution graph.

	(1) Family Income	(2) Income Share	(3) Cumulative Share	(4) Income Share	(5) Cumulative Share
Top	20%	40%			
	20%	25%			
	20%	20%			
	20%	10%			
Lowest	20%	5%			

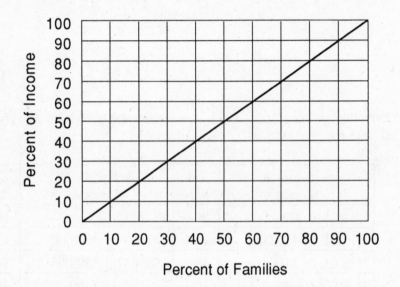

a) Assume that a tax to redistribute income reduces the income share of the highest income earning quintile by 10 percent and the next highest by 5 percent. The lowest quintile of families receives 75 percent of the proceeds and the second lowest quintile receives 25 percent. Fill in columns 4 and 5 in the table above.

b) Sketch a new Lorenz curve in the income distribution graph.

IV. CHALLENGE PROBLEMS AND POTENTIAL ESSAY QUESTIONS

a. Challenge Problems

1. The table below shows the income distribution for Canada and Mexico.

	Percentage of Total Income	
Income Quintile:	CANADA	MEXICO
Lowest 20%	4.7	2.9
Second quintile	10.2	7.0
Third quintile	16.5	12.0
Fourth quintile	24.8	20.4
Highest 20%	43.9	57.7

a) Using this information, draw a Lorenz curve for each country in the Figure below.

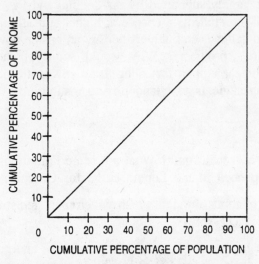

b) For which country is the distribution of income more equally distributed? How is a more equal distribution of income illustrated in terms of the Lorenz curve? How would perfect income equality graph? Has there ever been a country with perfect income equality?

c) What happens to the Lorenz curve for Canada after taxes and transfers are taken into consideration? What does that say about the equality of the distribution of income in Canada due to the existence of government taxes and transfers? Is that beneficial to society? What is the economic cost to society of government tax and transfer programs? Is it clear whether the benefits of government taxes and transfers outweigh the costs?

2. For *a – e* determine whether the tax would be considered progressive, proportional, or regressive.

a) Personal income taxes

b) Sales taxes

c) Property taxes

d) Gasoline, cigarette, and liquor taxes

e) Is a progressive, proportional, or regressive tax usually considered to be most "fair?"

3. Some people have advocated government subsidization of day-care centres to make day-care more affordable for the poor. Cheaper day-care, it is argued, would create a greater incentive for the non-working poor to seek out work, or schooling or some form of training to increase their skills, so they may find a decent-paying job to enable them to escape poverty. What effect would the subsidization of day-care centres have on the price and the number of children placed in day-care? Is there any difference between subsidizing the centres as opposed to subsidizing the parents? What would be a benefit and a cost of relaxing government day-care centre regulations instead?

4. Assume the working poor are paid their marginal revenue product. That is, they are getting paid what they are worth in the labour market. Generally, what type of policy may be most fruitful in increasing the wages and therefore the incomes of these working poor, reducing the percentage of our population living in poverty?

5. One of the major arguments in favour of publicly supported higher educational institutions is that because they are largely supported by tax-dollars, and therefore tuition is lower, they enable poor but deserving students a chance at higher education. Why do critics argue that government supported colleges and universities are an upside-down government transfer (an upside-down "welfare" program)? Why would some of these critics argue for the abolishment of government support for colleges and universities in favour of direct subsidies to poor but deserving students to attend private institutions?

b. **Potential Essay Questions**

1. What does a Lorenz curve illustrate? What are some limitations associated with a Lorenz curve? What has happened to the Lorenz curve for Canada over time?

2. What are two direct methods through which government redistributes income? Which has generally been more successful?

3. What's the difference between a progressive, proportional and regressive tax? Which tax is generally considered to be more "fair?" What are the most important sources of tax revenues for provincial and local governments? Which are progressive, proportional and regressive?

4. Summarize Canadian expenditure programs to redistribute income.

V. ANSWERS

II. Mastery Test

1. a	6. b	11. b	16. d	21. a
2. b	7. d	12. c	17. e	22. c
3. c	8. a	13. b	18. a	23. b
4. d	9. d	14. a	19. b	24. d
5. c	10. b	15. c	20. a	25. c

III. Short Answer Exercises and Problems

a. Short Answer Exercises

1. a) Size distribution of income—the relative distribution of total income
   b) Socioeconomic distribution of income—the allocation of income among relevant socioeconomic groupings

2. The bottom 20% of families received 4.7% of the income. The next 20% received 10.2%. The 3rd 20% received 16.5% of the income. The 4th 20% received 24.8% of the income and the 5th 20% received 43.9% of the income.

3. Between 1965 and 1980, the size distribution of income became more equal because of the redistributive measures instituted by the Canadian government between 1930 and 1970; i.e., welfare programs, unemployment insurance, social security, progressive taxation, and improved macro performance.

4. Families have relatively low income in their early years, relatively higher income in their middle years and relatively low income again after retirement. In particular, when the baby boomers age, this will affect the Lorenz curve.

5. Because poverty is a relative measure depending on family size, composition and location (urban, rural).

6. This is used by Statistics Canada to study the incidence of poverty in Canada. For example, the 1986 cut off says that people spending more than 56.2% of their income on food shelter and clothing are said to be in poverty.

7. When poverty is high, the incentive for crime is increased as people become more desperate.

8. a) An equally qualified man and woman apply for the same job, the man is hired. The woman is hired but paid less than the man would have been.
   b) A woman stays home to look after a sick child, or gives up a job to move with her family.
   c) A women's career in real estate begins to take off just when she has her first child.

9. Today the class structure looks like a diamond with a large middle class. It used to look more like a pyramind.

10. Since most Canadians don't view the distribution as that "unfair," there aren't cries for revolution, rather, Canadians look to affirmative action laws, pay equity laws, minimum wage laws, and social welfare programs.

11. Equality of opportunity for comparably endowed individuals to earn income. If equal opportunity of equals leads to inequality of income, that inequality in income is "fair."

12. a) The incentive effects of taxes may cause a switch from labour to leisure
    b) Taxes may cause people to avoid paying and to therefore understate their income
    c) People may try to appear more needy than they are

13. Because

    a) many poor don't vote believing one vote won't make a difference
    b) there is no organization amongst the poor to vote as a block
    c) voting rarely takes place on this issue
    d) elections require financing that comes from the rich who in turn persuade the poor to vote for them

14. a) Progressive
    b) Repressive
    c) Regressive

15. a) Canada Pension Plan
    b) Unemployment Insurance Program
    c) Canada Assistance Plan

16. A subsidy to income paid by government once income falls below a threshold level.

b. Problems

1.

	Percentage of Families	Income Share
Highest Income	20%	46.4%
Next	20%	24.1%
Next	20%	16%
Next	20%	9.6%
Lowest Income	20%	3.9%

2.

Family Income	Schedule A			Schedule B		
	Tax Burden	Marginal Rate	Average Rate	Tax Burden	Marginal Rate	Average Rate
$ 30,000	$ 2,000	10%	6.67%	$ 3,200	12%	10.67%
$ 75,000	$ 7,750	15%	10.33%	$ 9,100	14%	12.13%
$150,000	$21,500	20%	14.33%	$22,000	18%	14.67%

3.

	(1) Family Income	(2) Income Share	(3) Cumulative Share	(4) Income Share	(5) Cumulative Share
Top	20%	40%	100%	36%	100%
	20%	25%	60%	23.75%	64%
	20%	20%	35%	20%	40.25%
	20%	10%	15%	11.31%	20.25%
Lowest	20%	5%	5%	8.94%	8.94%

10% of the highest income share (40%) equals 4%.
5% of the next highest income share (25%) equals 1.25%.
4% + 1.25% = 5.25%.

75% of the 5.25% (3.94%) is distributed to the lowest income quintile:
5% + 3.94% = 8.94%.

25% of the 5.25% (1.31%) is distributed to the next lowest income quintile:
10% + 1.31% = 11.31%.

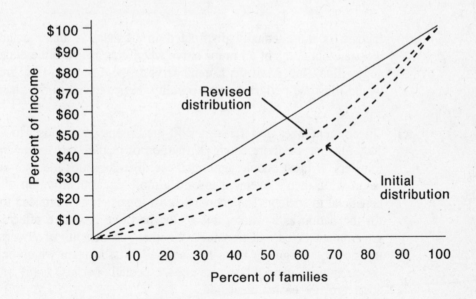

Challenge Problems and Potential Essay Questions

    a. **Challenge Problems**

        1. a) See the figure below.

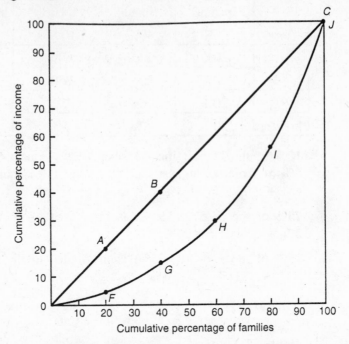

          b) Income is more equally distributed in Canada. A more equal distribution is illustrated in terms of a Lorenz curve which lies closer to the diagonal line (the 45 degree line). Indeed, if the Lorenz curve *is* the diagonal (45 degree) line then that would illustrate perfect income equality. No country has ever had perfect income equality.

          c) Government taxes *and* transfers shift the Lorenz curve closer to the diagonal line. This illustrates a more equal distribution of income due to government taxes and transfers. If most people agree that the distribution of income was not "fair" to begin with, then movement toward a more equal distribution of income may be beneficial to society. The economic cost to society is a reduced total income level for the nation as a whole, due to the negative incentive effects associated with government taxes and transfers. Whether the benefits of government taxes and transfers outweigh the costs is a normative issue upon which equally reasonable people may be expected to disagree—especially because many of the benefits and costs are not easily measured.

        2. a) Somewhat progressive. (A progressive tax is one in which the percentage of people's income paid as that tax increases as their income increases.)

          b) Slightly regressive. (A regressive tax is one in which the percentage of people's income paid as that tax decreases as their income increases.)

          c) Roughly proportional. (A proportional tax is one in which the percentage of people's income paid as that tax remains the same as their income increases.)

          d) Somewhat regressive

          e) Progressive

3. If government subsidized day-care centres, the supply would increase, the price would fall and the quantity of children placed in day-care would increase. If the parents were subsidized, there would still be a greater quantity of children placed in day-care because the demand for day-care services would rise. However, because demand will have increased, the price of day-care will be greater, but only for those who are not receiving subsidies. If day-care centre regulations were relaxed then the supply would increase more than demand would fall (there may be some decrease in demand if there was a decline in quality). The result would be a decline in the price and a greater number of children placed in day-care.

    The benefit of relaxing day-care regulations, as opposed to subsidization, is that no tax dollars are required (whereas, taxes are required to fund the subsidies). The cost to society of deregulating day-care could be the lower quality day-care services provided. It would be difficult to determine whether the benefits would outweigh the costs of relaxing the regulations (especially when one considers long-run costs).

4. In order to increase the wages of the working poor, their marginal revenue product (which equals their marginal product multiplied by the price of the output they produce) must increase. Therefore, finding a way to increase the productivity (marginal product) of the poor may be the best long-term policy the government could undertake to reduce the percentage of people living in poverty. Any investment in human capital (investment in people's skills, training, and education to increase productivity) will likely take time and may be expensive. Moreover, finding the right formula, especially given political constraints, has often proved difficult to find. Nevertheless, without doing so, there is little hope of substantially reducing the number of working poor living in poverty. The lesson is that any poverty relief program should have one eye on the long-run objective of increasing poor people's productivity while it sees to their more immediate needs.

5. The critics point out that the principle beneficiaries of the tax dollars paid by all citizens of the province or county to support colleges and universities accrue only to those who attend the institutions. These students and their families are usually in the middle and upper-income brackets. They are the ones who least need public assistance. Although there may be some social benefits associated with more individuals receiving college degrees (as well as other social benefits associated with the presence of public higher educational institutions), the critics argue that all of these benefits could still be experienced by simply subsidizing poor students to attend private schools. The bottom line: it would cost taxpayers less and the tax-dollars would go only to the poor but deserving students.

b. Potential Essay Questions

The following answers are annotated—they only indicate the general idea behind the answer.

1. A Lorenz curve illustrates the size distribution of income among families in a given country at a given time. The greater the inequality in the distribution of income the more the curve bows out below the diagonal line. Some of the limitations of a Lorenz curve include that it says nothing about the socioeconomic distribution of income (the allocation of income among relevant socioeconomic groupings), nor does it say anything about the way in which wealth is distributed among families. The Lorenz curve for Canada illustrates a decline in the amount of income inequality (the curve moved closer to the diagonal line) from 1965 to 1980. From 1980 to 1992 it increased at higher levels of income and decreased at lower levels of income. (See Exhibit 2, page 325 of the text).

2. The two methods are: taxation (policies that tax the rich more than the poor) and expenditures (programs that help the poor more than the rich). Spending on public assistance programs have accounted for most of the redistribution effects.

3. See the definitions in the margin of the text on page 336. The progressive tax is generally considered to be more "fair." See page 337 for the sources of tax revenues for provincial and local governments and their progressivity.

4. See Exhibit 9 on page 337 of the text and the discussion which follows on pages 337–339.

Chapter 17 THE ROLE OF GOVERNMENT IN THE ECONOMY

I. CHAPTER AT A GLANCE

Rip this page out for quick and easy reference.

1. **Two insights behind economists' support of markets are: e(1) if people voluntarily trade, that trade must be making them better off; and (2) excess profit generates competition and the price falls. (346)**

    But, economists agree there are some "market failures." However, they don't agree whether gov't intervention helps more than it hurts.

2. **Externalities are effects of decisions not taken into account by the decision makers. (348)**

    Can either be negative (undesirable side effects) or positive (desirable).

3. **Four arguments for government intervention are: (350)**

    1. *Agreements to restrain trade should be restricted.*
    2. *Informational and rationality problems necessitate government intervention.*
    3. *When there are externalities, marginal social costs and marginal social benefits should be equalized.*
    4. *When property rights are unfair, government should intervene to achieve fairness.*

    *Know these!

4. **Four arguments against government intervention are: (353)**

    1. *Preventing private restraints on trade creates even more restraints.*
    2. *Correcting informational and rationality problems creates even more problems.*
    3. *Correcting for externalities creates other problems.*
    4. *Preventing unfairness creates even more unfairness.*

    *Know these!

5. **Sin taxes are designed to discourage activities society believes are harmful to individuals. Milton Friedman would likely oppose sin taxes because they involve the government trying to direct individual's behavior. (355)**

    Taxes on producers ↓ supply, ↑ P and ↓ Q in the market.

6. a) **Licensing tends to prevent incompetents from practicing, providing information to consumers, and professionalize an activity. (357)**

    *Know about the "informational alternative" to licensure.

    b) **Licensing tends to restrict entry, restrict consumer choice, and cost money. (357)**

    Maybe its a way to restrict competition?

7. **Should government intervene in the market? It depends. (360)**

    Need to weigh the benefits against the costs on a case-by-case basis and need to remain as objective as possible!!

II. MASTERY TEST

1. Economists support market-based decisions because

   a) individuals freely participate to improve their welfare.
   b) markets always reach socially optimal solutions.
   c) government has no role in a market economy.
   d) All of the above.

2. In which case do laissez faire economic thinkers endorse government involvement in the economy?

   a) to improve the distribution of income
   b) to provide a legal framework for the functioning of markets
   c) to establish macroeconomic stability for improved market performance
   d) All of the above.

3. Proponents of activist government seek government intervention in the case of

   a) negative externalities.
   b) public goods.
   c) positive externalities.
   d) a, b, and c

4. Critics of government involvement in the economy reject the complaint about the unfairness of markets because

   a) unfairness cannot come about from marketplace decision making.
   b) property rights are always clearly defined in a market economy.
   c) government attempts at reducing unfairness create unfairness.
   d) central planning is considerably less fair than markets.

5. Laissez faire economists accept government efforts to reduce restraint of trade

   a) in the case of monopoly power.
   b) to improve the distribution of income.
   c) by licensure of professional services.
   d) in none of the preceding alternatives.

6. In the discussion of externalities, a third party is

   a) someone who enjoys a public good without paying taxes for its provisioning.
   b) government.
   c) a potential seller excluded from the market by monopoly power.
   d) a non participant in the market.

7. Some economists suggest placing effluent fees on goods

   a) that are considered sinful.
   b) to redistribute income to lower income families.
   c) that create pollution.
   d) to encourage positive externalities.

8. Which of the following statements about the imposition of a sin tax on a commodity is not true?

   a) The market supply curve shifts in.
   b) The market demand curve shifts in.
   c) Equilibrium price increases.
   d) Government generates revenue from the tax.

9. Which of the following statements about a sin tax is true?

   a) The more inelastic the demand and supply curves, the less output is reduced as a result of the tax.
   b) The more elastic the demand curve, the more revenue a sin tax generates for government.
   c) The more elastic the demand curve, the greater is the price increase as a result of the tax.
   d) The more inelastic the supply curve, the less revenue is generated by the tax for government.

10. Which of the following is not a statement in support of licensure?

    a) It provides useful information to consumers.
    b) It increases the rationality of consumer choices.
    c) It improves consumer sovereignty.
    d) It reduces monopoly power.

11. Almost all economists are advocates of laissez faire economics in the case of a

    a) nonbeneficent autocratic government.
    b) beneficent autocratic government.
    c) functioning democracy.
    d) non federal system of government.

12. Government in Canada which provides for national economic regulation is referred to as

    a) federal government.
    b) nonbeneficent autocratic government.
    c) non democratic government.
    d) provincial and local government.

13. A laissez faire philosophy of government is consistent with

    a) government oversight of property rights.
    b) anarchy.
    c) licensure of professional services.
    d) no government oversight of property rights.

14. Which of the following statements reflects economists' support of market decision making?

    a) Without markets, trading activity does not necessarily benefit both parties to a trade.
    b) The marketplace eliminates the occurrence of excess profits in the short run and in the long run.
    c) Markets represent the voluntary interaction of individuals seeking their own self interest.
    d) Markets assure that people at least start out with the same property rights.

15. Anarchy is a state which reflects

    a) excessive government intervention in markets.
    b) a collapse of institutions upon which markets are based.
    c) the ideal state for laissez faire economists.
    d) an institutional framework established by government to which laissez faire advocates are opposed.

16. While economists in Canada are generally in favour of market-based decision making, some believe that a case can be made for government intervention in all of the following scenarios except

    a) the need for government to defend competitive markets.
    b) the need for government to protect people from their own irrational choices.
    c) the need for government to shift in the demand curve when externalities arise.
    d) the need for government to promote equity when there is an unequal distribution of property rights.

17. A public good is an example of a good with an extreme positive externality which

    a) benefits only a few at a great cost to those who do not have access to the good or service.
    b) an individual can consume without prevention of consumption by everybody else.
    c) is provided for by a monopoly in restraint of trade.
    d) depletes a commonly held resource to the detriment of the group.

18. Which of the following is least likely to be characterized as a public good?

    a) national defense
    b) the interstate highway system
    c) public primary education
    d) long-distance phone service

19. An argument in favour of government intervention when an externality arises is

    a) the desirability of a marketplace outcome where marginal social costs equal marginal social benefits.
    b) the efficiency generated when unfairness is reduced by the redistribution of property rights.
    c) the relative ease of adjusting demand and supply curves to reflect their true social costs and benefits.
    d) the threat to the market system by anarchy if externalities are allowed to expand unchecked.

20. The serious flaw apparent in the arguments in favour of government intervention is the belief that

    a) the government has the ability to correct problems and not make them worse.
    b) the assumption that the current distribution of property rights is not ideal.
    c) monopoly is a problem rather than a blessing.
    d) such things as unfairness and externalities occur in market economies.

21. What problem arises, according to laissez faire advocates, from the attempt to correct for externalities?

    a) the elimination of necessary public goods
    b) disincentives for markets to create positive externalities
    c) discouragement of efficient market solutions to externalities.
    d) the inevitable replacement of market goods with public goods.

22. An alternative to government regulation to deal with effluent resulting from marketplace activities suggested by Paul in his debate against Milton is for government

   a) to simply outlaw effluent thereby eliminating the need to assess marginal costs and marginal benefits.
   b) to back off and allow market remedies to the problem to evolve from market interactions.
   c) to eliminate the property rights of those perpetrating the problem.
   d) to create pollution rights and foster a market structure to reduce pollution.

23. The proposal to legalize hitherto illegal drugs

   a) is endorsed by Milton Friedman and rejected by Bill Bennett.
   b) is not cost-effective and would only increase the problem according to Bennett and Friedman.
   c) would be cost-effective and reduce related criminal activity according to Bennett and Friedman.
   d) is endorsed by Bill Bennett and rejected by Milton Friedman.

24. An alternative to the drug policies favoured by Friedman and Bennett is for government to

   a) decriminalize drugs but create a government monopoly for their distribution to generate revenues and to better control their use.
   b) create more severe economic penalties for those involved in the drug trade.
   c) decriminalize but establish stiff taxes on their trade.
   d) retain the illegal status on the drug trade but to eliminate law enforcement activities to permit the market to develop a solution to the problem.

25. Which of the following is an accurate statement regarding the black market in drugs?

   a) Market price is a function of seller risk rather than production cost.
   b) Drug dealers and distributors generate only normal profits as a result of stiff market competition.
   c) Legalization of drug sales and use would have negligible impact on the illegal market for drugs.
   d) A sin tax would generate little revenue but would be an effective deterrent to consumption.

26. The informational alternative to licensure is:

   a) allow anyone to practice medicine as long as they have a medical degree.
   b) allow anyone to practice medicine but require that they be certified by government to practice.
   c) allow less qualified people to replace doctors.
   d) allow doctors to provide success rate information to patients.

27. Opponents of government intervention in the economy agrue that

   a) property rights need to be fair to achieve a fair distribution of income.
   b) only when property rights are unfair should government intervene to achieve fairness.
   c) government's attempts to correct informational problems are not necessary because efficiently operating markets always ensure that adequate information will be provided.
   d) externalities cannot be efficiently corrected by government due to the influence of special interest groups and other factors.
   e) All of the above.

28. Which of the following is an argument used by advocates of a laissez-faire policy?

   a) Because government represents the people, then more government intervention in the economy creates a more socially desirable outcome.
   b) Preventing private restraints on trade often creates even more restraints.
   c) Some market transactions involve very large externalities.
   d) Information is not always equally available to all of the participants in a market transaction.
   e) Overuse of a common access resource is the result of an inefficient market.

29. When negative externalities exist in the production of a good then the

   a) good is underproduced at the free market equilibrium.
   b) marginal social cost of producing the good equals the marginal cost borne by the firm.
   c) marginal social cost of producing the good equals the marginal cost borne by the firm plus the marginal external cost resulting from the production of the good.
   d) the marginal social benefits of production are greater than marginal social costs of production.

30. If a positive externality results from the consumption of a good

   a) the marginal social benefit is equal to the marginal social cost at the free market equilibrium.
   b) government should tax the good.
   c) the marginal social benefit is greater than the market place.
   d) then there are undesirable social consequences associated with the good.
   e) then the good is overproduced at market equilibrium.

III. SHORT ANSWER EXERCISES AND PROBLEMS

a. Short Answer Exercises

1. Provide the terms for the following definitions.

   a) the belief government should intervene in the economy as little as possible

   b) the existence of lawless confusion and general disorder

   c) the effects of decisions that are not taken into account by decision makers

d) a good an individual can consume without diminishing the amount of it other people consume

e) charges imposed by government on pollution

f) the right of the individual to make choices about what is consumed and produced

2. What term is used to describe the combination of federal, provincial, and municipal agencies whose officials are elected by the people or appointed by elected officials?

3. Which level of government is responsible for national defense, income security, national economic regulation, and macroeconomic stability?

4. Which level of government is responsible for education, roads, and welfare?

5. State the two arguments that form the basis for economists' support of marketplace decision making.

6. List four arguments for government intervention.

7. List four criticisms of government intervention.

8. What is the name given to a tax placed on a good to reduce its consumption? State why Milton Friedman would likely disapprove of it.

b. **Problems**

1. Assume the marketplace prices antilock brakes as a $1000 option on automobiles. This market scenario is pictured below. Further assume that an additional $200 of social benefit is generated per purchase of antilock brakes as a result of corresponding reduction in critical accidents.

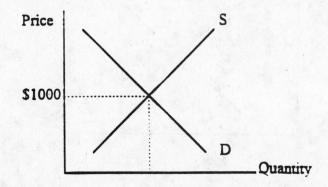

a) Sketch a new demand curve reflecting the social demand for antilock brakes as a result of third-party benefits.

b) Label the price needed to attract sufficient buyers to purchase the socially optimal quantity of antilock brakes P_b. Label the price sellers have to receive to produce the socially optimal level of antilock brakes P_s.

c) How might an activist government encourage the socially optimal level of air bag production and consumption?

2. In order to generate revenues for provincial government operations two excise taxes are considered: a one dollar per litre fee on hard liquor or a one dollar per ticket fee on movie tickets. (Excise taxes are paid by sellers.) Models for these goods, in the absence of taxes, are illustrated below.

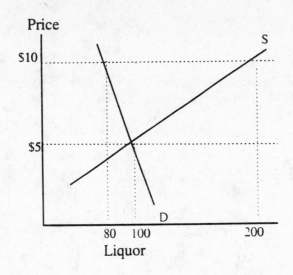

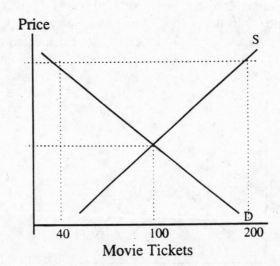

a) Sketch a curve reflecting the sin tax in both models.

b) On each model, shade in the area which reflects the amount of revenue the government generates from the tax on each good.

c) Which commodity is more appropriate to tax for purposes of revenue generation to finance government's operations?

IV. CHALLENGE PROBLEMS AND POTENTIAL ESSAY QUESTIONS

a. Challenge Problems

1. Determine which of the four justifications for government intervention in markets is most likely the reason for the existence of each of the following government actions. (It is not necessary for you to determine whether the government should, or should not be undertaking the action described, but simply to try to think about what may have motivated the government action.)

   a) Government regulation of Cable T.V. services.

   b) The Food and Drug Department of the federal government.

   c) The Department of Transportation regulates the airline industry.

   d) The Nuclear Regulatory Commission licenses and regulates nuclear power plants.

   e) Equal Opportunity Employment Agency regulates labour markets.

   f) The Occupational Health and Safety Department regulates the work environment.

   g) Labelling requirements set by the Food and Drug Department of the federal government.

   h) Provincial regulatory boards oversee rates charged by local electric utility companies.

   i) The federal government sets the minimum wage.

   j) The federal government provides for price supports on some agricultural commodities.

   k) Municipal government sets rent controls (controls rental rates).

2. Most credit card users have complained at one time or another about the high interest rates they are charged on their credit card balances. Many people believe they aren't "fair." Some people have argued that because high interest rates are especially hard on the poor, the government ought to limit the interest rates credit card customers are charged by banks. What impact would such a limit have? (Hint: an interest rate limit would be a price ceiling on those interest rates.)

3. Assume a community has decided that there are some substantial social benefits associated with certain goods and services being made available to the youth in the community. Let's suppose that the figure below represents the supply of after-school organized recreational activities provided to latch-key kids by some private recreational firms in the community. (Latch-key kids are children who are alone from the time school gets out until their parent, or parents get home from work.) The figure below also shows the private demand and society's demand for those services—that is, the marginal benefits (private benefits) and the marginal social benefits (private plus social benefits) respectively.

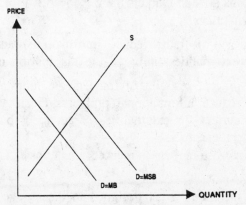

   a) Indicate the efficient level of output in the figure above. Why would this be an efficient output level?

    b) Assume the government is interested in a policy to increase the number of children spending time at these facilities. What policy would you recommend?

   4. Many people have advocated making abortion illegal because of the negative externalities associated with abortion. What would be the economic impact on the market for abortion services if those services were banned?

b. **Potential Essay Questions**

   1. What is an externalilty? How does government deal with externalities?

   2. What is a public good or service? What are some examples of public goods and services? What is the economic justification for government providing a public good or service?

   3. Why will there likely always be some debate among equally reasonable and well-intentioned people (including economists) concerning the appropriate role for government to play in the economy?

   4. What are the arguments for and against licensure?

V. ANSWERS

II. Mastery Test

1. a	6. d	11. a	16. c	21. c	26. b
2. b	7. c	12. a	17. b	22. d	27. d
3. d	8. b	13. a	18. d	23. a	28. b
4. c	9. a	14. c	19. a	24. c	29. c
5. d	10. d	15. b	20. a	25. a	30. c

III. Short Answer Exercises and Problems

a. **Short Answer Exercises**

   1. a) laissez faire   b) anarchy   c) externalities
      d) public good   e) effluent fees f) consumer sovereignty

   2. government

   3. federal government

   4. provincial and municipal government

   5. Individuals participate in markets of their own volition to make themselves better off; If excess profits arise in markets there is incentive for new sellers to enter the market, driving down prices.

   6. prevent restraint of trade; reduce informational and rationality problems; adjust markets for externalities; improve the distribution of property rights

   7. attempts to prevent restraint of trade create long-term restraints on trade;
      attempts to reduce informational problems create large, inefficient bureaucracies;
      attempts to correct for externalities create inept bureaucracies that tend to serve special interest groups;
      attempts to increase fairness in markets create instead disincentives for innovation and hard work

   8. Sin tax. A sin tax is a tax designed to discourage activities society believes are harmful to individuals. Milton Friedman would likely oppose sin taxes because they involve the government trying to direct individuals' behaviour.

b. Problems

1.

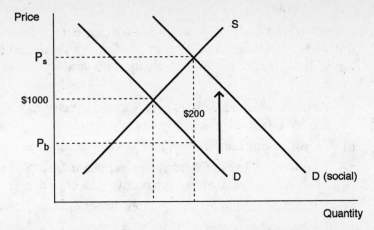

Government could offer a tax credit equal to the difference between P_s and P_b to encourage the purchase of automobiles with airbags

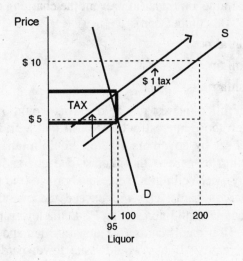

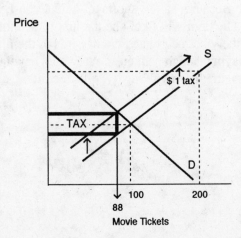

2.   The tax on liquor would be more appropriate for the generation of revenues.

IV. Challenge Problems and Potential Essay Questions

a. Challenge Problems

1. (There may be other motivations for government involvement than those mentioned below, or a combination of the four justifications listed in the textbook—which is very likely. However, I have tried to mention the justification which seems most likely to me.)

   a) To prevent restraints on trade (to prevent the charging of unnecessarily high prices due to a lack of competition).

   b) To offset problems of information and rationality.

   c) To offset problems of information and rationality; maybe also to correct (negative) externalities (from either perspective the objective is to ensure safety).

   d) To correct (negative) externalities (to ensure environmental safety).

   e) To prevent unfairness.

   f) To offset problems of information and rationality.

   g) To offset problems of information and rationality.

   h) To prevent restraints on trade (to prevent the charging of unnecessarily high prices due to a lack of competition).

   i) To prevent unfairness.

   j) To prevent unfairness.

   k) To prevent unfairness.

2. A government controlled interest rate below what would otherwise exist in the market is a price ceiling on those interest rates. (Recall that a price ceiling is a legal limit on the price which is set by government below equilibrium, such as at P_c in the figure below. The price in this case is the interest rate charged on outstanding credit card balances.) Like any price ceiling, it creates a shortage (the quantity demanded of funds to be placed on credit cards, Q_d, will exceed the quantity of funds supplied, Q_s). Compared to the equilibrium interest rate, P_e, at the lower, controlled interest rate more debt will be placed on credit cards (the quantity demanded increases as the price—interest rate— decreases). Banks would issue fewer cards, and/or place more strict credit limits on those cards (the quantity supplied of funds made available to credit card users would fall). Because of the shortage, banks can be more "picky" about who holds their cards. The poor will likely be the first to be more closely scrutinized. Many poor people will likely not be granted credit cards in the first place. The poor may have been better off paying "high" interest rates and having access to credit, than not having any access to this revolving type of credit at all.

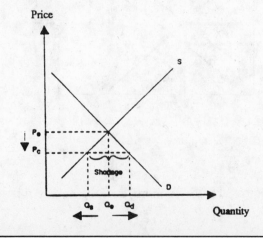

3. a) The efficient level of output (services provided in the community) is where the marginal social benefits equal the marginal social costs. This occurs at that output level where the MSB curve intersects the supply curve. (It is reasonable to assume there is no difference between the private and social costs. So marginal social costs are given by the supply curve.)

   b) The private demand and/or the supply needs to be increased. This could be accomplished by subsidizing parents (increasing demand) and/or subsidizing the facilities (increasing supply). Either one of these options would increase the output level toward the efficient level where MSB = MSC. It may be much easier to administer the subsidization of the facilities.

4. Demand would decrease somewhat. Supply would decrease significantly (the opportunity cost for Doctors getting caught performing an illegal procedure would be very high). Because supply would likely decrease much more than demand, the price would rise significantly. (The price would also rise significantly because the demand for abortion services is inelastic, and because the supply of services which would be made available after abortion was declared illegal would likely be very inelastic.) The equilibrium quantity of abortion services would fall. The extent to which the quantity would fall depends on the extent to which demand and supply shifts, and the inelasticity of demand and supply after abortion is made illegal. Abortion services would become accessible only to those whose financial resources would be sufficient to cover the high price of the procedure. Finally, as historical experience indicates, there would likely be a significant decline in the quality of the service which can be predicted to increase the probability of life-threatening medical complications for the women involved. These are the predicted economic consequences of making abortion illegal. This says nothing about the subjective value judgement concerning whether it should, or should not be banned. That is a normative issue for each individual to grapple with.

b. Potential Essay Questions

The following answers are annotated—they only indicate the general idea behind the answer.

1. Externalities are effects of decisions not taken into account by the decision makers. They can either be negative or positive. Negative externalities are undesirable social side-effects associated with the production and/or consumption of a good or service. Goods and services which have negative externalities associated with them are overproduced from society's perspective. To try to bring about a more efficient output level from society's perspective, government can ban them, tax them, or regulate their production and/or consumption. Positive externalities are desirable social side-effects associated with the production and/or consumption of a good or service. Goods and services which have positive externalities associated with them are underproduced from society's perspective. To try to bring about a more efficient output level from society's perspective, government can subsidize their production and/or consumption.

2. A public good or service is a good or service provided by government to everyone (at least if you are eligible to receive it from government). Examples include national defence, social security and other "welfare" programs, public parks, roads, police and fire service. The economic justification for government providing these goods and services is that there are very large positive externalities (desirable social side-effects) associated with them. In the absence of government providing them they would be grossly underproduced by the free enterprise system (if they would be provided at all).

Therefore, government provides for them. Note that most people like the goods and services provided them by government. However, few people like paying for them with taxes. Society must decide what is considered the optimal amount to be provided based on their benefits and costs.

3. Because the benefits and costs associated with government involvement are not easily measured. As such, there is much room for debate. Moreover, there are some cases in which the benefits and the costs are more obvious than in other cases. Therefore, one is well advised to take each case on its own merits. That is, don't necessarily conclude that government policy is always doomed to failure or that it can always help. Try to be as objective as possible in the measurement of the benefits and costs based on the best available objective evidence in each case. In some instances one will likely find that government may do more good than harm. At other times the best policy may be laissez-faire. So, when should government intervene in the economy? It depends.

4. For: Licensing tends to prevent incompetents from practicing, providing information to consumers, and professionalize an activity. Against: Licensing tends to restrict entry, restrict consumer choice, and cost money.

Chapter 18 POLITICS, ECONOMICS, AND AGRICULTURAL MARKETS

I. CHAPTER AT A GLANCE

Rip this page out for quick and easy reference.

1. **The good/bad paradox is the phenomenon of doing poorly because you're doing well. (363)**

    Because of the inelastic D for farm goods a good harvest ($\uparrow$ in S) means revenues (incomes) to farmers fall.

2. **Two reasons a persistent agricultural slump started in 1920 were: (365)**

    (1) post World War I demand for agricultural products declined, and
    (2) farm costs increased when Canada placed tariffs on imported manufactured goods.

    The major thrust of government involvement in agriculture was during the Great Depression.

3. **The general rule of political economy states that small groups that are significantly affected by a government policy will lobby more effectively than large groups that are equally affected by that same policy. (369)**

    The farm lobby has been successful in generating higher prices and incomes for farmers even though consumers and taxpayers are worse off.

4. **Four methods of price support are: (372)**

    1. Regulatory methods.
    2. Economic incentives to reduce supply.
    3. Subsidize the sale.
    4. Buying up and storing the good. The distributional effects are shown in Exhibit 4, on page 371.

    *Know these! Know who benefits the most and who is hurt the most for each of these—evaluate them.

5. **Price supports cause inefficiency and loss compared to a competitive solution. However, it is likely that, in the absence of price supports, private cartels would have been the outcome, and the price supports are the least inefficient practical solution. (376)**

    It is not clear whether we would have been better off never involving government in farming. A cartel situation could be worse.

II. MASTERY TEST

1. Agricultural markets resemble perfect competition but are not considered so because

   a) agrifirms exercise control over prices in most agricultural markets.
   b) agricultural commodities are mostly standardized.
   c) commodity prices are rigid in a downward direction.
   d) pricing in farm markets is influenced by government policy.

2. In the short run the elasticity of demand for farm products is _____. In the long run it is _____.

   a) inelastic, inelastic
   b) inelastic, elastic
   c) elastic, elastic
   d) elastic, inelastic

3. "Competition" in agriculture has meant that most of the benefits from large productivity increases in farming have gone to

   a) producers in the form of higher prices.
   b) consumers in the form of higher prices.
   c) producers in the form of lower prices.
   d) consumers in the form of lower prices.

4. If all farmers have a good year, output is high, then

   a) the farming industry as a whole will have a bad year.
   b) the farming industry as a whole will also have a good year.
   c) farm incomes will increase.
   d) the price will rise.

5. In order to avoid the good/bad paradox

   a) individual farmers should produce as much as possible.
   b) farmers should organize and each agree to reduce production.
   c) farmers should organize and agree on a plan to maximize joint production.
   d) it is impossible to avoid the good/bad paradox given that farmers operate in a perfectly competitive market.

6. The Great Depression marked an important change for agriculture because

   a) this was when agrifarms were born.
   b) this was when prices for farm products finally began their upward trend.
   c) the Canadian government stepped into agriculture.
   d) farmers were able to arrange privately to limit supply.

7. The Canadian Wheat Board

   a) through their policy, ensures that price = costs of production for farmers.
   b) follows a policy which puts a lower limit on wheat farmers income.
   c) limits the amount of wheat farmers can grow.
   d) essentially offers farmers a price ceiling—a maximum price when they deliver their wheat to grain elevators.

8. The Canadian Dairy Commission

    a) is a provincial agency.
    b) supports dairy prices at 90% of their price over the previous 5 years.
    c) makes payments to producers under a quota system.
    d) controls the activities of the Agricultural Stabilization Board.

Answer the following 3 questions (9–11) based on the figure below. The jagged line shows what wheat prices would have been from 1990–1995 had there been no stabilization program.

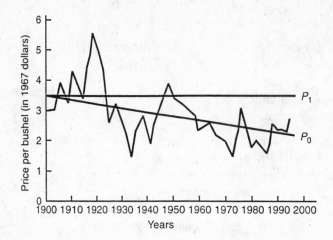

9. In order to minimize fluctuations in price at minimum cost to government, at what price should government agree to buy and sell wheat?

    a) At the price of $6 where the jagged line reaches a peak.
    b) At the price of $1.25 where the jagged line reaches a minimum.
    c) P_1
    d) P_0

10. At a price of P_0

    a) surpluses will exceed shortages.
    b) surpluses will roughly equal shortages.
    c) shortages will exceed surpluses.
    d) there will never be shortages or surpluses.

11. To support the price, government will agree to buy and sell wheat at

    a) P_1
    b) P_0
    c) whatever level is indicated by the jagged line.
    d) a price lower than P_0.

12. A price support program

    a) maintains price above the trend.
    b) allows price to fluctuate around the trend.
    c) ensures that shortages and surpluses will net out.
    d) is the same as a stabilization program.

13. Relative prices of agricultural goods cannot fall under

    a) a price support program.
    b) a price stabilization program.
    c) a marketing board arrangement.
    d) a price parity program.

14. The good/bad paradox occurs whenever the

    a) short-run decrease in price overwhelms the short-run increase in quantity.
    b) demand curve increases over an inelastic range of the supply curve.
    c) demand curve and supply curve are both inelastic.
    d) increase in demand brings about a relatively greater increase in quantity than decrease in price.

15. The goal of a price-support policy is to

    a) accomplish price parity.
    b) reduce surpluses.
    c) stabilize long-term prices.
    d) improve prices.

16. The farm lobby has evidently been successful at raising farm prices higher than the competitive level because

    a) agricultural commodities are often in surplus.
    b) the price parity ratio is greater than one.
    c) farm income and producers have increased.
    d) prices received by farmers exceed their costs.

17. The general rule of political economy states that

    a) small groups suffer at the hands of the majority.
    b) small groups lobby more effectively than large groups.
    c) in the long run the interests of the many prevail.
    d) market power is more influential than political power.

18. In general it can be said that price-support programs benefit farmers

    a) and cost consumers and taxpayers.
    b) and consumers and taxpayers.
    c) and consumers but cost taxpayers.
    d) without hurting consumers and taxpayers.

19. Without government farm programs, there likely would be

    a) fewer farmers.   b) more agrifirms.
    c) higher farm prices.   d) a, b, and c

20. Giving surplus wheat away results in

    a) domestic farmers being hurt by lower prices.
    b) foreign farmers being hurt by lower prices.
    c) domestic demand for farm goods increasing.
    d) a and b
    e) b and c

21. It is in the interests of producers to limit production when

 a) a cartel problem exists.
 b) demand is inelastic.
 c) supply is inelastic.
 d) demand and supply are elastic.

22. An increase in supply over the inelastic portion of a demand curve results in a

 a) price increase and a loss in seller revenue.
 b) price decrease and a gain in seller revenue.
 c) price decrease and a loss in seller revenue.
 d) price increase and a gain in seller revenue.

23. A price stabilization program is designed to

 a) eliminate long-run price fluctuations for agricultural commodities.
 b) establish a parity price guaranteeing farmers an income level commensurate to that of non farmers.
 c) maintain price stability in the long run and for the near term.
 d) reduce short-run fluctuations in the prices of farm goods.

24. Farmers generally prefer a price support program because

 a) it allows income in excess of the parity price of agricultural goods.
 b) price stabilization over the long run is targeted.
 c) farm prices are maintained at the long-term trend regardless of short run price fluctuations.
 d) prices are maintained at a level higher than the long-run trend.

25. Which of the following statements best describes the price parity concept?

 a) It is the ratio of the market prices of an index of agricultural goods to an index prices paid by farmers
 b) It is the ratio of the average income of farmers to the average income of non farmers.
 c) It is the price that maintains the ratio of prices received and paid by farmers at the same ratio as in a base year.
 d) It is the price for farm goods that maintains the long-term trend of agricultural prices in the absence of short-run fluctuations.

26. The most expensive price support option for taxpayers is

 a) subsidy, the one that provides the greatest benefit to consumers.
 b) regulation, which benefits both farmers and government the least.
 c) government purchasing farm output then storing it for later sale.
 d) government purchasing farm output then destroying it.

27. The least expensive price support option for taxpayers is

 a) subsidy, the one that provides the greatest benefit to consumers.
 b) regulation, which benefits both farmers and government the least.
 c) government purchasing farm output then storing it for later sale.
 d) government purchasing farm output then destroying it.

28. A price support creates downward pressure in price. All but which of the following will offset that pressure?

   a) Law preventing sale or purchase at a lower price
   b) Subsidize the sale to consumers
   c) Destroy the excess supply
   d) Provide economic incentives to reduce demand

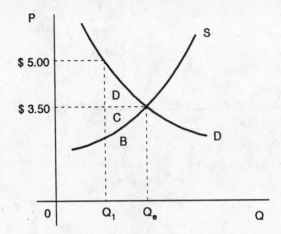

29. The diagram above represents a legal price of $5.00. The triangle made up of areas D and C represents

   a) lost income to farmers.
   b) savings to consumers.
   c) deadweight loss to society.
   d) revenue for the government.

30. A support program which restricts entry of new farmers is said to

   a) grandfather out new suppliers.
   b) grandfather in new suppliers.
   c) grandfather out existing suppliers.
   d) grandfather in existing suppliers.

31. When economic incentives to reduce supply are provided to existing wheat farmers, incomes go up for all but one of the following reasons.

   a) They get payments not to grow wheat
   b) They get higher prices for the wheat they do grow
   c) They can grow something else on the land taken out of wheat
   d) They get rid of excess burden

32. Giving away surplus food to the poor doesn't work because

   a) it lowers the price and leaves an even greater surplus.
   b) it raises the price even higher so fewer people can buy it.
   c) it creates a black market.
   d) it is forbidden by the Canadian Wheat Board.

33. Which option to increase farm incomes costs the least but is least beneficial to farmers?

    a) Regulation
    b) Subsidies on sales
    c) Destroying the foods
    d) Economic incentives

34. All but one of the following are disadvantages of cartelization of the agricultural industry.

    a) Higher prices
    b) Safety regulations
    c) Lower production
    d) Less efficiency

35. In 1995, GATT was replaced by _____ whose mission is to reduce tariffs and trade barriers among all countries.

    a) NAFTA
    b) Canada US Free Trade Agreement
    c) WTO
    d) G7

III. SHORT ANSWER EXERCISES AND PROBLEMS

a. Short Answer Exercises

1. Provide the appropriate expression for each of the following statements.

   a) The best interest of the individual producer is different from the best interest of a group of producers.

   b) Firms that own and operate large-scale farms in the same manner that nonfarm corporations operate their businesses.

   c) The price that would keep farmers relatively as well off as they were in a specified base year.

d) Government programs established to encourage farmers to take land out of production.

e) Government program designed to eliminate short run fluctuations in prices.

f) The phenomenon of doing poorly because you are doing well.

g) A vested interest group promoting the interests of farmers politically.

2. What event initiated government farm programs as they exist today?

3. What are the two goals of farm programs?

4. How can farmers get around the good/bad paradox?

5. Name and describe the two types of government programs designed to help farmers avoid the good/bad paradox.

6. What is the name given to the idea that small groups are better able to protect their interests than large groups are?

7. List the four options discussed in the text which are available to government to implement price supports.

8. What does "grandfather in" refer to?

9. Name the type of price support program that fits each of the following descriptions.

a) Costs the government the least, benefits farmers the least.

b) Benefits both consumers and producers but would be the most costly to taxpayers.

c) Leaves the government with a surplus.

10. Name three interest groups that affect and are affected by farm policy.

11. Describe four ways in which agricultural markets approach the model of perfect competition.

12. How might agriculture in Canada have been different without government support programs?

b. **Problems**

1. Evaluate the distributional consequences of the different approaches to price supports using the market model and the fictitious commodity "granolaoats".

   a) Government imposes a floor of $10 per bushel for granolaoats and restricts new entry. The market clearing price is $5 per bushel.

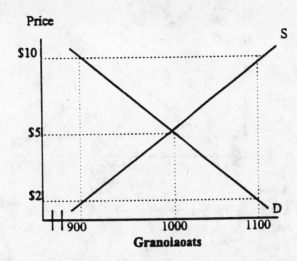

   (i) Indicate on the model the area of excess burden.

   (ii) What is the value of farmers' net gain from the price support

b) The government pays granolaoat farmers to cut back on production in order to reduce supply at a support price of $10 per bushel. As a result market quantity decreases to 900.

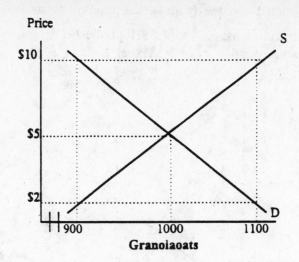

(i) How much do farmers get from the government to cut back on production?

(ii) What do farmers get from consumers in the form of higher payment?

c) Government establishes a support price of $10 per bushel and subsidizes consumers so they absorb the entire farm output at $2 per bushel.

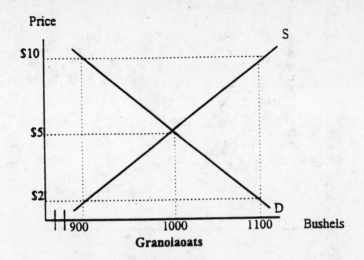

(i) Indicate on the model the benefit to farmers and to consumers.

(ii) What is the cost of this program to the government?

d) Which program is the most costly to taxpayers?

2. Refer to the following market for soybeans and respond to the questions below.

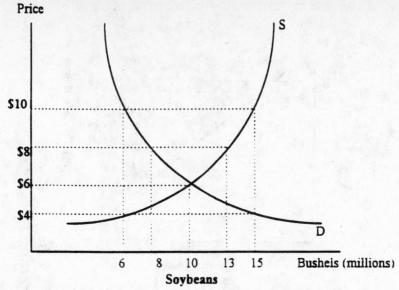

a) What is the equilibrium price and quantity for soybeans?

b) At what price does an excess of demand of 9 million bushels of soybeans occur?

c) If government guarantees soybean producers $10 per bushel what is the result in the soybean market?

d) What is the impact on the market for soybeans if growers produce 13 million bushels of soybeans?

e) Describe the situation if consumers are willing and able to purchase the entire soybean crop for $5 per bushel?

IV. CHALLENGE PROBLEMS AND POTENTIAL ESSAY QUESTIONS

a. Challenge Problems

1. Suppose the unregulated market for fluid milk in the fictitious country of Jersey can be described by the demand and supply schedules found in the following table.

Price (P) (dollars per litre)	Quantity Demanded (Qd) (millions of litres)	Quantity Supplied (Qs) (millions of litres)
$1	6,000	2,000
$2	4,000	4,000
$3	2,000	6,000

   a) Plot this information on a graph. That is, derive the demand and supply curves for milk.

   b) Identify the equilibrium price and quantity of milk on your graph. What are those numbers? What is the revenue (price multiplied by quantity) received by dairy farmers?

   c) Suppose there are 1 million dairy farmers in Jersey and that the minimum revenue necessary for dairy farmers to maintain a reasonable standard of living is $18,000. Suppose also that the government of Jersey establishes a plan to support dairy farmers' incomes. The government guarantees dairy farmers a price of $3 per litre; but these farmers are responsible for selling their milk at whatever price the market would determine, with the government making up the deficiency in any price below $3 with a cash payment. What is the quantity of milk supplied, the price that consumers will pay for this milk, and the cost of this plan to the government?

   d) What are the benefits and the costs of this plan? Is this the cheapest or most expensive plan, from taxpayers' perspective, the government could have come up with to support farmers' incomes?

   e) Assume you have been given the responsibility of finding the least expensive way, from taxpayers' perspective, of maintaining milk prices for dairy farmers at $3 per litre. What would you recommend?

2. Read the following article from the *Wall Street Journal*, May 1, 1990. Although this article refers to an American situation, the points to be made are not specific to this situation.

   As you will see, government involvement in a market can create numerous side-effects which economic reasoning can help us to predict. After reading the article briefly answer the questions which follow.

Peanut Quota System Comes Under Attack For Distorting Market

Limits on Output and Imports Raise Ire of Processors; Congress Weighs Changes

The Mansion Peanuts Built

By BRUCE INGERSOLL
Staff Reporter of THE WALL STREET JOURNAL

ALBANY, Ga.–Here in south Georgia, some of the best investments are made for peanuts.

Atlanta shopping center developer John Varner rambles around the countryside in a pickup, buying up swatches of timberland and crop land. Total acquisitions: 40,000 acres. He's the Donald Trump of farming around here," says one farmer, adding: "No, he's more like a Howard Hughes. He's very reclusive."

But it is what came with much of the land that made it so appealing: peanut quotas that amount to a government license to sell millions of pounds of peanuts a year in the U.S. market. Says Mr. Varner: "It's an added asset."

Peanut production is nearly a no-lose proposition. Even as the U.S. faults Japan for protectionism, it maintains a federal program that limits the number of farmers who can sell peanuts in the U.S. and all but forbids peanut imports. What's more, the government not only guarantees that the quota owners will recoup their production costs each year. It sees to it that the minimum selling price for their so-called quota peanuts is about 50% higher thant he world market.

Peanuts, Relatively Speaking

The program costs the federal Treasury about $4 million a year. But critics say the government isn't the only one that has to shell out.

Who else pays? Every mother feeding her children peanut-butter sandwiches, say peanut processors, and every baseball fan munching on ballpark peanuts. One processor estimate has consumers paying an extra $369 million a year–a hidden subsidy to quota holders. The Agriculture Department, using different assumptions, comes up with $190 million a year. Take away the subsidy, processors assert, and consumers could save as much as 40 cents on an 18-ounce jar of peanut butter priced at $1.79. Of course, much depends on whether cost savings would ever get passed on to the consumer.

Challenged Subsidies

But political forces now are building to challenge the peanut program, to the dismay of goober growers. The Bush administration is pressing Congress to limit the subsidies, and a coalition of conservative Republicans

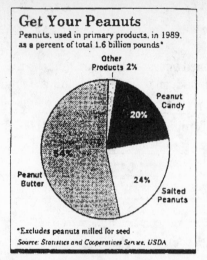

Get Your Peanuts
Peanuts, used in primary products, in 1989, as a percent of total 1.6 billion pounds*

Other Products 2%
Peanut Candy 20%
Peanut Butter 54%
Salted Peanuts 24%

*Excludes peanuts milled for seed
Source: Statistics and Cooperatives Service, USDA

and big-city Democrats intend to challenge the program when the 1990 farm bill reaches the floor this spring. Some peanut processors want to end this quota system altogether. They object to bureaucrats alloting production quotas each year–farm by farm, county by county, state by state–throughout the Peanut Belt, which stretches from Tidewater, Virginia to the New Mexico plateau.

"It's a blatant case of feudalism," asserts James Hintlian, an Everett, Mass., processor. "It spawns and protects privilege."

Not so, assert quota holders. It is a well-conceived program that stabilizes the economy of peanut-growing areas, maintains "the integrity of the family farm" and assures consumers an ample supply of nutritious peanut products at fair prices, says James Earl Mobley, the chairman of a national peanut-growers group.

No place is more threatened by the political assult than Early County, Ga., which leads the nation in peanut quotas with an allocation of 73 million pounds. Planting peanuts has been a way of life in the county since the 1920s, when cotton farmers, devastated by the boil weevil, took the advice of botanist George Washington Carver and tried the lowly legume.

Quota holders, many of them heirs to farmers who got peanut allotments four decades ago, tend to regard the peanut program as an entitlement, almost as their birthright. "Why anyone should attack it, I don't know,: says Guy Maddox, with an unlit Dutch Master between his lips. "The consuming public wants them cheaper, but it's out of the question. I think the people here are entitled to make a living."

Peanuts have been good to 88-year-old Mr. Maddox, who, by his own reckoning, is worth $4.5 million. He has a staff of servants, a white-columned mansion and control of the biggest bank in Blakely, the Early County seat. He used to own a big peanut mill in town, but these days he sticks to banking. He rents the family quota of 874,000 pounds of peanuts to two grandsons for $70,000 a year.

More than a third of the nation's 44,000 quota owners don't get their hands dirty

farming; they rent their quotas to farmers who do. Many owners are so-called allotment lords living in distant cities, such as Greenwich, Conn., and West Palm Beach, Fla. Says Gilbert Cooley, a Spokane, Wash., businessman whose wife inherited a peanut quota on about 35 acres in Oklahoma: "Oil wells would be better, but it isn't too bad."

The fact isn't lost on investors, either. Miss Brown's Busy Bee restaurant on the edge of Blakely is often abuzz with talk of the big money moving in. Fred Wenzel, an Anheuser-Busch Cos. director and the chairman of St. Louis apparel maker Kellwood Co., bought the Kolamoki Plantation a few years ago. That brought him a 1.2 million-pound peanut quota. Growing peanuts "looks like a better investment than any other crop you can raise," Mr. Wenzel says.

But Mr. Varner makes him look like small potatoes. The shopping-center developer says he and his partner, Earl Bass, own 12 million to 13 million pounds of quotas (worth $4 million according to agribusiness experts). Mr Varner's showplace: Wildfair Planation, a quail-hunting perserve south of Albany, Ga.

He commutes by private jet from Atlanta to oversee his rural empire out of a hangar at the Albany airport, his privacy protected by tight airport security and an uncommunicative staff. Many perceive him as a city-slicker bent on cornering the peanut market. The spectacle of 15 Varner-Bass mechanized peanut-pickers rumbling from one farm to another, followed by a mighty fleet of trucks, can be intimidating.

"People tell me it looks like a panzer division," says the 39-year-old Mr. Varner, who denies having monopolistic intentions: "If some other commodity makes more sense, I'm going to grow it. Peanuts just happen to be the best way to maximize investment."

While the peanut program has prevented peanut glut and propped up quota holders' income, critics say the success has come at the cost of stifled industry growth, market distortions and higher costs to consumers.

U.S. peanut consumption remains flat at 2.2 billion pounds a year, with the industry barely making enough gains in sales to offset losses to cheaper snacks like pretzels. In the meantime, unfettered California almond growers and Hawaii macadamia-nut growers are expanding to meet demand.

"We're captives of the program," complains Larry Pryor, the top purchasing agent for snack-food maker Lance Inc., in Charlotte, N.C. "We can only buy whats produced for quota, and we can't really import peanuts." Only 1.7 million pounds of imports–a tiny fraction of U.S. consumption–are allowed in each year. "That might keep Skippy running for one afternoon," says James Mack, lobbyist for the Peanut Butter and Nut Processors Association. "It's a virtual embargo."

The peanut program benefits only peanut farmers who have a "green card"–government issued proof of quota–to flash at peanut buyers and shellers. "That's their ticket to happiness," says Mr. Hintlian, the processor. It entitles the quota holders to the perks of the peanut program, and it guarantees them a so-called support price for their crop that is four times higher than the minimum given to farmers without quotas.

Under current law, card-carrying farmers qualify for a support price of $631.47 a ton, more than enough to cover their average costs of production and ensure a profit or $100 to $200 a ton. If they can't get higher prices, the government will buy their quota peanuts at that floor price. If their production costs rise, the government raises the floor price the next year.

As for the quota-less farmers, they are free to grow so-called additional peanuts, but only for the lower-priced export market for edible peanuts or the domestic market for peanut oil and meal. The result: Foreigners can buy U.S. peanuts a lot more cheaply than American consumers can.

If the growers of the additional peanuts fail to sell their crop, they must turn it over to the government at $149.75 per ton—too little for most quota-less farmers to make a go of it. So, too, must quota holders who produce peanuts in excess of their quotas.

The government has what amounts to a peanut-police to keep people from diverting additional peanuts from their overseas destinations and passing them off on the U.S.

market as more expensive quota peanuts. In Blakely, Ga., Lamar Lindsay of Opp, Alta., an inspector for a marketing association deputized to supervise the peanut program, is on the beat, hovering over the bagging and shipping of 300 tons of government-owned additionals at the Birdsong Inc. mill.

"If any of these peanuts move, the government wants to know about it," the burly Mr. Lindsay shouts over the roar of forklifts. "I've got to make sure they don't put [additional] peanuts on a load of quota peanuts."

States That Lose Out

Critics contend that Congress, in repeatedly reauthorizing the peanut program over the years, has legitimized cartels. The right to grow peanuts for the U.S. market is still limited to just those states and countries that were growing peanuts in 1949 when allotments were passed out. Thus, farmers in Maryland and Kansas don't grow peanuts today because none of their fathers and grandfathers grew them with other subsidized commodity prices.

The proposals have members of Congress from the Peanut Belt fuming. At a recent hearing, several lawmakers wondered why the administration would, as Republican R. William Dickinson of Alabama put it, "want to fool around with a true success

story." Democratic Rep. Charles Rose of North Carolina, chairman of the tobacco and peanuts subcommittee, surmised that there must be some Marxist policy-making "beavers" in the Agriculture Department trying to figure how to "screw it up."

For these lawmakers and their constituents, few issues are more important or emotional than protecting the status quo in peanuts. Thomas "Gene" Miller, a Republican Party leader who used to grow peanuts in Lumpkin, Ga., joined a 1961 effort to kill the peanut program outright. For his audacity, he says, he was "semi-ostracized" by his neighbors, and a suspicious fire burned his barn.

Peanuts are a cash crop a farmer can count on—and bank on. The peanut quota is collateral a farmer can get a loan with. The quota enhances land values and enriches the tax base in rural counties. It gives farmers a sense of financial security.

Says Rep. Bill Grant, a Florida Democrat who spent 20 years in banking before his election: "I forclosed on a lot of poor farmers growing corn and soybeans and just about everything else, but...I never foreclosed on a peanut farmer, never, never did."

a) What type of price support option (or combination of options) is used with peanuts?

b) Who is hurt from government involvement in the peanut market?

c) Who benefits from governement involvement in the peanut market?

d) Why are all but a tiny fraction of imports not allowed into the country?

e) Who is "grandfathered in" the peanut farming business?

f) How has the government created a cartel in peanut farming?

g) If you wanted to construct a new factory to produce peanut butter for American consumers, would you want to build this factory in the United States or Canada? Why?

b. Potential Essay Questions

1. What explains the long-run decline in farm incomes?

2. What accounts for the short-run fluctuations in farm prices and farm incomes?

3. What are the benefits and the costs of government involvement in agricultural markets? That is, who benefits and who hurts?

4. Explain, using supply and demand curves, the distributional consequences of four alternative methods of price supports.

V. ANSWERS

II. Mastery Test

1. d	6. a	11. a	16. c	21. b	26. a	31. d
2. a	7. b	12. a	17. b	22. c	27. b	32. a
3. d	8. c	13. d	18. a	23. d	28. d	33. a
4. a	9. d	14. a	19. d	24. a	29. c	34. b
5. b	10. b	15. d	20. d	25. c	30. d	35. c

III. Short Answer Questions and Problems

a. Short Answers

1.
   - a) cartel
   - b) agrifirms
   - c) parity price
   - d) acreage control program
   - e) price stabilization program
   - f) good/bad paradox
   - g) farm lobby

2. the Great Depression

3. price stabilization, price support

4. By limiting supply. Since there are so many farmers, this would be hard to arrange privately so government has established programs that limit production or hold the price high.

5. Price stabilization—program designed to eliminate short-run fluctuations in price but allowing prices to follow the long term trend.
   Price support—program that maintains price at a level higher than the trend of prices.

6. The general rule of political economy

7. legal and regulatory force, economic incentives to reduce output, subsidizing food prices consumers pay, buying the excess agricultural output

8. When a support price is introduced farmers already producing will benefit but more people will want to supply at the higher price. In order to prevent this from happening (which would make the surplus situation worse) only those farmers who were producing at the beginning of the support program are allowed to produce. Furthermore, they are only allowed to produce what they produced before the program went into effect. This is grandfathering-in existing suppliers.

9.
   - a) regulation
   - b) subsidies on sales to keep prices down
   - c) buying up surplus goods

10. farmers, taxpayers, consumers

11. many independent sellers who are price takers, many buyers, individual farmer' commodity is interchangeable with that of other farmers, prices vary with demand and supply conditions

12. Because of the inelastic demand and fluctuating supply, cartelization would likey have developed. Agricultural prices might be higher and agricultural production lower than they currently are. Profits would have been high. Farm workers would have demanded safe working conditions and limited hours. Pension plans would exist for farmers as they do in the manufacturing industry.

b. Problems

1 a)

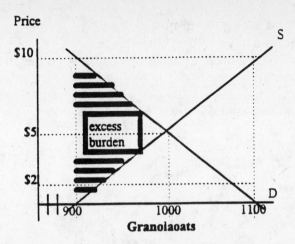

(ii) $(900 \times \$10) - (1000 \times \$5) = \$4000$

b)

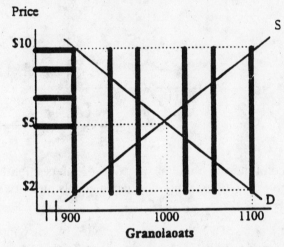

(i) $10 per bushel not produced times 200 bushels equals $2000

(ii) $5 per bushel times 900 bushels equals $4500

c)

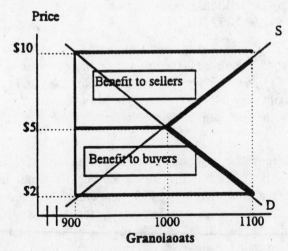

(ii) $(\$10 - \$2) \times 1100$ bushels $= \$8800$

d) Program c) at a cost of $8800 b) is $2000, a) is $1000

2. a) $6, 10 million bushels

   b) $4

   c) excess supply of 9 million bushels

   d) excess supply of 5 million bushels

   e) at $5 per bushel quantity demanded is greater than quantity supplied and price increases

IV. Challenge Problems and Potential Essay Questions

a. Challenge Problems

1. a) Refer to the figure below.

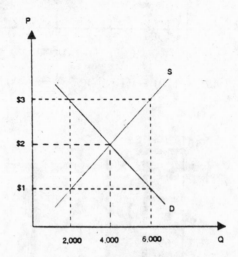

   b) Equilibrium is found at the point of intersection between the demand and supply curves; where quantity demanded equals quantity supplied. Price = $2. Quantity = 4,000. Revenue = $8,000.

   c) At a price of $3, the quantity supplied by dairy farmers will be 6,000. The price in the market will be $1 because when 6,000 litres of milk (in millions of litres) are supplied, consumers are only willing to pay $1. The cost to the government is $2 per litre, or $12,000 ($2 × 6,000). But, because the units of measurement for litres is in millions, then the cost to the government is really $12 billion ($12,000,000,000).

   d) (This is the third option discussed in the textbook—subsidizing the sale of the good.) The benefits are that consumers (demanders) get more milk at a lower price ($1) and suppliers get a higher price ($3) and can supply all they want. They're both very happy. The catch is that taxpayers foot the entire bill ($12 billion). That is the cost. This option of supporting farmers incomes is the most expensive from taxpayers' perspective.

   e) Impose the regulatory option. That is, impose regulation on existing milk producers to limit or shift the supply curve to the left until the price of $3 per litre is established. Do not allow any other producers to enter the market—including foreign imports. See Exhibit 4a, p. 371. However, keep in mind that this program, like all of them, will likely have some economic, social and political costs associated with it.

2. a) This is a combination of option #1 (regulatory force—government allotting production quotas which can be inherited) and option #4 (buying up the commodity). The government is mainly using regulatory controls (the quota system) to limit supply.

   b) Taxpayers and consumers in the form of higher taxes and higher prices for peanut products. It also stifles industry growth.

   c) Farmers and possibly politicians.

   d) To limit the supply of peanuts in order to prop up their prices.

   e) The peanut farmers at the time of the program's inception.

   f) The government has, in essence, created a cartel in the peanut producing business. This has been accomplished by government doling out acreage allotments (or quotas) to peanut farmers four decades ago. Those existing farmers were "grandfathered in." Any additional peanut farmers have been discouraged from entering the market. For example, quota holding farmers have their prices supported above the non-quota farmers' prices. The barrier to entry into this cartel is the ability to get a government quota.

   g) Canada, because peanuts can be purchased cheaper outside the United States.

b. **Potential Essay Questions**

The following answers are annotated—they only indicate the general idea behind the answer.

1. The significant technological advances associated with the production of agricultural products has increased the supply of agricultural commodities much more than the growth in population has increased their demand. This has put downward pressure on the prices and therefore farm incomes. (This is the good/bad paradox.) Moreover, the inelastic demand for farm commodities has resulted in a particularly acute decline in farm incomes (recall that a price decrease when demand is inelastic results in a decrease in total revenue—farmers' incomes). (See Exhibit 1, p. 364.)

2. Just as in the long run, the short run fluctuations are due to the good/bad paradox. There are significant changes in supply due to changing weather conditions, etc. Moreover, demand is even more inelastic in the short run. Hence, prices and therefore farm incomes fluctuate widely from year to year.

3. The benefit is more stable prices and farm incomes, as well as higher prices and farm incomes. Farmers benefit. The costs to society are the higher prices consumers must pay for food and fiber. Taxpayers are also hurt by having to pay higher taxes to support farm prices and incomes. The government also may have to deal with the surplus production in some manner. This too can be costly.

4. Four methods of price support are:

   a) Regulatory methods.
   b) Economic incentives to reduce supply.
   c) Subsidize the sale.
   d) Buying up and storing the good.

   The distributional effects are shown in Exhibit 4, p. 371. See also the accompanying discussion on pages 370-373.

Chapter 19   MICROECONOMICS, SOCIAL POLICY, AND ECONOMIC REASONING

I. CHAPTER AT A GLANCE

Rip this page out for quick and easy reference.

1. Economists views on social policy differ widely because (1) their objective economic analyses are colored by their subjective value judgements; (2) their interpretations of economic issues and of how political and social institutions work vary widely; and (3) their proposals are often based on various models that focus on different aspects of problems. (381)

    Analysis should still be as objective as possible.

2. Liberal and conservative economists agree on many policy prescriptions because they use the same models, which focus on incentives and individual choice. (383)

    There is more agreement among economists than most laypeople realize because they all use <u>cost/benefit analysis.</u>

3. Economists believe many regulations are formulated for political expediency and do not reflect cost/benefit considerations. (384)

    Keep regulating until marginal benefits of regulation just equal marginal costs.

4. Cost/benefit analysis is analysis in which one assigns a cost and benefit to alternatives, and draws a conclusion on the basis of those costs and benefits. (385)

    Unfortunately, not all costs and benefits (especially social and political) can be easily quantified.

5. Economists disagree about minimum wage policy because of differences in empirical estimates of direct and of side effects. (388)

    Much disagreement among economists stems from inconclusive empirical evidence (because it's imprecise there is room for differences in interpretation).

6. Applying economics is much more than muttering "supply and demand." Economics involves the <u>thoughtful</u> use of economic insights and empirical evidence. (390)

    This requires a careful consideration of all views: radical, liberal and conservative.

II. MASTERY TEST

1. Economists have differing views about what is appropriate social policy because

   a) they are experts in economics and have no specialized knowledge about social policy.
   b) policy proposals incorporate positive analyses and normative judgments.
   c) they fail to take into account empirical data.
   d) All of the above.

2. A Pareto optimal economic policy

   a) benefits no one.
   b) benefits some while hurting no one.
   c) benefits everyone, although not the same.
   d) benefits everyone equally.

3. The choice of an economic model to apply to a policy proposal

   a) reflects a value judgment by an economist.
   b) does not matter in the long run since economic models are objective representations of reality.
   c) does not affect the conclusions reached by economists.
   d) is a political decision not an economic one.

4. Economists' advice about public policy proposals

   a) incorporates cost/benefit analysis.
   b) stresses the importance of incentives and individual choice.
   c) focuses on the long-run effects of policies.
   d) All of the above.

5. Economists place quantitative values on the costs and benefits of everything

   a) because economics is a logical science which does not pertain to assessments regarding morality.
   b) because market prices are the true reflection of people's values.
   c) to estimate the relative worth of alternatives to improve decision making.
   d) because these are readily available and agreed upon.

6. Economists endorse public policy proposals when

   a) marginal benefits exceed marginal costs.
   b) total benefits exceed total costs.
   c) average benefits exceed average costs.
   d) marginal benefits are increasing and marginal costs are decreasing.

7. In modern economies, public policy options should be scrutinized by

   a) neoclassical analysis.
   b) radical analysis.
   c) institutional analysis
   d) All of the above.

8. Economists are in favour of a "count from 1 to 10" approach because

a) government decision making processes are too slow to deal with problems quickly.
b) politicians are too secure in their elected positions to react to the immediate interests of their constituencies.
c) hastily drawn short-run solutions often have negative long-run consequences.
d) a and b

9. Which of the following statements best reflects Pareto optimality and the real world?

a) Pareto optimal policies occur seldom, if ever, in the real world.
b) Pareto optimality is a positive economic concept which does not have relevance to normative issues.
c) A Pareto optimal short run policy is not likely to be Pareto optimal in the long-run.
d) By definition any policy proposal that receives political approval is Pareto optimal.

10. On what do liberal and conservative economists agree upon with respect to social policy?

a) Markets should supplant government provisioning of goods and services.
b) Unions are an inefficient intrusion in labour markets.
c) If something cannot be quantified then it has no role in an economic assessment of a policy.
d) Policy prescriptions need to incorporate individual choice and incentive structures.

11. Noted economist Herbert Stein argues that

a) it is cheaper to compensate traffic victims than it is to install and maintain traffic lights.
b) traffic lights just barely pass the cost/benefit test as a safety system.
c) economists tend to use empirical data selectively to support their views.
d) economists need to make more use of cost/benefit analysis.

12. Economists appear to look at the world cold heartedly because

a) economists objectively consider a policy's long-run incentive effects as well as short run effects.
b) they use cost/benefit analysis.
c) they make extensive use of statistics.
d) All of the above.

13. Which of the following statements is true concerning economic models?

a) Public choice economists use economic models that focus on individuals trying to use government to protect their monopoly power.
b) Neo-classical economists use economic models that focus on the tensions among the social classes and the exploitation of workers by capitalists.
c) Marxist economists use economic models that focus on the tendency of markets to achieve equilibrium.
d) Economic models do not involve value judgements because they are purely mathematical.
e) There is very little general agreement among the different economic models.

14. Which of the following statements is *false*?

   a) Empirical evidence takes all guess work out of policy analysis because it is so precise.
   b) Economists' suggestions for social policy are determined by subjective value judgements as well as by their objective economic analysis.
   c) Usually economists provide advice for policy makers whose values are similar to their own.
   d) Economists are trained to be as objective as they can be.
   e) Economists have had problems getting their ideas fairly expressed in public because economists' arguments are often long-run arguments and the press and the public usually focus on short-run effects.

15. Assume that 100 deaths are expected from the faulty design on an automobile and each death is valued at $600,000. Then:

   a) the manufacturer is expected to redesign the automobile at any cost.
   b) the manufacturer is expected to redesign the automobile if the cost is $55,000,000.
   c) the manufacturer is expected to redesign the automobile if the cost is greater than $60,000,000.
   d) the manufacturer would redesign the automobile if the marginal costs exceed the marginal benefits.
   e) economists would recommend the government impose a regulatory requirement on the manufacturer to avoid the deaths no matter what the cost.

16. Cost/benefit analysis:

   a) requires empirical estimates of costs and benefits to determine whether or not a given policy is worthwhile, even though personal values may influence that approach.
   b) requires only direct and explicit costs and benefits to be measured.
   c) implies that a decision should be undertaken if the costs exceed the benefits.
   d) should not be applied, according to economists, to the value of a person's life.
   e) implies that the optimal, or best amount of any activity is that quantity in which the marginal benefits exceed the marginal costs by the greatest amount.

17. The assessment that higher minimum wages increase unemployment in unskilled labor markets is

   a) general equilibrium analysis.
   b) normative economic analysis.
   c) Pareto optimal economic analysis.
   d) partial equilibrium analysis.

18. The minimum wage

   a) creates some unemployment for workers—the extent of unemployment is empirically difficult to estimate.
   b) is an efficient method of ensuring that everyone has a decent standard of living.
   c) will create more unemployment the more inelastic is the demand and supply of labor.
   d) is an example of a price ceiling.
   e) All of the above.

19. A policy proposal has been suggested that government fund a medical vaccination that costs $100 to eliminate the possibility of a medical syndrome that arises in 1 out of every 100,000 first year university students. The syndrome only affects college freshman and costs $10,000 to cure if it does occur. Should the policy proposal be instituted?

a) The marginal cost of $100 does not justify the marginal benefit of 10 cents.
b) The marginal benefit of $10,000 justifies the marginal cost of $100.
c) It depends upon the number of first year university students who take the test.
d) It should be instituted because marginal analysis is not appropriate for health issues.

20. A liberal economist would argue that when analyzing a minimum wage proposal

a) the focus should be on partial equilibrium analysis.
b) the focus should be on general equilibrium analysis.
c) the floor wage should be no higher than the competitive market equilibrium level.
d) that both a wage floor and a wage ceiling needs to be established.

21. A conservative economist may criticize a minimum wage proposal on the grounds

a) that general equilibrium costs exceed the partial equilibrium gains.
b) there will be a redistribution of income from higher wage earners to lower wage earners.
c) that it will create unemployment.
d) there will be an increase in government borrowing to finance the program.

22. General equilibrium analysis refers to the interactions between

a) all markets.
b) the government and the private sector.
c) buyers and sellers in a given market.
d) inflation and unemployment in the macroeconomy.

23. Low income housing projects in Canada create all but which of the following problems?

a) Once in a unit a family has an incentive to remain low income and retain the unit.
b) Landlords have no incentive to keep rents low because occupants always pay 30% of their income while the government pays the rest.
c) There will be no incentive to build cheaper housing outside the government provided housing.
d) There will be an excess supply of expensive units.

24. John Doe is a heavy drinker and a chain smoker. He has been advised that if he quits drinking he will reduce the risk of a fatal heart attack by 5% and if he quits smoking he will reduce his risk by 3%. He is willing to pay $2000 for treatment program to help him stop drinking but is unwilling to pay a similar fee to quit smoking. Assess his decision.

a) John is irrational because the implicit value of quitting smoking is higher than quitting drinking.
b) John is rational because the marginal benefit of treating his habits justifies the drinking treatment but the cost at the margin of treating his smoking habit exceeds the marginal benefit of doing so.
c) John implicitly values his life at more than $40,000 but at less than $66,667.
d) John explicitly values his life at $2000.

25. Along with the above (#24) information assume if John quits both smoking and drinking at the same time he reduces his risk of heart failure by 10%. John decides to spend $4000 on the treatment programs to rid himself of both habits. Assess his decision.

    a) He values his life at $40,000.
    b) He values his life at a minimum of $66,667.
    c) He values his life at more than $100,000.
    d) He places an explicit value of $4,000 on his life.

26. Social policy in the real world reflects

    a) emotion only.
    b) a balancing of cost/benefit analysis and special interest desires.
    c) special interest desires and political considerations only.
    d) None of the above.

27. Because economists see everything in a cost/benefit framework, they see that all but which of the following can occur?

    a) Well intentioned policies often are prevented by individual self-seeking activity
    b) Policies that have short term benefits may have long term costs
    c) Politicians act on different incentives apart from cost/benefit analysis.
    d) Politicains act on the basis of cost/benefit analysis alone.

III. SHORT ANSWER EXERCISES AND PROBLEMS

a. Short Answer Exercises

1. List three types of economic models that are used to support public policy choices.

2. In the design of social policy, what two characteristics do economists tend to agree should be incorporated?

3. Explain why liberal and conservative economists often agree in their views on social policy.

4. What is the typical economist's view of many regulations?

5. List the aspects of economic reasoning which become apparent from the reading of the text examples of the application of cost/benefit analysis.

6. Explain why economists disagree about whether the minimum wage should be raised.

7. Why does Professor Colander take issue with Thomas Carlisle's assessment of what it takes to be an economist?

b. Problems

1. Assume a major metropolitan hospital receives a $1,000,000 grant from the estate of a philanthropist for the expressed purpose of saving lives. You are hired as a consulting economist to identify the most cost effective way to allocate the grant money. Your empirical research has determined four projects warrant consideration for use of the funds: expanding helicopter life-flight capabilities, upgrading ambulance services, modernizing emergency room facilities, and expanding the pre natal and post natal educational unit.

   The table below describes the projected benefits (lives saved) from outlays of the grant money.

Lives Saved

Project Outlay	Life-flight capabilities	Ambulance services	Child care educational unit	Emergency room services
$250,000	10	5	4	6
$250,000	4	4	4	5
$250,000	2	3	3	2
$250,000	1	3	2	1

a) If the hospital were to allocate all of the money to a single project, which one would be selected if the goal is to save lives?

b) How should the hospital allocate the funds in order to save the greatest number of lives?

c) What real-world obstacle may prevent the allocation of funds as (b) suggests?

2. Given below is a model depicting a labour market and two sets of demand and supply curves. Use the model to respond to the questions regarding a minimum wage that follow.

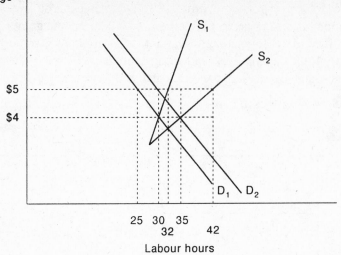

a) What is the equilibrium wage and quantity given D_1 and S_1? ...Given D_2 and S_2?

b) What is the impact on the market of a minimum wage of $5 per hour if D_1 and S_1 are the appropriate curves? ... If D_2 and S_2 are the appropriate curves?

c) Which scenario creates more unemployment in the labour market, D_1 and S_1 or D_2 and S_2, with the minimum wage at $5 per hour?

What is the difference?

d) Which set of curves, D_1 and S_1 or D_2 and S_2 is more elastic? Explain

IV. CHALLENGE PROBLEMS AND POTENTIAL ESSAY QUESTIONS

a. Challenge Problems

1. Assume economists have undertaken cost/benefit analysis of a problem and are unanimously in favour of a particular policy proposal over all other proposals. Why might this policy recommendation not be enacted as policy?

2. Suppose an automobile producer discovers that a faulty design or part may result in a low probability of explosion when the vehicle is struck from a particular angle. If the verhicle does explode on impact then the passengers may be seriously injured or killed. Under what circumstances could the manufacturer use cost/benefit analysis to conclude not to recall this model for repairs? Under what circumstances would the manufacturer conclude that the vehicle should be recalled?

3. Why does it often appear to the lay public that economists never agree on social policy?

4. Why do politicians sometimes wish for a one-armed economist?

b. Potential Essay Questions

1. Discuss three reasons why economists sometimes differ in their views on social policy.

2. What is cost/benefit analysis? How is this related to why economists often find themselves united with one another but at odds with the general public?

3. How can the presence of the three invisible forces in all real-world economies and economists' use of benefit/cost analysis help explain the disagreement among economists concerning what is considered "appropriate" social policy? Even if economists all agreed upon what is "appropriate" policy, why might it not become policy?

V. ANSWERS

II. Mastery Test

1. b	6. a	11. c	16. a	21. c	26. b
2. b	7. d	12. a	17. d	22. a	27. d
3. a	8. c	13. a	18. a	23. d	
4. a	9. a	14. a	19. a	24. c	
5. c	10. d	15. b	20. b	25. b	

III. Short Answer Exercises and Potential Essay Questions

a. Short Answer Exercises

1. neo-classical, Marxian, public choice

2. long run goals and individualized incentive structures

3. Liberal and conservative economists agree on many policy prescriptions because they use the same models, which focus on incentives and individual choice.

4. Economists believe many regulations are formulated for political expediency and do not reflect cost/benefit considerations.

5. Costs and benefits are an underlying determinant in making assessments about policy proposals;
   Economists focus on competitive pressures;
   Economists do not always favour the market solution;
   Economists recognize all of the invisible forces;
   Economists use empirical evidence.

6. Economists disagree about minimum wage policy because of differences in empirical estimates of both direct and side effects.

7. Repeating demand and supply is not how economists resolve all problems that arise; they integrate economic insights and empirical evidence in their analysis of problems and solutions.

b. Problems

1. a) life-flight helicopters—17 lives saved projected
   b) 26 lives saved: $250,000 to helicopter, 10 lives; $250,000 to ambulance services, 5 lives; $500,000 to emergency room services, 11 lives.
   c) Pressure from the child care staff not to be left out of the funding or any number of other political influences may make it difficult to implement funding allocations based solely on costs and benefits at the margin.

2. a) $D_1 S_1$ – Wage $4, Quantity = 30 labour hours; $D_2 S_2$ – Wage = $4, Quantity = 35 labour hours
   b) Quantity supplied exceeds quantity demanded by 7 labour hours;
      Quantity supplied exceeds quantity demanded by 12 labour hours
   c) $D_1 S_1$—at the minimum wage the quantity demanded is 2 labour hours less than the quantity demanded at the equilibriuim wage;
      $D_2 S_2$—at the minimum wage the quantity demanded is 7 labour hours less than the quantity demanded at the equilibrium wage.
   d) $D_2 S_2$—the relative change in the quantity demanded for a given percentage in price is greater with $D_2 S_2$ than with $D_1 S_1$.

IV. Challenge Problems and Potential Essay Questions

a. Challenge Problems

1. Because the policy-makers (e.g, politicians) may weigh the non-quantifiable social and political costs and benefits of the policy recommendation differently than did the economists. They may have a tendency to be "short-sighted"—to focus more on the short run rather than the long run effects. The policy makers, because they may place more weight on the short-run political or social benefits and costs of a policy, may decide that the social and political costs outweigh any other benefits. What makes sense from an economic perspective may not be deemed politically, or socially acceptable.

2. The manufacturer could conclude that it may be cheaper to pay damages to those injured or killed in auto accidents than incur the costs of repairing the vehicles. Most of us would find this highly unethical. However, once in awhile there are reports of this kind of business behaviour. On the other hand, the manufacturer may well decide that the long-run benefit of preserving the reputation of the company, and its ethical standards, outweigh the high cost of recalling and repairing the cars or trucks. There may be a difference in terms of how forward-looking the manufacturer is; or how long they believe the memory of consumers to be. Some companies think in terms of the short-term while others think long-run. When does self-interest end and social or moral obligation begin? Ethical standards differ among people because they weigh the benefits and costs of "moral" behaviour differently.

3. Economists often disagree on social policy because of their differing subjective value judgements, because of imprecise empirical evidence and because they focus on different aspects of a policy or problem. However, economists agree upon more than the lay public often realizes. Most people usually observe or recall the disagreements reported in the media because it is the disagreements which are often relevant; or because they sell better. Moreover, most often the questions economists are asked to address are policy questions which are normative in nature. Answers to these types of questions inevitably require some subjective value judgements pertaining to the non-quantifiable benefits and costs associated with the policy. Equally reasonable and well-intentioned economists can be expected to weigh these benefits and costs differently—especially if they focus on different aspects of the policy.

4. Economists are trained to weigh both the benefits and the costs associated with any policy or course of action. On the one hand, there are the benefits. On the other hand, the costs. Politicians only want to hear the benefits. But, unfortunately, "there ain't no such thing as a free lunch."

b. Potential Essay Questions

The following answers are annotated—they only indicate the general idea behind the answer.

1. Economists views on social policy differ widely because (1) their objective economic analyses are colored by their subjective value judgements; (2) their interpretations of economic issues and of how political and social institutions work vary widely; and (3) their proposals are often based on various models that focus on different aspects of problems.

2. Cost/benefit analysis is analysis in which one assigns costs and benefits to alternatives, and draws a conclusion on the basis of those costs and benefits. Note that it is marginal costs and marginal benefits which are relevant. Economists try to quantify those costs and benefits—to use empirical evidence to help reach a conclusion. The general public often does not.

3. The three invisible forces are the invisible hand (economic forces), the invisible handshake (social forces), and the invisible foot (political forces). Policy-makers take into consideration the economic, social and political consequences associated with a policy. Not all the costs and benefits associated with a particular policy are quantifiable with respect to each of those three invisible forces. This leaves some room for subjective value judgements with respect to what the benefits and costs of a policy are. Moreover, empirical evidence is not exact. There is also some room for focusing on different aspects of a problem. Finally, if the policy is undertaken in a political environment, as is usually the case, then political considerations may take precedence over the social and economic considerations.

Chapter 20   ECONOMICS AND THE ENVIRONMENT

I. CHAPTER AT A GLANCE

Rip this page out for quick and easy reference.

1. **Four ways in which economists' approach to environmental problems differs from noneconomists' approach include: (1) their understanding of the problem; (2) their opposition to explicit regulation; (3) their dubiousness about voluntary solutions, and (4) their methods for paying. (393)**

    There's no fundamental difference in terms of beliefs or concerns about the environment. The difference is in approach.

2. **Correlation does not necessarily imply causation. (393)**

    Just because 2 things occur together does not necessarily imply causation.

3. **Economists are likely to oppose direct regulation because it does not achieve the desired end as effectively and as fairly as possible. (399)**

    Economists favour market incentive programs (a program that makes the price of the good reflect the negative externality).

4. **If a policy isn't optimal, resources are being wasted because the savings from reduction of expenditures on a program will be worth more than the gains that will be lost from reducing the program. (400)**

    The optimal level of pollution control (or any policy) is that amount at which the marginal social benefits (MSB) equal the marginal social costs (MSC).

    If MSB > MSC ⇒ Do more

    If MSB < MSC ⇒ Do less

5. **Economists believe that a small number of free riders will undermine the social consciousness of many in the society and that eventually a voluntary policy will fail. (401)**

    Economists are skeptical of voluntary solutions.

6. **If a program requires people to pay a price that reflects the cost of an externality, it will be in their interest to change their behaviour until marginal social benefits equal marginal social costs. (402)**

    So, economists favour policies that make the price people pay reflect the cost of the externality, as opposed to direct regulation or voluntary conservation.

7. **Economists' reasoning involves a general approach to all problems in which a cost/benefit analysis is taken and the program with the least cost is chosen. (409)**

    Economists search for optimal solutions.

II. MASTERY TEST

1. When a change in one data point causes another data point to change, then the data points are

   a) correlated.
   b) causally related.
   c) corroborated.
   d) not necessarily related.

2. Global warming statistics indicate

   a) an increase in temperature during the 20th century.
   b) temperature will continue to rise into the next century.
   c) fossil fuel use is responsible for the temperature change.
   d) All of thr above.

3. The interpretation of statistical evidence is

   a) unambiguous because it is merely a collection of data.
   b) influenced by one's normative stand on any given issue.
   c) ambiguous in the hands of politicians but unambiguous in the hands of scientists.
   d) largely irrelevant to the study of social behaviours.

4. Concern that resources will be depleted assumes that

   a) there will be new discoveries of proven resources.
   b) conservation efforts will increase.
   c) technology will remain the same.
   d) the price of the resource will increase.

5. If a shortage of resources is expected in the future then

   a) there will be a surplus now.
   b) the price of those resources will go up now causing people to conserve.
   c) the price of those resources will go down causing people to be more wasteful.
   d) expectations will not affect market price.

6. Economists contend a natural resource is not being exhausted if

   a) its real price is decreasing.
   b) its real price is increasing.
   c) the rate of resource consumption is declining.
   d) proven reserves are unknown.

7. Economists believe the data regarding proven reserves for a resource is misleading because

   a) of the markets ability to provide more of a resource at a lower price over time.
   b) proven reserves reflect current technology and prices.
   c) it is only an estimate of the ability of the development of new technology to access future reserves.
   d) it assumes that prices will increase in the future making it more costly to search and find more reserves.

8. How does the marketplace serve to reduce the concern that the world is running out of resources?

    a) Fear of resource exhaustion reduces demand, decreases resource prices, and stimulates innovation.
    b) The marketplace provides incentive structures which guarantee that if a profit can be made a resource will be forthcoming.
    c) Supply reductions cause higher prices, substitution on the part of buyers, and increased incentive for sellers to find the resource or an alternative.
    d) The marketplace has always provided members of society with an ever improving quality of life.

9. Economists believe direct regulation over the occurrence of negative externalities

    a) is inefficient.
    b) is efficient.
    c) improves market performance.
    d) is justified.

10. If the current price of a resource is steady or falling

    a) it indicates the market has failed to take into account the availability of proven reserves.
    b) future shortages are likely as demand decreases today in anticipation of inadequate future reserves.
    c) the marketplace suggests there is little current concern regarding future resource availability.
    d) no prediction can be made regarding the status of proven reserves or future reserve availability.

11. The problem with direct regulation from an economists point of view is that

    a) it forces consumers to equate the marginal costs of conservation with the marginal benefits.
    b) it results in too much being produced.
    c) it doesn't result in those producers who can reduce pollution at the lowest cost, making the largest adjustment.
    d) it does not allow for voluntary reduction of production.

12. Economists consider direct regulation to deal with economic problems inefficient because

    a) they believe market incentive programs can accomplish the same goals at less cost.
    b) the marketplace will resolve any problem in the long run without government policy.
    c) sellers self-regulate voluntarily in the short run more quickly than government can impose regulations.
    d) the invisible foot has no economic role to play in the economy.

13. The market mechanism to deal with shortages is

    a) a decrease in demand to conserve resources and encourage conservation.
    b) a decrease in price to stimulate innovation and supply increase.
    c) government subsidy to stimulate research and development of alternative resources.
    d) an increase in price to encourage conservation in use and incentives to increase production.

14. A tax incentive program initiated to push the costs of a negative externality onto those responsible for it

   a) increases the market price of the good creating the externality.
   b) generally is absorbed by the seller without affecting the price buyers pay.
   c) is an example of direct regulation.
   d) decreases market quantity but does not affect the market price.

15. A tax on gasoline to encourage conservation is considered fair by economists because

   a) it places a larger burden on the income of lower income people than it does on the income of higher income people.
   b) lower income people have access to public transportation and can avoid the tax while higher income people typically have to drive and have to pay the tax.
   c) the people who choose to buy less gasoline pay less tax than do those who choose to buy more.
   d) economists are generally prosperous and their policy proposals reflect their value structures.

16. From an economic perspective an efficient solution to the problem of pollution

   a) is one that generates the largest net social benefit.
   b) pushes the costs onto sellers without increasing prices to buyers.
   c) reaches its goal with the lowest cost possible in resources.
   d) cannot be achieved without direct regulation.

17. An optimal level of pollution control occurs when the

   a) total benefits exceed the total costs of control.
   b) marginal benefit exceeds marginal cost.
   c) level of pollution is not measurable.
   d) marginal cost equals the marginal benefit.

18. If a negative externality occurs from a market activity, the marginal social cost curve

   a) is identical to the marginal cost curve.
   b) lies above the marginal cost curve.
   c) lies below the marginal cost curve.
   d) reflects the firm's private costs of production.

19. Economists who have environmental concerns are likely to

   a) support the same policy recommendations as environmentalists without an economics background.
   b) endorse policies that rely on voluntary solutions so as to not distort marketplace decision making.
   c) propose policies that give polluters an economic incentive to reduce undesirable behaviour.
   d) reject taxation of polluters as a remedy.

20. A textile mill is located on a river that is also an important source of fish—food for people in the area. The textile mill is dumping waste in the stream which is harming the fish stock. Suppose the government grants the fishermen the right to a pollution free river. This right is marketable.

   a) The fishermen would never sell this right and the textile mill would be forced to clean up.
   b) A tax on the fish caught would now be necessary to ensure an efficient solution to the pollution problem.
   c) The textile mill would be willing to pay anything to get the right from the fishermen.
   d) The textile mill will not dump its wastes if the fishermen value the stream more than the textile mill values the pollution right.

21. Suppose all factories are issued the same number of tradeable permits for pollution. The equilibrium price of each pollution certificate is $100 per ton of emissions. Factory A has a marginal cost of $200 per ton to reduce emissions while factory B faces a marginal cost of $100 to reduce emissions. If both factory managers seek to maximize profit; then

   a) Factory A will sell pollution rights to factory B.
   b) Factory B will sell pollution rights to factory A.
   c) There will be no incentive for either factory to either buy or sell the right to pollute.
   d) Both firms will try to buy up as many permits as they possibly can.

22. An optimal corrective tax on polluters would

   a) force them to equate MSC and MSB.
   b) not generate revenue.
   c) reduce pollution to zero.
   d) result in an inefficient amount of pollution reduction.

23. Economists are dubious of voluntary solutions to problems because

   a) they have no faith in the ability of people to work together for the common good.
   b) it is not a market-based approach.
   c) the incentive for people to become free riders is so great voluntary solutions fail.
   d) philosophically it is a group effort while economists favour individual incentive structures.

24. NIMBY is an acronym which infers

   a) a community should not have the right to give political expression to their collectivized self-interest.
   b) that in the political marketplace the interests of prosperous communities is superior to the interests of less prosperous communities.
   c) the idea of regulating toxic and solid wastes is popular unless one's own town is chosen as a collection site.
   d) a, b, and c

25. If price in the marketplace is flexible then a shortage

   a) cannot exist in the long run.
   b) can be eliminated by government subsidy.
   c) can be eliminated by a corrective tax.
   d) is corrected by an increase or decrease in supply.

26. Opportunity costs measure

   a) the explict costs of an activity.
   b) the implicit costs of an activity.
   c) the external costs of an activity.
   d) the cost to government per unit of reducing pollution to the optimal amount.

27. The free rider problem occurs when

   a) the marginal benefit of pollution control exceeds the marginal cost of controlling it.
   b) direct regulation of pollution is used instead of voluntary controls.
   c) government replaces voluntary controls with market incentive programs.
   d) people who do not pay get the same benefit as those who do pay.

28. In a community with a volunteer fire department, there will likely be fewer resources devoted to fire protection than would be socially optimal because of

   a) the free rider problem.
   b) the NIMBY problem.
   c) the problem of relative externalities.
   d) the tax problem.

29. To solve the externality problem of trash generation, an economist would suggest

   a) government regulation of the externality.
   b) a reduction in the number of landfill sites.
   c) raising the private costs so MPC = MSC.
   d) introduce a program of mandatory sorting of trash into wet and dry.

30. Economists reaction to the theory of global warming is generally one of

   a) rejection of the hypothesis that the earth is warming up.
   b) acceptance of the theory's cause and effect assessment.
   c) acceptance of the correlation of the theory's variables but with a need for more corroboration.
   d) rejection of the corroboration of the evidence because the variables are not correlated.

31. Why may an economist be willing to accept the global warming theory and offer policy proposals to deal with it.

   a) The theory has been corroborated.
   b) There is no ambiguity in the data reflecting a trend toward global warming and the need to deal with it.
   c) Policy may need to be enacted to forestall possible problems before conclusive evidence verifies the theory.
   d) Economists have a professional incentive to practice the art of economics to enhance their reputations.

32. An optimal environmental policy

   a) has the minimum total cost to society.
   b) has the maximum total benefit to society.
   c) eliminates all environmental problems.
   d) accomplishes environment goals efficiently.

33. A tax on trash alleviates the solid waste problem by

a) encouraging recycling.
b) creating awareness of the problem and encouraging voluntary changes in consumption behaviour.
c) discouraging the creation of trash.
d) providing a source of revenues to subsidize the creation of more waste collection centers.

34. A marketable certificate program is a conservation incentive policy which

a) provides income tax credits to households and firms that recycle.
b) provides subsidies to firms that enter into a formal contract with the government to reduce pollution.
c) establishes property rights over a resource, or even pollution, which can be traded in markets.
d) imposes taxes on firms which pollute the air, water, and other public resources for which established markets do not exist.

35. The economic approach to environmental issues

a) recognizes that the business community has been wrongly vilified by environmentalists.
b) seeks to correct the propaganda being espoused by elementary and secondary educators.
c) contends that environmentalists are bent on the destruction of the market economy.
d) suggests an alternative which may be more efficient and effective than the regulatory approach.

III. SHORT ANSWER EXERCISES AND PROBLEMS

a. Short Answer Exercises

1. Provide terms for the following expressions.

a) more costly than necessary

b) costs of foregone resources

c) the joint movement of data points

d) resource reserves that have been discovered and documented to date

e) the result of a decision that is not taken into account by the decision maker

f) a policy whose marginal cost equals its marginal benefit

2. What is the global warming theory?

3. List four ways economists differ from non-economists in their approach to pollution problems.

4. What does the acronym NIMBY stand for?

5. Describe two concerns economists have with statistics that state the world is running out of resources.

6. Name two incentive-based policies meant to reduce the creation of negative externalities in the marketplace?

7. Explain why economists often oppose mandatory regulation of a good which has a negative externality associated with its production and/or consumption. What alternative would an economist likely favour?

8. What is the optimal amount of pollution control?

9. Discuss economists' concerns with voluntary programs.

10. Explain why economists believe that long-term solutions to environmental problems involve making people pay a price that reflects the cost of an externality.

b. Problems

1. The table below is a hypothetical statement of the costs and benefits associated with pollution reduction in an economy. Complete the table and respond to the questions that follow.

Pollution reduction	Social benefit	Marginal social benefit	Marginal social cost	Social cost
10%	$100 billion			$10 billion
20%	$188 billion			$35 billion
30%	$255 billion			$65 billion
40%	$305 billion			$100 billion
50%	$350 billion			$143 billion
60%	$380 billion			$193 billion
70%	$400 billion			$259 billion
80%	$405 billion			$359 billion
90%	$408 billion			$504 billion

a) Use marginal analysis to determine an optimal level of pollution.

b) On the graph below, model the marginal social costs and marginal social benefits depicted in the table above.

c) Assume that market-based incentive policies have stimulated breakthroughs in pollution control technologies. Illustrate on the above model the effect of efficiency improvement in pollution reduction and the impact on the optimal level of pollution.

2. Assume one dollar of non measured costs are created for every litre of gas that is burned in an internal combustion engine. Illustrate on the model below the impact of a corrective tax internalizing the negative externality.

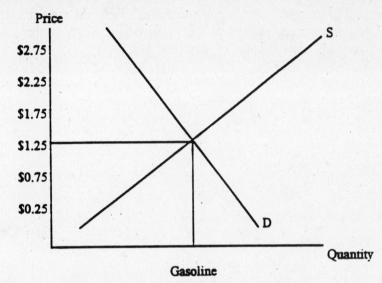

What happens to the market price and quantity of gasoline?

IV. CHALLENGE PROBLEMS AND POTENTIAL ESSAY QUESTIONS

a. Challenge Problems

1. The supply (marginal private cost), marginal social cost and demand (marginal social benefit) for gasoline are represented in the figure below. Suppose there are no restrictions on the purchase and consumption of gasoline.

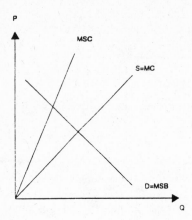

a) Assuming perfect competition, what is the market equilibrium price and quantity? Indicate this in the figure above.

b) Is there an external cost or benefit associated with gasoline? How do you know by looking at the figure above? What is that external cost or benefit associated with gas?

c) What is the socially efficient (optimal) quantity and price? Indicate this in the figure above.

d) Has the government taxed or subsidized gas in order to internalize the external cost or benefit associated with its consumption? What should the tax or subsidy be equal to in the figure above to arrive at the socially efficient quantity?

2. A small city located by a lake has been dumping its raw sewage into the lake. This has created a public outcry by those citizens who like to fish, swim and water-ski in the lake. The city council has surveyed the community and has estimated the benefits associated with different levels of pollution control. These benefits, as well as the costs of associated pollution control efforts are shown in the table below. What is the optimal level of pollution control? Will there be some pollution of the lake?

Units of Pollution Control	Total Benefits	Total Costs
1	$200,000	$ 40,000
2	$275,000	$ 75,000
3	$330,000	$110,000
4	$375,000	$145,000
5	$410,000	$180,000
6	$435,000	$215,000

3. Environmentalists are concerned about deforestation in Canada. Some of these environmentalists have advocated government regulating the number of trees which can be cut down. As an economic advisor to the Department of Natural Resources, you are asked to comment on this at a public forum. What do you say?

b. **Potential Essay Questions**

1. Scarcity of resources and prophets of doom have been around a long time. Why do economists generally believe that they are often overstating their case?

2. Many empirical studies suggest relative scarcity declining over time. How can scarcity decline?

3. Generally, what is the difference between environmentalists and economists?

4. What is "economic reasoning" as it is applied to real world issues and policies?

V. ANSWERS

II. Mastery Test

1. b	6. a	11. c	16. a	21. b	26. b	31. c
2. a	7. b	12. a	17. d	22. a	27. d	32. d
3. b	8. c	13. d	18. b	23. c	28. a	33. c
4. c	9. a	14. a	19. c	24. c	29. c	34. c
5. b	10. c	15. c	20. d	25. a	30. c	35. d

a. **Short Answer Exercises**

1. a) inefficient
    b) opportunity cost
    c) correlation
    d) proven reserves
    e) externality
    f) optimal policy

2. Theory that argues the earth is going through a period of warming due to the rise in carbon dioxide gases as the result of burning fossil fuels.

3. a) their understanding of the problem
    b) prefer incentive-based solutions
    c) do not have faith in voluntary solutions
    d) method of paying for the correction of externalities

4. not in my back yard

5. Statistics refer to proven reserves not the actual amount of the resource in existence. Resource use depends upon prices. Increased scarcity of resources increases its price and reduces its consumption.

6. tax incentive program
    marketable certificate program

7. Economists are likely to oppose direct regulation because it does not achieve the desired end as effectively (it does not get people to equate the marginal costs with the marginal benefits) and as fairly as possible. Economists would likely favour some type of a market incentive program (a program that makes the price of the good or service reflect the negative externality).

8. The optimal quantity of pollution control is that quantity in which the marginal social benefits (MSB) just equal the marginal social costs (MSC) of pollution control. If the MSB > MSC then keep doing it—its worth it; and vice versa.

9. Economists believe that a small number of free riders will undermine the social consciousness of many in the society and that eventually a voluntary policy will fail.

10. In most environmental issues, it is relatively easy to conclude that there is a negative externality. Thus, economists often agree with environmentalists that there is a social environmental problem that the current market structure doesn't solve. But the answer to that problem for an economist is seldom direct regulation nor is it voluntary conservation. Rather the economist's answer is to *find a program that makes the price people pay reflect the cost of the externality*. If a program requires people to pay a price that reflects the cost of an externality, it will be in their self-interest to change their behaviour until marginal social benefits equal marginal social costs.

b. Problems

1. a)

Pollution reduction	Social benefit	Marginal social benefit	Marginal social cost	Social cost
10%	$100 billion	$100 billion	$10 billion	$10 billion
20%	$188 billion	$88 billion	$25 billion	$35 billion
30%	$255 billion	$67 billion	$30 billion	$65 billion
40%	$305 billion	$50 billion	$35 billion	$100 billion
50%	$350 billion	$45 billion	$43 billion	$143 billion
60%	$380 billion	$30 billion	$50 billion	$193 billion
70%	$400 billion	$20 billion	$66 billion	$259 billion
80%	$405 billion	$5 billion	$100 billion	$359 billion
90%	$408 billion	$3 billion	$145 billion	$504 billion

At 50% pollution reduction MSC of pollution reduction comes closest to being equal to the MSB of pollution reduction without MSC exceeding MSB. Consequently, the optimal level of pollution would be approximately 50%.

b)

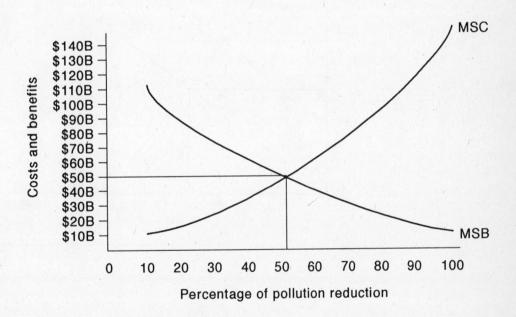

c)

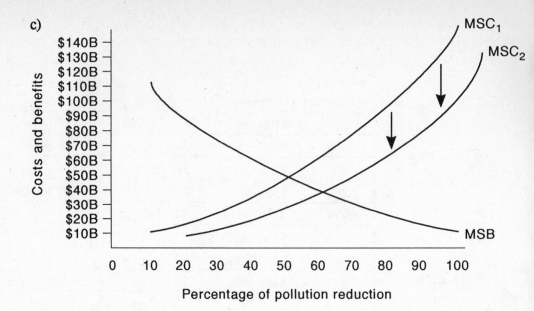

Percentage of pollution reduction

The incentive structure may serve to reduce the costs of pollution reduction which in turn increases the optimal level of pollution reduction.

2.

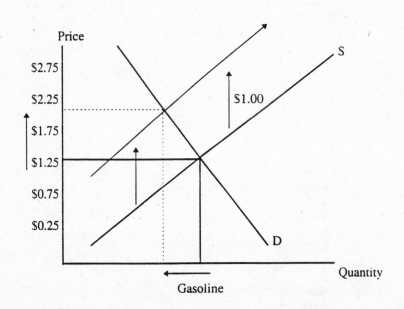

IV. Challenge Problems and Potential Essay Questions

a. Challenge Problems

1. Refer to the figure below.

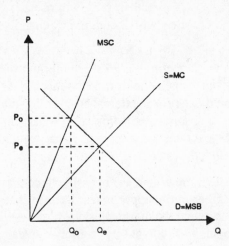

a) P_e and Q_e.

b) There is an external cost associated with the consumption of gasoline. We know this because the marginal social costs (MSC) is greater than the private marginal costs (S). The external cost associated with the consumption of gas is air pollution (it has been estimated that cars and trucks account for 30 percent of the nation's carbon dioxide emissions—a major cause of acid rain and the greenhouse effect).

c) P_o and Q_o because this is the quantity in which the marginal social benefits of consumption just equal the marginal social costs of production.

d) Government has taxed gasoline at the pump to internalize the external cost. This could be accomplished by imposing a tax equal to P_o minus P_e (just enough to increase the price consumers must pay per litre to reduce consumption down to Q_o).

2. See the table below. The optimal level of pollution control is 5 units, because this is the quantity of pollution control in which the marginal social benefits of the control just equals its marginal social costs. There will still be some pollution of the lake as evidenced by the increased marginal benefits associated with the 6th unit of pollution control—but that amount of pollution control is not worth it to the community given the marginal cost of the 6th unit of pollution control.

Units of Pollution Control	Total Benefits	Total Costs	Marginal Benefits	Marginal Costs
1	$200,000	$ 40,000	$200,000	$40,000
2	$275,000	$ 75,000	$ 75,000	$35,000
3	$330,000	$110,000	$ 55,000	$35,000
4	$375,000	$145,000	$ 45,000	$35,000
5	$410,000	$180,000	$ 35,000	$35,000
6	$435,000	$215,000	$ 25,000	$35,000

3. First, assuming a perfectly competitive market for lumber (which may not be the case), one must look carefully at the evidence to see if the marginal social benefits equal the marginal social costs at the current quantity of trees harvested in the timber industry. If they are equal then there is not a problem. After all, trees are a renewable resource. If they become more scarce then their price will rise and people will voluntarily conserve. Moreover, a higher price will increase the quantity supplied—more trees will be planted.

    However, if at the competitive market equilibrium quantity the marginal social costs exceed the marginal social benefits then too many trees are being cut down. That is, an external cost would exist. That external cost is often cited as the reduced ability of trees to clean the air—to absorb carbon dioxide. If we assume the external cost is sufficiently large to warrant government action then direct regulation by government often is not the most efficient approach.

    Instead, a typically more efficient proposal is to continue to impose a higher tax on the production of lumber until supply is restricted to that quantity in which the marginal social benefits just equal the marginal social costs. At the resulting higher market price for lumber people will voluntarily conserve trees. Another real possibility is to subsidize people or communities to plant more trees to absorb carbon dioxide (and to continue to require the timber industry to plant a new tree to replace each one cut down). This course of action may preclude the necessity to tax the timber industry.

b. Potential Essay Questions

The following answers are annotated—they only indicate the general idea behind the answer.

1. Prophets of doom do not take into account that there is a built-in market reaction to scarcity. Scarcity of anything increases its price. This causes the quantity demanded to fall (people voluntarily conserve) and the quantity supplied to rise (through such action as investment in new technologies that replace the resource with another resource). This eliminates the scacity over time. This is not to say that sometimes there isn't cause for concern.

2. Available resources depend on technology—and if technology increases faster than resources are used, relative scarcity declines.

3. There's no fundamental difference between environmentalists and economists in terms of beliefs or concerns about the environment. What difference there is involves initial approach. An environmental economist's initial thoughts are likely to focus on market incentives, while an environmentalist untrained in economics is likely to distrust the market's effectiveness and therefore favour regulatory approaches.

4. Economic reasoning can be applied to all problems and it involves a general approach in which a cost/benefit analysis is undertaken and the program to address the problem with the least cost is chosen (which could mean no program at all if the marginal costs of the least-cost program exceed its marginal benefits).

Chapter 21   GROWTH AND THE MICROECONOMICS OF DEVELOPING COUNTRIES

I. CHAPTER AT A GLANCE

Rip this page out for quick and easy reference.

1. **Seventy-five percent of the world's population lives in developing countries, with average per capita income of around $700 per year. (413)**

    Be careful in judging a Society by its income alone. Some developing countries may have cultures preferable to ours. Ideally, growth would occur without destroying the culture.

2. **The "dual economy" refers to the tendency of developing countries to have two somewhat unrelated economies—one an internationally-based economy, the other a traditional, often nonmarket, economy. (417)**

    There is a large discrepancy between the rich and the poor as a consequence. The challenge is to "modernize" the traditional sector.

3. **Six microeconomic problems facing developing countries are: (418)**

    1. Political instability.
    2. Corruption.
    3. Lack of appropriate institutions.
    4. Lack of investment.
    5. Inappropriate education.
    6. Overpopulation.

    *Know why these are problems!

    *The opposite constitutes the ingredients for growth—remember them!

4. **When rights to conduct business are controlled and allocated by the government, economic development can be hindered. (420)**

    Bribery, graft and corruption are a way of life in most developing countries. This increases the costs of investment and therefore less economic activity is undertaken and growth is hindered.

5. **With per capita incomes of as low as $300 per year, poor people in developing countries don't have a lot left over to put into savings. (422)**

    Savings (funds) are needed for investment. Without investment there's no growth.

---

6. **Four debates about strategies for growth are: (426)**

    1. Balanced vs. unbalanced growth.
    2. Agriculture vs. industry.
    3. Infrastructure vs. directly productive investment.
    4. Export-led growth vs. import substitution.

    Know these!

    Think about and list the ingredients for growth (e.g. must have political stability, investment in capital accumulation...)

7. **Economic development is a complicated problem because it is entwined with cultural and social issues. (427)**

    There's no easy solution. Only by having a complete sense of a country, its history, culture and norms can one decide whether it's the right time and place for this or that policy—the art of economics!

II. MASTERY TEST

1. The costs to developing countries of choosing not to grow would include all but which of the following?

   a) being overrun by the expansionary developed market societies.
   b) changed agricultural patterns.
   c) obliteration of culture.
   d) reduction in poverty.

2. When we compare incomes in developing countries with those in developed countries using _____ we find income differences that are _____.

   a) consumer price index; even more unequal.
   b) foreign exchange index; more equal.
   c) purchasing power parity; cut in half.
   d) purchasing power parity; double.

3. In a dual economy,

   a) one segment of the economy is traditional and nonmarket, the other is more like a developed market economy.
   b) one segment of the market is agricultural and the other is traditional.
   c) one segment of the market is market oriented, the other is wealthy and autocratic.
   d) one segment is interested in cultural events, the other is more interested in traditional events.

4. A country is defined as developing based on

   a) per capita GDP.   b) population growth rates.
   c) literacy rates.   d) a, b, and c

5. Which of the following has not made the transition out of the status of low income?

   a) Asian tigers
   b) oil producing/exporting countries
   c) sub-Saharan countries
   d) b and c

6. Which of the following contribute to political instability in developing countries?

   a) cultural and population homogeneity.
   b) disorderly transitions of governmental authority.
   c) international investment in the domestic economy contributing to foreign ownership of assets.
   d) a, b, and c

7. Which of the following statements about a highly inequitable distribution of income is not accurate?

   a) It contributes to political instability.
   b) It adversely affects domestic saving.
   c) It is typical under Marxist regimes.
   d) It lends support for radical change.

8. Political instability is an impediment to growth because it

   a) discourages saving by the wealthy.
   b) discourages agricultural activity.
   c) discourages foreign and domestic investment.
   d) encourages population growth.

9. When the development process becomes self-sustaining then we can say

   a) the economy is in disequilibrium.
   b) the economy is at a "steady state."
   c) the economy has reached an economic equilibrium.
   d) a state of economic takeoff.

10. The debates about strategies for growth include all of the following except

    a) whether to pursue balanced or unbalanced growth.
    b) whether or not to accept foreign aid.
    c) how to allocate investment between directly productive projects and infrastructure.
    d) whether to have export led growth or import substitution.

11. When education doesn't match the needs of society then degrees become more important than knowledge. This is called

    a) brain drain.
    b) economic takeoff.
    c) credentialism.
    d) unbalanced education.

12. The term infrastructure investment refers to

    a) foreign direct investment by multinational corporations.
    b) a conditional requirement set down by the IMF.
    c) non military foreign aid.
    d) spending on education, transportation, and communications.

13. Why have foreign aid packages not had a good record of developmental success?

    a) Corruption in government has led to misuse of funds.
    b) Most foreign aid is for military procurement, which does not do much for development.
    c) Aid earmarked for development is too small relative to the task.
    d) All of the above.

14. A developing country that uses aid to improve the efficiency of its export industries is using a

    a) balanced growth plan.
    b) unbalanced growth plan.
    c) an infrastructure investment strategy.
    d) diversification strategy.

15. Which of the following is not an example of an infrastructure investment?

    a) agricultural equipment
    b) transportation system
    c) educational facilities
    d) communications network

16. What a specified amount of consumer goods costs in different countries is determined by

    a) purchasing power parity.
    b) currency exchange rates.
    c) per capita GDP.
    d) per capita GDP ÷ price of a market basket.

17. The challenge of the dual economy facing developing countries refers specifically to the

    a) choice of maintaining cultural integrity or implementing growth policies.
    b) debate between use of central planning or markets for economic decision making.
    c) existence of a nonmarket traditional economy along with a market based international economy.
    d) choice between developing the nation's infrastructure first or its agriculture.

18. In most developing countries the traditional economy is

    a) a system of highly competitive bazaars reminiscent of early capitalism in Western Europe.
    b) the reason why unemployment is negligible even though per capita income is also low.
    c) the reason why per capita income is low.
    d) the primary source of savings and investment.

19. The problem of _____ occurs when _____ .

    a) unbalanced growth; students waste their potential.
    b) brain drain; developing countries lose their best and brightest young people to developed countries.
    c) political stability; when students learn agricultural skills abroad.
    d) brain drain; students skilled in occupations relevant to the development of their own countries return home.

20. Which of the following poses the biggest *threat* to the enforcement of property rights which are needed for effective market place interactions?

    a) Overpopulation
    b) Strong central government
    c) Foreign direct investment
    d) Political instability

21. From an economic point of view, the occurrence of graft in developing countries is

    a) morally and ethically wrong.
    b) not in the self-interest of participating parties.
    c) an impediment to growth.
    d) All of the above.

22. Domestic investment funded by domestic savings in developing economies is undermined by

    a) excessive taxation by government on middle and upper income families.
    b) profit withdrawals by global corporations sent to shareholders in developed countries.
    c) a combination of a large class of poor people and a small middle class.
    d) prosperous members of the middle class investing in the debt paper of the domestic government.
    e) All of the above.

23. The problem of inappropriate education in developing countries refers to

   a) the brain drain outflow of the most highly educated persons to developed countries.
   b) the failure to adopt Western educational institutions and approaches.
   c) the failure to teach population control methods in their school systems.
   d) the failure to emphasize broad-based education to improve basic skills.

24. The economic principle expressed by Thomas Malthus in the 19th century has relevance for developing countries today in the respect that

   a) productivity improvements in agriculture enable a society to sustain a larger, more productive labor force.
   b) growth in GDP does not imply economic success if the population growth is so great that per capita GDP declines.
   c) reliance on foreign, direct investment may provide short-run improvements in GDP, but will result in long run domination of the culture and economy by foreign imperialists.
   d) short-run problems seem insurmountable but long-run per capita growth is the historical norm.

25. A country is able to increase its per capita income if it is able to

   a) increase its food supply in the long run.
   b) reduce its population in the long run.
   c) increase its long-run income.
   d) b and c.
   e) a, b, and c.

26. Thomas Carlisle nicknamed economics the *dismal science* because

   a) he was a poet who did not appreciate the rigors of economic analysis.
   b) of Marx's projections about the enslavement of the proletariat under capitalism.
   c) of Malthus' projections that food production is outstripped by population growth.
   d) he agreed with Ricardo's **Iron Law of Wages** which predicted subsistence existence for workers.

27. The debate about "the Dueling Duals" concerns

   a) whether development should make use of a balanced approach or unbalanced approach.
   b) whether development should focus on developing domestic industry or agriculture.
   c) the choice between the Japanese neo mercantilist model of development or a more traditional market-based approach.
   d) the Malthusian contention that population growth is a negative and Julian Simon's belief that people are the ultimate source of economic growth.

28. An advantage of an export-led growth strategy is that

   a) it may benefit domestic agriculture and domestic industry equally.
   b) if it works, domestic industries are better able to compete in international markets.
   c) it stimulates domestic competitive pressures which increases innovation and efficiency.
   d) it reduces domestic consumption, freeing up resources for investment in the economy.

29. A directly productive investment strategy is one which concentrates on

a) infrastructure investment which stimulates increased domestic and foreign, direct investment.
b) investment in specific firms and industries.
c) import substitution polices which encourage domestic production rather than export production.
d) improving output in the traditional economy rather than the international economy.

30. Which of the following approaches is associated with an import substitution policy?

a) A balanced approach to include both industry and agriculture in the development effort.
b) Imposition of tariffs to secure protection of domestic industries providing for domestic production.
c) Providing subsidies to export industries in order to substitute export output for import output to encourage the development of the international economy and reduce the traditional economy.
d) Heavy taxation and reduction of consumption in the expectation that short-run suffering leads to long run economic growth as the result of increased investment.

III. SHORT ANSWER EXERCISES AND PROBLEMS

a. Short Answer Exercises

1. Identify issues developing countries are faced with regarding the relationship between economic growth and cultural integrity.

2. List six obstacles to economic growth in low-income countries.

3. Explain how markets can function in inappropriate ways when there is no well-defined public morality.

4. What are two external sources of funds for development?

5. What is the "conditionality" feature of loans from the IMF to developed countries?

6. Define per capita income.

7. Identify three reasons for population growth.

8. Identify two ways developing countries can increase per capital income.

9. What is the development debate regarding the "Dueling Duals"?

10. Discuss four debates about strategies for growth.

11. Why is the quest for economic growth and development a complicated problem?

b. Problems

1. Refer to the table below to respond to the questions that follow regarding purchasing power parity.

AVERAGE MONTHLY COSTS

Commodity \ Country	Aceland (dollars)	Deuceland (pesos)	Trayland (yen)	Jackland (cruzeiros)
Housing	1,000	100	1,000	
Transportation	500	75	100	
Food	500	25	50	
Health care	400	100	50	
Market Basket				

a) Identify the price of the market basket for each country. It takes two cruzeiros to purchase a dollar's worth of goods on average.

b) Express the purchasing power parity of the currencies in terms of the peso.
   Aceland:

   Deuceland:

   Trayland:

   Jackland:

c) In Jackland, it takes three times the cruzeiros for housing and three times the cruzeiros for health care as it takes dollars for those items in Aceland; Purchasing power parity for transportation between Deuceland and Jackland is one peso to four cruzeiros; Six cruzeiros in Jackland buys the amount of food that one yen purchases in Trayland. Fill in values in the table for Jackland.

d) In which country is food the cheapest?

e) In which country is food most expensive?

f) In which country is housing most expensive?

g) In which country is health care the cheapest?

2. Complete the table below which provides selected statistics on developing and middle-income countries.

Statistic / Country	Life expectancy	Infant mortality per 1000	Literacy rate (%)	Per capita GDP	Population per physician	Ag labour force (%)
Bangladesh						
Ethiopia						
Haiti						
Brazil						
Iran						
South Korea						
Thailand						

IV. CHALLENGE PROBLEMS AND POTENTIAL ESSAY QUESTIONS

a. Challenge Problems

1. Determine whether each of the following items is most associated with a high or low level of economic growth and development by placing a check in the appropriate column.

		High	Low
a.	High quality labour force	_____	_____
b.	Political stability	_____	_____
c.	Overpopulation	_____	_____
d.	High savings rate	_____	_____
e.	Inequitable distribution of income	_____	_____
f.	Low rate of investment and capital formation	_____	_____
g.	High level of technology	_____	_____
h.	Low per capita income	_____	_____
i.	High percentage of the population employed in agriculture	_____	_____
j.	Technological dualism	_____	_____
k.	Traditional society	_____	_____
l.	Low productivity	_____	_____
m.	Infrastructure in place	_____	_____
n.	Limited range of exports	_____	_____
o.	Limited social roles of women	_____	_____
p.	Military aid that does not release funds for the development of an infrastructure	_____	_____
q.	Brain drain	_____	_____
r.	Political corruption	_____	_____
s.	An outflow of financial funds	_____	_____

2. You are the chief economic advisor to a developing nation which is politically stable and possesses a culture that you believe is conducive to growth. Assume new evidence has just been brought forward which supports the argument that the Asian tigers' success has been primarily due to their governments' involvement in their economies. What economic policies would you recommend to the developing nation to promote its growth and development?

b. Potential Essay Questions

1. In what way is economic development the only choice for developing countries?

2. Define the dual economy and explain its relevance for developing countries.

3. Explain why it is so difficult for developing countries to generate investment.

4. Why are some developing nations suffering from the Malthusian fate?

V. ANSWERS

II. Mastery Test

1. d	6. b	11. c	16. a	21. c	26. c
2. c	7. c	12. d	17. c	22. c	27. b
3. a	8. c	13. d	18. c	23. d	28. b
4. a	9. d	14. b	19. b	24. b	29. b
5. c	10. b	15. a	20. d	25. d	30. b

III. Short Answer Exercises and Problems

a. Short Answer Exercises

1. Economic development often places stress on cultures based on traditions as markets supplant established ways of doing things; overpopulation and poverty also undermine culture as the stress placed on society by these forces also destroy traditional ways of doing things.

2. political instability, lack of investment, corruption, lack of appropriate institutions, overpopulation, lack of appropriate education

3. Bribery, graft, and corruption can cause payments to have to be made to undertake economic activity. The more it costs to undertake economic activity, the fewer the economic activities individuals will undertake. This inhibits growth and development.

4. foreign aid and foreign investment

5. The borrowing government must agree to establish formal policies, usually with respect to fiscal and monetary policies, which work against inflation and government borrowing.

6. GDP ÷ population

7. Infant mortality rates decline as death rates decline; higher income leads to expanded family size; children are a source of family income and production as well as being the parents retirement plan.

8. decrease in the population without decreasing national income; increasing income without increasing the population.

9. Should developmental efforts concentrate on agriculture and the traditional economy or should developmental efforts concentrate on the international economy and improving the ability of domestic industry to compete on international markets.

10. Four debates about strategies for growth are:
    1. Balanced vs. unbalanced growth.
    2. Agriculture vs. industry.
    3. Infrastructure vs. directly productive investment.
    4. Export-led growth vs. import substitution.
       (You should be able to evaluate them. See pp. 426–427 in your text.)

11. Economic development is a complicated problem because it is entwined with cultural and social issues. There does not exist any prescribed set of procedures that a nation— any nation—could simply follow if it wishes to grow and develop. It's not that simple. Possibly, only by having a complete sense of a country, its history, and its cultural, social, and political norms can one decide whether it's the right time and place for this or that policy to promote economic growth and development.

b. Problems

1.

AVERAGE MONTHLY COSTS

Commodity \ Country	Aceland (dollars)	Deuceland (pesos)	Trayland (yen)	Jackland (cruzeiros)
Housing	1,000	100	1,000	3,000
Transportation	500	75	100	300
Food	500	25	50	300
Health care	400	100	50	1,200
Market Basket	2,400	300	1,200	4,800

    b) Aceland: 8 dollars = 1 peso
        Deuceland: 1 peso = 1 peso
        Trayland: 4 yen = 1 peso
        Jackland: 16 cruzeiros = 1 peso

    d) Trayland

    e) Aceland

    f) Trayland

    g) Trayland

2.   See Exhibit 2 in the textbook, chapter 21 p. 416.

IV. Challenge Problems and Potential Essay Questions
a. Challenge Problems

			High	Low
1.	a.	High quality labour force	√	
	b.	Political stability	√	
	c.	Overpopulation		√
	d.	High savings rate	√	
	e.	Inequitable distribution of income		√
	f.	Low rate of investment and capital formation		√
	g.	High level of technology	√	
	h.	Low per capita income		√
	i.	High percentage of the population employed in agriculture		√
	j.	Technological dualism		√
	k.	Traditional society		√
	l.	Low productivity		√
	m.	Infrastructure in place	√	
	n.	Limited range of exports		√
	o.	Limited social roles of women		√
	p.	Military aid that does not release funds for the development of an infrastructure		√
	q.	Brain drain		√
	r.	Political corruption		√
	s.	An outflow of financial funds		√

2. While keeping your fingers crossed, you might generally recommend greater government involvement to promote an export-led growth strategy. That is, the country should generally try to promote the growth of those industries in which the country already has, or might potentially have, a comparative advantage. To achieve growth, you might recommend:

a) Continue to preserve political stability (absolutely necessary). Minimize corruption. Promote and create incentives to enhance the work ethic, high savings, and a reliance on trading through markets.

b) Government should pursue expansionary monetary policy to keep interest rates down. This should help promote investment and capital formation and accumulation. Capital accumulation should increase productivity and provide for growth.

c) Government should pursue fiscal and monetary policy measures to keep the country's exchange rate low. A cheap (weak) currency will make exports relatively cheaper to the rest of the world, increasing their competitiveness.

d) Government should subsidize or provide low interest loans to those industries which show some promise for growth and produce products which can be exported.

e) Government should protect its expanding "infant industries" from foreign competition by imposing tariffs, quotas and other import restrictions—but only for as long as the protected industries show improvement in their ability to compete with foreign companies.

f) Government should invest in the infrastructure. Build better roads, power plants, etc. This will help to attract foreign investment (foreign companies to locate in the country).

g) Possibly most importantly, the country should invest in human capital—its people's skills, training and education. It should try to educate as many people as possible in the basic skills of reading, writing, math and science. Most international businesses are looking to locate in countries where the lowest level worker has a firm grasp of the basics in education. So the focus of education should be on the many; not the few.

b. Potential Essay Questions

The following answers are annotated—they only indicate the general idea behind the answer.

1. Given market societies' expansionary tendencies, the cultures in economically poor countries that do not grow would simply be overrun and destroyed by cultures of market societies. This means that the choice is not between development and preservation of existing culture; rather, the choice is between economic development with its attendant wrenching cultural transitions, and continued poverty with exploitation by developed countries and its attendant wrenching cultural transitions.

2. The "dual economy" refers to the tendency of developing countries to have two somewhat unrelated economies—one an internationally-based economy, the other a traditional, often nonmarket, economy. The internationally-based economy usually promotes growth and people who participate in it usually earn incomes similar to those found in the developed countries. The traditional economy is not very conducive to growth or high incomes. One of the greatest challenges for developing nations is trying to find a way to "modernize" the traditional economy without destroying the nation's culture.

3. If a country is to grow it must somehow invest (investment in capital—plant and equipment—increases productivity and therefore growth), and funds from investment must come from savings. Developing nations, because they are poor usually have little savings to invest. What savings does exist among the higher income individuals is usually put in developed countries. These people are justifiably afraid to save in their own countries because of the very real possibility of a government overthrow where their savings could be lost.

Another way to generate funds for investment is from external savings, either foreign aid or foreign investment. The problem with foreign aid is that it usually comes with strings attached. For example, most foreign aid is military aid; helping a country prepare to fight a war isn't a good way to help it develop. Foreign investment usually takes the form of a global corporation locating in the country. For that to occur, the developed nation needs political stability, a government conducive to business, adequate infrastructure, a motivated and cheap labour force...Most developed countries have difficulty measuring up. Even if they do, the competition among developing nations for the foreign investment often results in offers to the global corporations that are so lucrative few benefits accrue to the developing nation.

4. Because diminishing marginal productivity has exceeded technological change. See p. 425 in your textbook.

Chapter 22 SOCIALIST ECONOMIES IN TRANSITION

I. CHAPTER AT A GLANCE

Rip this page out for quick and easy reference.

1. The theory of modern socialist economies originated in the early 1800s when a group of writers reacted to the excesses of unregulated capitalism. (430)

   Unbridled capitalism of the past and its abuses gave rise to the birth of socialism. Welfare capitalism of today has blunted some of the sharp edges.

2. In a centrally planned economy, central planners decide the general direction the economy will take. They make the what, how, and for whom decisions. (430)

   Central planners in a Socialist economy don't have to take consumers' desires into account. They follow whatever set of principles they think best.

3. Most Soviet-style socialist countries suffered from consistent shortages of goods because the planners chose too-low prices relative to demand. (434)

   Planners set prices at levels they believe are "fair" or reflect the "social worth" of the product--in short, at whatever level they want. But economic forces are still present.

4. Five problems that tend to undermine central planning are: (435)

   1. *Nonmarket pricing and perverse incentives.*
   2. *Inability to adjust prices quickly.*
   3. *Lack of accurate information about demand.*
   4. *Ambiguous production directives.*
   5. *Inability to adjust plans quickly to changing situations.*

   *Know why these are problems. They are the same kinds of problems facing many large firms.

5. The problems faced by transitional economies include the lack of political will to decide on an institutional structure, determining initial property rights, and developing a legal and physical infrastructure within which the economy can function. (440)

   Markets aren't going to solve many of the political and social problems that most transitional economies face. Markets require solutions to political problems before they can operate.

6. Four cautionary lessons for transitional economies are: (442)

   (1) the Nirvana caution,
   (2) the QWERTY caution,
   (3) the tombstone caution, and (4) the transplant caution.

   There are always the 3 invisible forces present--economic, political and social. The challenge for the transitional countries is to develop economic institutions that reflect each country's unique political and social sensibilities as well.

II. MASTERY TEST

1. The idea of socialism as it was originally espoused was that

    a) the workers of the world needed to unite in order to achieve their rightful claim on production.
    b) there should be an equal distribution of income among all people.
    c) unemployment should be eliminated by job guarantees.
    d) the right to vote in the political arena should be available to all adult males, not just property owners.

2. The French socialist who believed that everyone who wanted a job should be able to get one was

    a) Louis Blanc.
    b) Karl Marx.
    c) Thomas More.
    d) Robert Owen.

3. By the end of the 19th century the focus of socialist thought had evolved to

    a) practical efforts at reforming the rough edges of capitalism through democratic political reform.
    b) guaranteeing that everyone who wanted a job would get one.
    c) the creation of an economy in which government controlled production.
    d) creating a fairer society by the redistribution of income from the wealthy to the poor.

4. The model of a socialist economy during much of the 20th century has been

    a) Soviet-style centralized planning.
    b) the Chinese planning/market mix.
    c) Scandinavian democratic socialism.
    d) Robert Owen's utopian socialism.

5. A market economy differs from a centrally planned economy because

    a) market economies must deal with the issues of *what, how* and *for whom.*
    b) planning does not occur in a market economy.
    c) the demand for goods and services drives production decisions.
    d) government has no role in a market economy.

6. The best way to describe *Utopia* as it was originally construed is that

    a) it was Thomas More's vision of an ideal society.
    b) it was Robert Owen's attempt at creating a cooperative, working community.
    c) it was Karl Marx' dream of a workers' paradise.
    d) it was Adam Smith's model of a market economy.

7. The formal technique of designing an economic plan so that the inputs needed to produce outputs at different production stages were coordinated under Soviet-style socialism is called

    a) materials balance.
    b) linear programming.
    c) nonmarket coordination.
    d) centralized planning.

8. The technique established to provide for feedback to planners higher up in the hierarchy from below in the Soviet-style system is referred to as

   a) linear programming.
   b) input-output analysis.
   c) materials balance.
   d) counterplanning.

9. In Soviet-style economies prices and production for necessities and luxuries were established so that

   a) necessities could be afforded while luxuries were discouraged.
   b) necessities were affordable but unavailable while luxuries were available but not affordable.
   c) both were affordable but only necessities were available.
   d) both were affordable but neither was available to the extent people wanted.

10. Shortages were common for most goods in Soviet-style socialist economies because

   a) low interest rates made credit easily accessible to finance consumer purchases.
   b) prices were generally set so low that the quantity demanded exceeded production.
   c) established prices were not high enough to create incentives for increased production.
   d) production quotas exceeded the quantity demanded at the planned prices for most goods.

11. Which of the following expresses a motivation for the pricing decisions of central planners?

   a) Prices need to be high enough to provide revenues to finance government operations.
   b) Prices cannot be too high so as to create inflationary pressures.
   c) Shortages are a more serious imbalance than are surpluses.
   d) Prices for necessities must be affordable by the mass of people.
   e) All of the above.

12. In centrally planned economies it is not uncommon that necessities which are priced low to be used for purposes for which they are not designed because

   a) consumers tend to behave irrationally in socialist economies.
   b) prices that do not reflect costs create perverse incentives.
   c) there is a general lack of consumer awareness about appropriate use of modern consumer goods in those countries.
   d) self-interest creates perverse incentives for individuals to behave in a manner that damages the general social well-being.

13. Soviet-style economies are characterized by prices which adjust slowly, the outcome of which is

   a) quantity demanded and quantity supplied generally at or near equilibrium.
   b) excessive profits for sellers who are able to keep prices high relative to their costs.
   c) surpluses for some commodities and shortages for others.
   d) reduced production incentives for producers.

14. A lack of accurate information about demand is a problem in centrally planned economies because

   a) illegal markets provide the quantity of goods desired when legal prices create shortages.
   b) illegal markets provide a market for goods for which legal prices create surpluses.
   c) producers do not have an incentive to react to the quantity demanded at legal prices.
   d) no mechanism exists for producers to inform planners about the relationship between production and demand.

15. The wages established by central planners in a socialist economy tend to be

    a) just sufficient to purchase the output of the economy at the legal prices and no more.
    b) inadequate to purchase the output of the economy at the set prices leading to surpluses and chronic unemployment problems.
    c) excessive in some regions of the country creating shortages and inadequate in other regions creating surpluses with respect to the prices set.
    d) excessive relative to the set prices creating chronic shortages.

16. The problem of ambiguous production directives refers to

    a) certain industries receiving inputs in excess of their production quota needs and others having inadequate inputs to meet quotas.
    b) the failure of central planners to provide complete specifications for the goods producers are responsible to generate.
    c) producers receiving different specifications and quotas for the goods they are to produce from the different planning agencies overseeing their work.
    d) the general failure of linear programming and input-output analysis techniques to provide for effective materials balances.

17. What does the marketplace provide to adjust to changing circumstances that central planning does not?

    a) Skilled managers proficient in creating well-reasoned projections regarding consumer demand
    b) Consumers
    c) Information and incentives
    d) Research facilities to provide innovative goods and services.

18. In a market economy, an increase in demand for a particular good in the short run results in _____ while in a socialist economy it is likely to result in _____.

    a) increased supply, decreased production
    b) higher prices, longer lines
    c) lower prices, increased production
    d) increased quantity supplied, increased quotas

19. Concern that transitional economies may attempt to prematurely try to establish markets in their societies before more pressing problems are dealt with is called the

    a) Nirvana caution.
    b) Qwerty caution.
    c) tombstone caution.
    d) transplant caution.

20. Soviet-style socialist countries did not make use of democratic political institutions because

    a) they had no previous experience with democracy before adopting their totalitarian system.
    b) democracy has always been inconsistent with the aims of socialism: full employment and an equitable distribution of income.
    c) centralized authority over economic decision making is inconsistent with political power distributed over a broad base of the population.
    d) with economic egalitarianism democratic political institutions are irrelevant.

21. Which of the following statements is a criticism of the non economic record of socialist countries?

a) Socialist economies failed to distribute income equally among the members of their societies.
b) Alleged concern for the well-being of society did not prevent socialist countries from being among the most environmentally degraded on earth.
c) Soviet-style socialist countries experienced the most dire infant-mortality rates and rates of illiteracy in the world.
d) a and b
e) a, b, and c

22. A necessary prerequisite for countries engaged in economic transition before they can hope to realize improvements in economic performance is

a) the establishment of democratic institutions.
b) the establishment of social and political stability.
c) elimination of all bureaucratic planning structures.
d) the realization of cultural homogeneity.
e) All of the above.

23. After 40 or 50 years of Soviet-style socialism, a major problem that transitional economies face in establishing market-based decision making is

a) the lack of a literate populace.
b) the absence of an economic infrastructure.
c) the lack of well-established property rights.
d) the absence of people with governing experience.

24. Concern that transitional economies may add to their existing problems the problems that now exist in the Western economies that they wish to emulate is called the

a) Nirvana caution.
b) QWERTY caution.
c) tombstone caution.
d) transplant caution.

25. Concern that transitional economies may try to incorporate institutions that exist in the Western economies they wish to emulate, but which may be counterproductive to their own unique social and cultural needs, is called the

a) Nirvana caution.
b) QWERTY caution.
c) tombstone caution.
d) transplant caution.

III. SHORT ANSWER EXERCISES AND PROBLEMS

a. Short Answer Exercises

1. What is a Soviet-style socialist economy?

2. How has socialist planning differed from market planning?

3. What is Utopia?

4. Identify two mathematical techniques developed to aid socialist planning that have been useful to capitalist businesses?

5. Identify two criteria that central planners may use to set prices.

6. List five problems that tend to undermine central planning.

7. What is the lesson of microeconomic theory to central planners concerned with formal adjustment methods and contingency plans?

8. Why is it that Central Planning may be inconsistent with Democracy?

9. List four cautionary lessons for transitional economies as they move to adopt western institutions.

10. Summarize some transition problems former Soviet-style socialist economies are experiencing.

11. Why do the authors consider their advice to Bulgarians ''contingent'' advice?

12. Why were the authors referred to as the TANSTAAFL professors in Bulgaria and why does it seem appropriate to wrap up the course on that theme?

b. Problems

1. Given the demand for widgets in Redland, a Soviet-style socialist country, respond to the questions that follow.

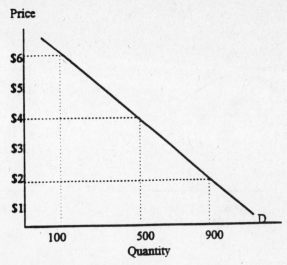

a) Identify three possible pricing and production scenarios where neither shortages nor surpluses for widgets arise in Redland.

b) If widgets are a necessity in Redland, what is the most appropriate pricing and production policy?

c) If widgets are a luxury and only sufficient resources are made available to produce 100 units, explain the difference between pricing widgets at $1 and pricing widgets at $5.

d) Widgets are priced at $10 and 250 are produced. Assess this policy.

2. Respond to the following questions on the basis of the production possibilities curves provided for Redland, a centrally planned economy, and Greentopia, a market economy.

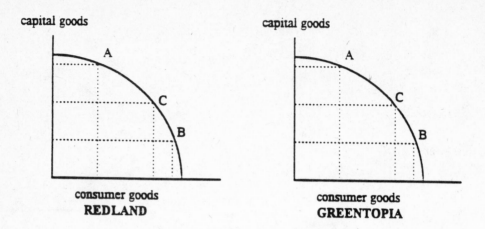

a) What is the most appropriate combination of production in order to enhance future production possibilities for Greentopia? ... for Redland? Explain your choice.

b) Assume that Redland and Greentopia are each operating at combination "C" on their respective production possibilities curves. Compare or contrast their respective future production possibilities as the result of currently producing at C.

IV. CHALLENGE PROBLEMS AND POTENTIAL ESSAY QUESTIONS

a. Challenge Problems

1. Why is the study of the problems facing central planners in centrally planned economies relevant for Canadian firms operating in a market economy?

2. Why has modern capitalism adopted some degree of "socialism" (government intervention in economic affairs)? What are some examples? Why have the Soviet-type socialist countries moved to adopt a more market-oriented or capitalist system?

3. Why do firms introduce profit-sharing into their compensation packages offered to employees? Why do firms decide to "downsize"?

4. Why is the economic principle "there ain't no such thing as a free lunch" relevant for transitional economies to keep in mind as they transform their economies?

b. Potential Essay Questions

1. Summarize the historical roots of socialism.

2. How does a centrally planned economy like that of the old Soviet Union differ from a market economy like that of Canada?

3. Summarize how a centrally planned economy works.

4. Explain why most Soviet-style socialist economies suffered consistent shortages of most goods.

V. ANSWERS

II. Mastery Test

1. c	6. a	11. d	16. b	21. d
2. a	7. a	12. b	17. c	22. b
3. c	8. d	13. c	18. b	23. c
4. a	9. d	14. c	19. c	24. a
5. c	10. b	15. d	20. c	25. d

III. Short Answer Exercises and Problems

a. Short Answer Exercises

1. Centrally planned economies in which the state owns most of the means of production

2. Socialist planning is hierarchical where a central planning agency establishes broad directives for answering economic questions which are developed as they flow down through planning bureaucracies. Planning in market economies is decentralized among the individual producing and buying units in the economy: businesses and households. Planning in market economies is reflected in the behaviour of demand and supply conditions in markets.

3. Utopia is the name of the fictitious country described by Thomas More that epitomized the values and virtues that More believed were ideal. Utopia has come to represent an ideal society, whose characteristics depend upon the values and ideals of the person describing the perfect society.

4. input/output analysis and linear programming

5. Central planners may establish prices which are designed to cover the explicit costs of production but are likely to reflect attitudes of fairness and affordability which the planners hold.

6. Nonmarket pricing and perverse incentives, an inability to adjust prices quickly, the lack of accurate information about demand, ambiguous directives regarding product specifications, an inability to adjust plans to changing situations.

7. Market prices transmit information effectively; market prices incorporate incentives for acting on the information.

8. Critics of socialism argue, and history tends to support the idea, that centralized economic authority is inconsistent with the distribution of political power among a broad electorate. Economic power concentrated in government reduces any leverage that an electorate may have to deny government the ability to eliminate political freedoms.

9. Four cautionary lessons for transitional economies are: (1) the Nirvana caution, (2) the QWERTY caution, (3) the tombstone caution, and (4) the transplant caution.

10. The problems faced by transitional economies include the lack of political will to decide on an institutional structure, determining initial property rights, and developing a legal and physical infrastructure within which the economy can function.

11. Decisions that Bulgarians made regarding their economic directions had to incorporate the unique fabric of Bulgaria's society and culture; only Bulgarians would have the insights into their society to design paths that are appropriate for Bulgaria.

12. As the authors have emphasized from the start, economics deals with the recognition of the foregone choices when any decision is made. The gains from any option undertaken must be weighed against the opportunities lost by not choosing alternative solutions.

b. Problems

1. a) 100 widgets at $6, 500 widgets at $4, 900 widgets at $2

   b) The highest level of production that is feasible at a price that is as low as possible.

   If shortages and waiting lines are to be avoided an attempt must be made to coordinate the production quota to the price which will create a corresponding demand for widgets?

   c) If 100 widgets are produced, then regardless of a price of $5 or $1, that is all that will be purchased; However, a price of $1 leads to a shortage situation while a price of $5 will ration the commodity to those who can afford it, leaving those who cannot afford it without an opportunity to purchase a widget.

   d) A surplus occurs because at $10 the quantity demanded is far less than the 250 widgets produced.

2. a) Combination A for both countries allocates more resources for the production of capital goods that may serve to enhance future production possibilities than do the alternatives identified.

   b) Market economies have exhibited superior ability to coordinate spending and saving decisions so that resources allocated towards future production are more effectively translated into expanded levels of future production. It is likely that Greentopia will realize greater growth than Redland.

IV. Challenge Problems and Potential Essay Questions

a. Challenge Problems

1. Because their problems are very similar. Canadian firms are continually looking for better ways to match the goals of workers and the goals of the firm; to increase their ability to respond to change in consumers wishes more quickly and efficiently; to find out what consumers want; to reduce the ambiguity associated with production directives to ensure quality; and to reduce bureaucratic inefficiencies.

2. Modern capitalism has adopted some degree of socialism (government intervention in economic affairs) because of the experience of "market failures." Historically, in all capitalist systems, citizens have called upon their governments to try to correct for these market failures—growth of monopoly power, presence of external costs and benefits, lack of public goods and services, an inequitable distribution of income, and macroeconomic instability—in differing degrees reflecting their differing political and social sensibilities.

   Some examples of government action directed at moderating some of these problems include, respectively; anti-trust enforcement and regulation; taxing, regulating and subsidizing externalities; providing public goods and services; redistributing income through taxes and welfare programs; and the use of fiscal and monetary stabilization policies. (Economic reasoning tells us that the government should be involved only if the "benefits" outweigh the "costs.") Because of government involvement, modern capitalist systems are often characterized as "welfare capitalist" systems.

   The Soviet-style socialist countries are opting for more capitalism because of the failures of too much government involvement. Historically speaking, there appears to be a convergence. Could it be a case of all things in moderation?

3. Both of these are examples of firms trying to become more efficient and therefore successful in meeting the needs of their customers in order to increase profits. The idea behind profit-sharing is to create incentives that will motivate workers to pursue the same goals as those of the firm by giving workers a stake in the outcome. Downsizing, at least ostensibly, is designed to reduce bureaucratic inefficiency.

4. You are strongly encouraged to re-read the box in Chapter One, "Economic Knowledge in One Sentence." TANSTAAFL (There Ain't No Such Thing As A Free Lunch) means nothing is free. A price must be paid for everything. The price that must be made for change is sometimes very high.

   Moveover, all costs are really opportunity costs (what must be given up in order to get something else). As the transitional economies settle on a more market-oriented economy they will have to give up what many will likely argue were the advantages of the previous system. For example, the Soviet-style job security. The transitional economies will realize that even though the new more market-oriented economies they will develop for themselves will be much better in many ways than their old system, new challenging problems will present themselves. "You can't have your cake and eat it too." That is, "there ain't no such thing as a free lunch"—a fault-free economic system.

b. Potential Essay Questions

The following answers are annotated—they only indicate the general idea behind the answer.

1. Socialism grew up in response to the excessive abuses of unregulated capitalism during the industrial revolution (poor working conditions, an inequitable distribution of income, high unemployment and starvation). Some intellectuals at the time argued there must be a better way. At first, Socialists placed emphasis on ensuring full employment. Later, concern focused on redistributing income and then to creating an economy in which the government controlled production. Socialists are still looking for a better way. However, they agree that the Soviet-style socialist approach is not the way to go.

2. The difference is not that in one there is planning and in the other there is not. The difference lies in who does the planning, how many planners there are, and what motives guide planners' decisions.

    A centrally planned economy has one central agency for economic planning, while a market economy has many planners. In a market economy, the various branches of government control and plan about 25 percent of the economy which is periodically ratified by the public through regularly scheduled elections. In the rest of the economy (the private sector) the planners are business executives, and their decisions are guided by the profit motive, which in turn reflects consumer sovereignty (the consumers' wishes expressed in the demand for products).

    The multitude of planners in a market economy makes it difficult to say exactly who decides what, how and for whom to produce. See Exhibit 1 on page 432.

    There's a big difference in the motivation behind planning in a socialist economy and in a capitalist economy. In a capitalist economy firms must take the consumers' desires into account. Central planners in a socialist economy don't have to take consumers' desires into account.

3. In a centrally planned economy, central planners decide the general direction the economy will take. They make the what, how, and for whom decisions.

    Planning in practice begins with a group of planners deciding what to produce, which will likely reflect the goals of the planners and not necessarily what is desired by consumers. This is followed by many specifics, including production quotas for each factory. Managers of factories are allowed to modify the production quotas or goals if they were unrealistic (counterplanning). Then the coordination of inputs and outputs among various segments of the economy followed (material balances). This entails the use of linear programming and input-output analysis. Central planners also have to decide what prices to charge for the goods produced.

4. Central planning requires that the planners decide what prices to charge for the goods produced. This can reflect their subjective value judgements regarding what is "fair" or what they believe to be the social worth of the product—in short, at whatever level they want. In the old Soviet Union often "necessities" were priced low while "luxuries" were priced high without regard to costs or other economic criteria—like the laws of demand and supply. The result was shortages of some products (prices were set too low) and surpluses of others (prices were set too high). Shortages were particularly acute because prices were set too low relative to demand. Shortages were one of the people's biggest complaints. When shortages exist an alternative rationing system must be established to determine who gets what. Sometimes those who were members of the Communist party, or some other in-group got the goods while others didn't.